Torn between the career paths of two illustrious relatives, Max Born, the Nobel Prize Winner in Physics and his granddaughter, Olivia Newton-John, Lois Pryce abandoned her interest in Quantum Theory at the age of 16, left school and spent the next couple of years as a carrot picker, painter and decorator and failing an audition as a kiss-o-gram before bowing to the inevitable and going into rock 'n roll. After various underpaid jobs in record shops and as a product manager in the Beeb, she decided to jack it all in and ride her trail bike from Alaska to Tierra del Fuego. Her on-line diary of her journey became a cult hit and led to her first book, *Lois on the Loose*. When not on her bike she is at home on her houseboat with husband Austin.

Praise for Lois Pryce

'Lois Pryce knows what it takes to be a fun, fearless female. She rode solo from London to Cape Town, with the barest of essentials.' *Cosmopolitan*

'A natural storyteller, she brings the African landscape to life in this funny, fast-paced travelogue.' *Sainsbury's Magazine*

'A gutsy tale of one woman and her bike, told with vigour and honesty she manages to make the journey an enjoyable experience and a solid read. There are the usual chaotic scenes of jumble in border towns, and heart-warming tales of help en route. But there are also some genuinely chilling episodes and these make the book, and perhaps the journey, all too authentic.' *Irish Times*

'Lois Pryce defied convention when she decided to travel from London to Cape Town by motorcycle. *Red Tape and White Knuckles* reads like a non-fiction chick-lit adventure as the pasty skinned, heatstroke prone Pryce deals with cultural differences, Africa's troublesome roads and the company of various travellers she meets along the way.' *Metro*

To Austin, the unsung hero of this journey

RED TAPE AND WHITE KNUCKLES

Lois Pryce

One Woman's Motorcycle Adventure through Africa

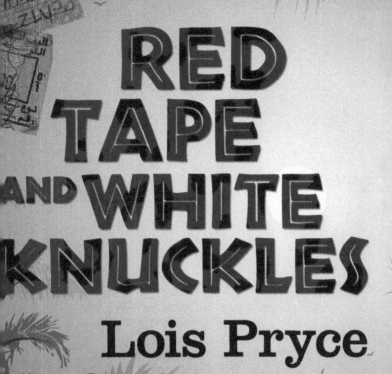

Originally published by Century, June 2008
under ISBN 978-1846052439

Octane Press, Edition 2.0, February 2013
Copyright© 2013 by Octane Press

ISBN 1937747131
ISBN-13 978-1-937747-13-8

OCTANE
PRESS
octanepress.com

Printed in the United States of America

Acknowledgements

A solo trip relies on others for its success, and my journey was enhanced in many ways by the following people, to whom I am extremely grateful

To Austin for his love, unconditional support and the beautiful maps – I could not have done it without you. Thank you to everyone who waved me off from home – Nat, Lisa, Nikki, Sarah and Ken, Sophie, Angie and Trundle, Sarah Bradley and Doug Brown, Janine, Gerald, Loretta, Carole and Ray, David Boyer, P.W., Stuart 'Reggie' Martindale, Paul Mules, Bob Chapman, Charlie Benner and Tina, Lawrence Hamperl, Jason Simmons, Greg and Sharon Taylor, Suzi and Simon Harby, Andy Miller, Walter Colebatch and especially to Andrew and Collette for the fab home-sewn banner.

To Geoff and Phyllis Vince, Elaine, Paul and Liam Kenchington, Nigel, Gerry, Sam and everyone from Southampton Advanced Motorcyclists for the surprise send-off, to Gary and Carole Lamsdale for appearing at Portsmouth out of the blue, Kate Pryce for Nigerian visa assistance, Ahmad Ahmadzadeh for putting me in touch with Ekoko and Nadya Mukete who welcomed me into their home and treated me like royalty – thank you both for your generosity. Much admiration and gratitude to Jasia Ward for her patience and professional webmastery, to Lisa Hall for being the best impulsive friend a girl could have, to Si, Mel and James at Trail Bike Magazine for all their support. Many thanks to Paul and Zoe for their pre-departure advice and for giving me my first taste of a hookah pipe, to Rachel, Simon and Patrick for their kindness and hospitality on my way through France, to David Lambeth, Reg, Jez, John, Rupert and Tamsin for their fine company on the El Chott Rally – thanks for having me along. Thank you to the Kusserow family in Niger for their much-needed warmth and hospitality, to Eric and Sherry-kay for a fun night out in yaounde and for their helpful tips, to David in Luanda, for taking me under his wing. Thanks, as ever, is due to Chris Scott and Susan and Grant Johnson for inspiration and practical assistance by way of the Adventure Motorcycling Handbook and HorizonsUnlimited.com

At Random House I am forever grateful to Oliver Johnson for not being Superbri, to Charlotte Haycock for her endless patience and efficiency and to Louise Campbell for all her work and infinite good cheer. As always, enormous gratitude is due to my agent Faye Bender for her positive words and enthusiasm and to Jenny Meyer for all her hard work in making this book happen.

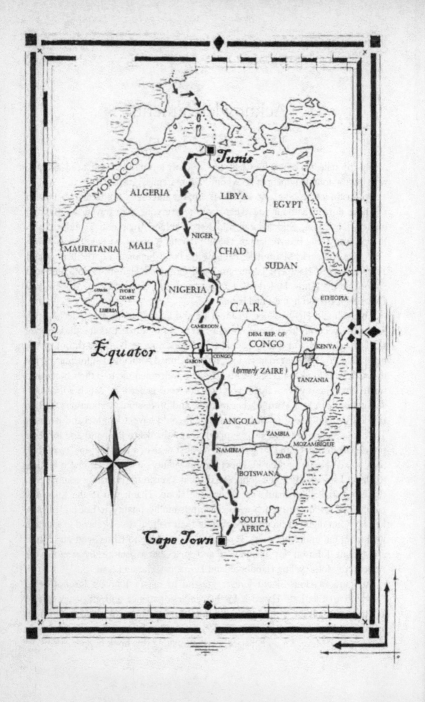

Prologue

If ever there was a continent I wasn't cut out for, it's Africa, and my first visit to its shores almost put me off for good. The problem is that I am whiter than white, not morally I'm afraid, but quite literally. Where some women blossom in the heat, I wilt; and while those other ladies might drape a sarong around their tanned bodies and throw on a stylish sunhat and designer shades, I'm the one with the frizzy hair and the bright pink face. Tennyson may have dreamed of fair women and Milton may have waxed lyrical about the 'divinely fair', but the pasty reality is far from poetic – less English rose, more Romanian vampire, and you don't see many of them in Africa.

I am also troubled by extremely itchy feet, although in this case, not literally (rest assured, this book is not the misery memoir of an albino woman's battle with athlete's foot). For as long as I can remember I've fantasised about grand adventures, and I remain unashamedly seduced by images of khaki-clad explorers, parchment maps and the hopelessly quixotic notion of 'wayfaring'. Aged twenty-two I bought myself a narrow-boat to live on in London, hoping that as well as providing me with a cheap home, a life afloat would inject a dash of romanticism into my daily grind. This it did in spades; I discovered a hidden world of fascinating characters, of self-sufficiency and beautiful decay; a veritable soap opera tucked away from London's rat runs, and for many happy years the Regent's Canal was my oyster, allowing me to live in postcodes that would under normal circumstances have laughed me out of town. (Although, while the great and the good of NW1 or W9 were quaffing fine wines on a Sunday lunchtime, I was more likely to be found emptying my chemical toilet.)

But I relished every moment of my watery life; it sprinkled my workaday existence with happy holiday dust; even the tedium of the 9 to 5 was made bearable by the potential of ever-changing surroundings, but by my late twenties my feet were itching worse than ever and the 9 to 5 had become the 9.30-ish to when can I go home? Even the convoluted system of transporting my motorcycle aboard my boat (thus enabling me to wake up in different places and ride to work) couldn't stave off the urge to hit the road.

So I jacked in my dreary office job at the BBC and rode my 225cc trail bike from Alaska to the tip of South America, a 20,000 mile journey. Rather than curing my itch, this most excellent adventure only made it worse, and as soon as I returned home I dug out my map of the world and started dreaming about the Next Trip – that life support system of all house- (or even boat-) bound travellers.

Africa called to me for some reason, not in any concrete,

explainable way, but in a way that summoned the heart, not the head. It wasn't about following in the footsteps of some famous explorer or tracing my ancestry; I wasn't even running away from anything, or trying to 'find myself'. It just seemed to me that Africa might be the last place on earth where I could still have a real, proper, old-fashioned adventure. And it had to be real: just me and my bike, no support trucks or organised tours or satellite phones or any of that malarkey. I'm not a foreign correspondent, or a Dakar racer, or a hard-bitten war reporter. I'm a thirty-three-year-old fair-skinned English woman who's five foot and four inches tall, reasonably fit (but could probably do with losing a couple of pounds), and, quite simply, I wanted to see what would happen if I jumped on my dirt bike and pottered my way down the African continent.

I wasn't fooling myself, though. Compared to my ride through the Americas, I knew Africa was going to be a whole lot trickier, especially as the route I was planning took me straight through the heart of the Sahara, and then further south, across the seething pit of jungle madness that is the Congo Basin, followed by Angola, a nation whose recently ended civil war has left the country in ruins and littered with landmines. There were easier routes, true, but I was intrigued by these places, where the only news is bad news and the bad news never seems to end. Could it really be so terrible? I wanted to find out for myself.

With stupendously poor timing, I had managed to fall in love just before I set off on my trip of the Americas, but upon returning home, Austin, the object of my desires, proposed and we were married a year later, prompting us to trade in my small boat for a larger, marital vessel. Thankfully my new husband was a fellow globetrotting motorcyclist and a man for whom the expression gung-ho was invented, so when, in the spring of 2006, I suggested we escape the dregs of the English winter and dip our toes into Africa by riding our bikes to the Moroccan Sahara for a three-week jolly, he agreed without hesitation.

We rode through Spain to catch a boat to Melilla, with dreams of palm trees, sand dunes and lush oases awaiting us on the other, exotic, side of the Mediterranean. Two days later we were deep in the desert, and I was lying in a nomad encampment, delirious, hallucinating and vomiting. We hadn't had much of a plan, but this was definitely not part of it.

The idea had been a three-week holiday of desert biking, but in forty-five-degree heat, with a pale-and-interesting complexion, it seemed that I might not be up to the job, a thought that had not even crossed my mind until it was too late. We had ridden through the desert all day, along sandy pistes and rocky trails, but it wasn't until late afternoon, when we took a break under the straggly shade of a thorn tree, that I noticed I felt slightly woozy. But with nothing but miles upon miles of empty sand stretching out in every direction, all we could do was keep going. We had set off late and ridden through the hottest part of the day, and now we were ploughing on towards sunset, aiming for a small village marked on the map where we could replenish our waning supplies of water and food.

Darkness was almost upon us, and I was feeling increasingly queasy and light-headed when the bikes' headlights picked out a camp of Berber nomads. They were an arresting sight: a group of dark-skinned men, dressed in flowing robes and elaborately wrapped blue turbans that covered their entire face except the eyes. We stopped to greet them, and as soon as I dismounted from the bike I knew there was something very wrong. I was staggering around, blathering and bewildered, until Austin decided I was dehydrated and poured a bottle of Coke down my neck. I promptly threw up all over him and then, for the first time in my life, I fainted.

When I came round, I was lying on the dusty ground staring up at several sets of kindly brown eyes peering out from folds of indigo cloth, and one pair of twinkly blue ones belonging to a worried husband. I was thoroughly disorientated, but I have a vague recollection of being carried into a fly-infested hut where I spent a long feverish night, convinced, in my confused state, that if I fell asleep I would never wake up again.

This Saharan sickbed seems an unlikely place in which to come up with the idea of motorcycling from London to Cape Town on my own. Africa had a very clear message for me: *You're not made for this continent! You're not meant to be here!* But once I started to recover, I knew I had to conquer the demons that had been spawned in Morocco. Back home, as the memory of delirium, vomit and squalor metamorphosed from humiliation and misery into amusing dinner-party yarns, my urge to tackle the Sahara returned stronger than ever (although this probably says more about the kind of dinner parties I get invited to than anything else). I was determined to go back for another go, and once I'd decided to return to the Sahara, well, I thought, why not go the whole hog and keep going, right down to the bottom?

When I shared these far-fetched plans of mine with Austin he didn't waver (well, he did, but he only told me many months later).

'You've got to go!' he declared immediately. We both knew that he wouldn't be able to come with me due to the demon

5

Work, but there was no doubt in his mind that I should go for it, and on the odd occasion that I did make doubtful noises he was the last person who was going to let me off.

'What about the heat, what about malaria, what about the landmines . . .?' I was fretting one night, in the dark hours, when the cold grip of fear sneaks in, twisting and churning your innards.

'The thing is,' he pointed out, 'you're never really ready to do a trip like this until you've done it.'

He was right; there was only way to prepare for a ride across Africa, and that was to ride across Africa.

What with the bike and the visas and the luggage and all the other things that take over one's life in the run-up to a long motorcycle journey, I had plenty to get on with, but my ill-fated Moroccan trip still loomed large in my memory. I spent most of my time worrying about the brutal African heat and eventually I came up with a novel way to prepare my pallid skin for the African sun: I would book a session on a sun-bed. I had never entertained such a notion before, it had always seemed, well, slightly trashy, but I was willing to try anything.

After ten minutes of UV glare I was pink as a fillet of farmed salmon, and by late afternoon I was back home in bed, reliving my Moroccan experience in full Technicolor glory, although minus the flies and nomads on this occasion. At this point I decided to give up on getting a tan, but why, oh why (after getting heatstroke from a sun-bed for crissake!) did I still feel compelled to return to the Sahara and then continue all the way to Cape Town, alone?

Well, I guess that's the lure of Africa. Like so many Europeans before me, the Dark Continent had got well and truly under my pasty skin.

ONE

I had set my departure date as 14 October 2006 in order to be crossing the Sahara during the northern hemisphere winter, when the desert was at its coolest. As the date loomed, everything was in place: my bike was ready, my luggage was packed, my paperwork was as ready as it ever would be, having spent several days traipsing around posh, and not so posh parts of London, gathering as many visas as possible from the African embassies. But I still didn't feel ready, and I didn't think I ever would.

To ease my ragged nerves I often found myself turning to a book I had discovered a few months earlier, entitled *The Rugged Road*, by a British woman named Theresa Wallach. It told the incredible story of a trans-African motorcycle trip made in 1935 by Miss Wallach and her splendidly named friend Florence Blenkiron. Together they rode a 600cc Panther motorcycle and sidecar combination, pulling a trailer, from London to Cape Town, straight across the Sahara, through equatorial Africa and then down the eastern coast to the Cape. As the book declared merrily on the back cover, 'no roads, no back-up, not even a compass!' It made for an inspiring read, and I was mightily impressed by the spirit and skill of the two women as they tackled the kind of hurdles I have nightmares about: rebuilding the engine in the middle of the Sahara, raiding wrecked vehicles for nuts and bolts to fix their bike and surviving on stale bread and lashings of good ol' Blighty spirit.

In comparison to my imminent journey, I had the clear advantage over them when it came to the motorcycle itself, thanks to the giant leaps in engineering and technology over the last seventy years. Environmentally, not much has changed for the motorbike traveller in Africa; it's still insufferably hot and physically gruelling. But it was interesting to see that culturally and logistically, African travel was an easier business back in the colonial heyday of 1935. Britannia not only ruled the waves, but a big chunk of the Dark Continent too, and the remainder of Africa was governed by the other European empires. Theresa and Florence's route took them through French, Belgian and English controlled colonies, where Foreign Legion soldiers and safari-suited colonels saluted them at every border post. The indigenous natives, although treated with great respect by the ladies, were merely an anthropological curiosity. However, seven decades later, despite the collapse of the British Empire and the improvements in motorcycle design, there was one theme that united our respective journeys, as relevant now as when it was written by Theresa Wallach on New Year's Eve, 1934, as she listened to the chimes of Big Ben resonating from a Foreign Legion wireless post in Algeria: 'In my mind I could picture the crowds, culture, cuisine, concrete and the folk at home, secure in a challenging world . . . I would rather grapple with the sands of the Sahara than the sands of contemporary society.'

You and me both, sister!

Contemporary society probably breathed a sigh of relief on 14 October 2006 as I boarded a Brittany-bound ferry from Portsmouth. I had been given a royal send-off from home by friends and family, many of whom had braved chilly motorways on all manner of bikes, from every corner of Britain. Austin had even made button badges for everyone, with a cartoon of me on my bike, waving cheerily – but that cheerful, happy-go-lucky image couldn't have been further from how I was feeling. As I made a few final checks and buckled up my crash helmet, I was riddled with nerves and choked-up emotions. Why was I leaving all this behind: Austin, my wonderful husband, truest companion and favourite person in the world, my dear friends, my cosy floating home, the gentle climes of southern England? Why on earth? To ride a motorcycle alone across a dangerous, inhospitable, friendless continent. At that moment, I don't know if I could have explained it even to myself. My mouth was as dry as the desert that awaited me as I made a short, croaky speech and kissed Austin an unbearable farewell. As I mounted my bike and fired up the engine, two friends unfurled a giant hand-sewn banner bearing the missive 'CAPE TOWN OR BUST!' I had to go now; they'd brought it all the way from Walthamstow on the Tube, it was the least I could do.

Motorway riding in England is not the finest of motorcycling experiences, and is generally to be avoided on a loaded 250cc trail bike, but it does give one the opportunity for contemplation, and on this occasion the slow lane provided me with a place to gather my thoughts about the adventure that lay ahead. The old adage that a journey begins with a single step was never truer as I headed for Portsmouth on that cool October evening. The best way to view my impending expedition, I decided, was to think of the whole thing as a series of single steps. For now, I was just going to Portsmouth. Tonight I was taking a boat to St Malo, the next day I was visiting some friends in Brittany, after that I was off to Marseille, and so it went on. As I set off on my trans-African journey, Cape Town had never been further from my mind.

As a linguistic warm-up, it was useful that the first leg of my trip took me through France. Most of the African countries on my itinerary were Francophone territories and these first few days would give me an opportunity to practise my sub-GCSE French. It would be the language of the trip until I got to Angola, a nation of Portuguese-speakers, and Lord only knew how that would work out. But like the miniature Portuguese phrase book that I had buried at the bottom of my panniers, I shoved these qualms to the back of my mind, to be dealt with at a later date, and decided to put my efforts into brushing up my Franglais.

It is almost compulsory as an English person that you have to nail your colours to the mast on the subject of our Gallic neighbours. There is no middle ground; you either love 'em or loathe 'em. For members of the latter category, it usually seems to have something to do with Paris not being bombed in the war, rude waiters and an aversion to garlic. I am most definitely in the opposite camp, and, were it not for their lame attempts at pop music, could quite happily adopt France as my spiritual homeland. I can only attribute this fondness to nostalgic recollections of school trips and family holidays, for like many folk of my age growing up in southern England in the 1970s and 80s, a childhood trip to France was our first taste of foreign travel. The food was weird, the toilets were even weirder, people went to sleep in the afternoon; it was all very strange and exciting.

Although these outings were filled with plenty of traipsing around the palace of Versailles and brass-rubbing at Notre Dame, twenty years on, the passage of time and rose-tinted pince-nez have worked their magic, and these dreary events have faded away to leave the more significant memories of buying flick-knives and Mace in Parisian street markets or sneaking out of the Louvre to smoke soft-pack Lucky Strikes. I can't quite believe that my school trips were really this much fun, but it does go some way to explaining why France holds such a place in my heart – it's where adventures start. And as I rode off the ferry, it seemed fitting that here I was again, setting off on the biggest one yet.

I was heading for the town of Nantes in Brittany, where I was visiting my friends Rachel and Simon. Like the Argentinian sheepskin on my bike's saddle, our lives had entwined on the road in South America. Rachel and I had first met in Los Angeles when we were both about to head south into Mexico. She too was travelling on a dirt bike, and together we set off on a Thelma-and-Louise-on-motorbikes adventure south of the border (although sadly without the Brad Pitt scene). We met up again in Chile a few months later, from where we made a testing 2,000-mile ride across Patagonia to the tip of South America. Little did Rachel know, as we bumped and crashed our way across the wilderness, that she was in fact pregnant by her boyfriend, Simon, with their son, Patrick. Fast forward to

11

the present, and Patrick, Rachel and Simon are all happily ensconced in Rachel's home town of Nantes, where the family transport is, naturally, a motorcycle and sidecar.

During these early days of my journey it was reassuring to be among people who knew what it meant to be setting off on such a venture. Between them, Rachel and Simon had covered most of the world on their bikes, although neither of them had ticked Africa off the list yet.

'It's never really appealed to me,' admitted Simon, as we pored over my map, spread out on the floor, while Patrick crawled and dribbled over Kenya and Sudan.

'Nor me,' agreed Rachel. 'It's pretty scary.'

I was a bit knocked back. These two were no *Daily Mail*-waving scaremongers. They were well-travelled, intelligent, educated, level-headed folk.

'So what is it exactly about Africa that scares you?'

'Big black men with guns,' said Rachel simply, with a Gallic shrug.

'The mud!' declared Simon, speaking from a motor-cyclist's perspective. 'Oh, the mud! You must have seen the pictures?'

I knew what he was talking about. There were a few photos in motorcycle travel books of riders covered head to toe in thick red mud, pushing their bikes through knee-deep swamps or sinking up to the axles on the churned-up 'mud motorways' of central Africa. With tarmac roads thin on the ground in this part of the world, the rainy season turns every other highway and byway into a sticky quagmire and makes many routes impassable. I had to admit it wasn't very appealing, but as usual I was taking the ostrich approach – I would worry about it when the time came. As for the big black men with guns?

Well, it wasn't really the people that scared me either; when it came to my fellow human beings I have found that old-fashioned politeness and lots of smiling will diffuse all sorts of tricky situations, and if that doesn't work, then hard cash will certainly do the job.

'It's not the mud or the natives that worry me,' I said, 'it's the heat, the sun, it's so fierce, and I'm not very good in extreme heat.'

'Oh well, that's the problem with being an English rose!' said Rachel, being kind.

'Hmm, I think pasty is probably a more accurate description of my complexion.'

'You'll get used to the heat after a while.'

'I'm not so sure,' I said, and I filled them on the details of my Moroccan disaster.

'Lois, are you sure this trip across Africa is a good idea?' asked Simon after I had finished. He said this in a slightly sardonic manner, but his question was serious.

'Well, I don't know if it's what you'd call a good idea exactly, but for some reason, I still want to do it.' It wasn't much of an explanation but it was the only one I could give.

Rachel and Simon made a good show of being supportive and positive about my African adventure, and I made a good show of being confident and upbeat. But after a few days I knew I had to move on, as it would be all too easy to linger here, enjoying their hospitality and the genial banter in my mother tongue, all the time putting off the inevitable. No, it was time to get out there and start talking the lingo.

This turned out to be harder than I expected, not just because of my linguistic ineptitude but because I kept meeting my fellow countrymen. Somewhere in central France, near

Lyon, it was raining hard, and towards the end of the day I followed one of those promising signs bearing the words 'Chambres d'Hôtes'. A winding, poplar-lined track led me to an old farmhouse of grey stone, where Jeff and Angela of Worcester were, like many other disillusioned English folk, making a new life as proprietors of a guesthouse in rural France. All the rustic ingredients were in place – chickens clucked around the courtyard, the breakfast consisted of local organic produce, the plaster walls were peeling just enough to be charming rather than decrepit, and all was well in this brave old world. Jeff and Angela were more than pleased with themselves and wasted no time in describing their escape from the horror that is twenty-first-century Britain.

'It was the immigrants,' said Angela.

'And the speed cameras,' added Jeff.

'Yes,' they cried together, 'the immigrants and the speed cameras!'

'Too bloody many of both of them,' confirmed Jeff, in case there had been any confusion.

'So are you enjoying your new life in France?'

There was lots of cooing and gushing from Angela about good schools and cheap wine before she warmed to her favourite subject.

'But, the French driving is TERRIBLE! They drive round the town as if it was a racetrack, they go through red lights all the time, it's outrageous – I mean, there was one day I was driving to the airport and this car pulled out on me, it must have been doing a-hundred-and-fifty . . . er, kilometres, that is,' she added with a pitying smile for the non-metric guest.

'Sounds like you could do with a few speed cameras,' I suggested, but she was already on to another tale of dastardly

French driving. Jeff, who had clearly heard it many times before, began talking over her with his own French driving story and for a while I sat there in silence while the two of them battled it out in stereo. Jeff had the louder voice, so he won.

'. . . But, I don't care what you say, you couldn't pay me to go back to England. Couldn't pay me,' he concluded.

'Well, they're all coming over here, aren't they?' twittered Angela.

'Oh yes, that's the only problem really.'

'Apart from the driving . . .'

'What's the only problem?' I asked quickly, before another episode of French driving unfolded.

'The English, they're all moving over here. When we first came out we were the only ones in this area, now they're everywhere. You go to the airport and it's all English cars in the car park, they're buying up all the properties, they're all over the place.'

'There's a delicatessen in town that's started selling Marmite!' added Jeff, his voice rising in indignation.

'Tch!' I tutted. 'Imagine that? Foreigners trying to make a better life in another country, outrageous! Darn immigrants.'

But Jeff and Angela weren't listening; they were telling me about the couple from Kent who had bought a nearby château for far too much money. Much more than it was worth, more than they should have paid for it, but they're making a TV show about it – we were on the TV, weren't we, love? When we first came out here, we were the first ones here, you see . . .

I made for my bedroom with excuses about being tired and having wet feet, and slipped off to sleep among crisp cotton sheets, aromatherapy candles and second thoughts about adopting France as my spiritual home.

Marseille was just one day away now, and as I rode through the south of France warm air blasted my face, reminding me of the joyous fact that I was escaping the gloom and drudgery of another northern hemisphere winter. Southern Europe had been scorched by a fiercely hot summer that year, leaving the land a parched, pale yellow. The sun-bleached buildings and faded paintwork of the little towns along the way, with their pavement cafés and Gauloise-scented *tabacs,* spoke of warmth, civilisation and familiarity, even to a displaced Brit like me. I wallowed in the comfort and ease of it all, for in a couple of days I would be leaving the safe confines of Europe, the mores and culture I knew so well, for the alien world of Muslim North Africa, where white girls on motorbikes were about as common as a well-thumbed copy of *The Female Eunuch*.

In Marseille I pitched up at a pleasingly shabby hotel on the Corniche, the road that runs along the Mediterranean coast, with a top-floor view over what E. M. Forster so accurately described as 'that exquisite lake'. I had fond memories of my last visit to this melting-pot city on the edge of Europe. Austin and I had come here as part of our motorcycling honeymoon, to catch the ferry to Corsica. Full of outdated fears about a city splintered by racial tension, we had approached with caution, but were pleasantly surprised to discover what was in fact, the French San Francisco – a hilly city buzzing with life, music and sunshine. When we found an entire street devoted to motorcycle shops, our love affair with Marseille deepened, and upon mentioning to one of the shop's staff that we were on our honeymoon, we were presented with complementary inner tubes. Our romance was sealed.

As I lugged my bags up five floors of hotel stairs, the friendly and slightly fey chap on the reception loped along behind me, inquisitive about travel plans that involved a crash helmet and two bulging pannier bags. His English was almost as bad as my French but we bumbled our way through something resembling a conversation.

'You come from England, all zee way on zee moto?'

'Yes,' I panted as I turned the final twist of the staircase.

'And where do you go from Marseille?'

'I'm taking the ferry tomorrow morning to Tunis.'

'Oh!' He threw up his hands in horror and pushed his floppy hair aside to reveal a pale, worried face.

'Alone? You go alone to Tunisie?'

'Er, yes.'

'Oh, *non*! But Madame, Tunisie is not a good place for a . . . for a . . .' He struggled to remember the right word. 'For a wife!'

I tried not to laugh, but his rusty translation of the word '*femme*', meaning both wife and woman in French, had come out sounding like a dire warning to all married women. I assured him that it would be fine, while I fiddled nervously with my wedding ring, hoping he wasn't right.

Early the next morning, with his words still ringing in my ears, I made my way to the port to discover a scene of African-style mayhem being played out in Marseille docks. Despite arriving with hours to spare, I couldn't even make it as far as the gates due to the gridlock of cars, vans and trucks that were jamming up the entrance. Some of the vehicles seemed to have been driven backwards and were mounted on the pavement at all sorts of unlikely angles. People were shouting and honking their horns, someone was driving the wrong way round a roundabout, the port officials were flapping their arms and blowing their whistles, but nobody was taking any notice. Fortunately, as a motorcyclist, there was no need for me to join this unholy rabble and I squeezed my way through the gaps, into the port, and followed the smell of burning clutches and exhaust fumes to find hundreds of vehicles in a giant, slow-moving queue, all waiting to sail to Tunisia.

I went to collect my ticket from the port office, where I was unwittingly launched into another indecorous scrum. The punters were pushing and shoving and yelling, and Tunisian men swapped effortlessly between French and Arabic insults, depending on who they were shouting at. The office was hot, dirty and airless, and behind two glass windows marked 'Tunis' were two weary clerks, issuing tickets with exaggerated slothfulness, occasionally pausing to scream in a chillingly controlled manner at the mob that banged on the glass and literally fought each other for their attention.

'A queue! A queue!' I bemoaned silently. 'It works, I promise you, we do it all the time in England.'

It was only a week ago that I had left London and I was still in polite British mode, so I took my place at the back of the rabble and waited patiently. But after a steady stream of Tunisian men had pushed in front of me or, in some cases, literally shoved me out of the way, I realised it was a case of 'when in Rome . . .' Sure enough, as my turn at the window finally came around, a middle-aged man sporting a greasy moustache and a shell-suit came hurtling in from the side and, with a smile that somehow managed to be both sleazy and threatening, shouldered his way in front of me, clutching a handful of crumpled Euros, which he threw down on the counter.

'*Excusez-MOI!*' I said, giving him a similar shoulder-budge back to regain my rightful place. He stared at me, surprised for a moment, and then broke into what he thought was a charming plea. But when I stood my ground, the niceties were abruptly switched off and he grabbed my arm, shouting at me in Arabic. I had no idea what he was saying but his tone of voice was enough for me to get the message, and by now his mates had gathered round to back him up. As he made a final bid for the front of the queue it occurred to me that I probably didn't want to spend twenty-two hours on the ferry with these chaps, but at this rate I was never going to get my ticket at all.

Then a booming French voice startled us all. We turned round to find a tall, immaculately dressed elderly gentleman, complete with overcoat, hat and walking cane, who put his arm round my shoulder in a protective manner and roared at the Tunisian men, waving his cane at them until they backed away hissing and muttering. I was steered back to the ticket window by my saviour.

'*Merci monsieur, merci beaucoup,*' I said gratefully.

'*De rien!* You travel by motorcycle?' he asked, pointing at my crash helmet.

I nodded.

'And where do you go after Tunisia?'

'I am riding to South Africa.'

'*Non! Mon Dieu!* On a moto, all alone?'

The rest of the punters, who had witnessed my dramatic rescue, were listening to every word and gave a collective 'Oooh!' As soon as I got my ticket, the old man swept me out from the crowd, twirled me round on the ticket office floor, grasped my shoulders and planted a continental kiss on each cheek.

'*Bonne chance, ma chérie, bonne chance!*' he bellowed, to the delight of the other customers, who began clapping and cheering. He gave me a giant bear hug, and with that, he was gone. I wished he was coming to Cape Town with me.

It had taken so long to get my ticket that I was worried the boat would be leaving without me, so I pegged it out of the office towards my waiting bike, almost knocking over a port official.

'Have I missed the boat to Tunis?' I asked him in a panic.

He gave a short jaded laugh.

'Mademoiselle, the boat is five hours late.'

I breathed a huge sigh of relief and surprise.

'Five hours late!'

'This boat is always late. It runs on African time,' he added with a very French raise of the eyebrows.

Although it was only mid-morning, the day was already sweltering, so I left my bike in the queue of sizzling, frustrated vehicles and cowered in the shade of a nearby building from where I could observe my fellow passengers. The majority of them were Tunisian men returning to the motherland in unfeasibly tatty vehicles, all of them straining under the load of luxury goods from the free West. With just a quick scan I spotted several fridge freezers, a three-piece suite, an electric oven, an exercise bike (broken) and countless Chinese laundry bags strapped on the roof, bulging with Allah knows what. The remainder of the passengers were French rally drivers, heading off into the Sahara for a desert adventure in their immaculate 4 × 4s, complete with sand ladders, winches and support crews. The rallyists all had a certain look – well-heeled but rugged, wearing quasi-military, sand-coloured desert outfits with lots of functional pockets. I noticed there was even a rally equivalent of the WAG – tough blonde women, trim and tanned but a little weatherbeaten; an outdoor version of the footballer's wife.

The five-hour delay raised the hackles of the more lively passengers further, which culminated in a mass horn-honking protest that made no difference to anything, except to make the participants feel better. As the impatient Tunisians around me blasted their horns, yelling and complaining in Arabic, I noticed that the French rally drivers were just sitting it out in patient, resigned silence. Maybe they had made this journey many times before. I sat it out too, chatting to the rally teams to pass the time, until eventually by mid-afternoon everyone was on board. My bike was squeezed in and strapped down among the shiny Land Rovers and decrepit minibuses, and at last we set sail for Africa.

As I stood on deck, watching Europe disappear into the distance, I wondered if today's events had been a taster for what lay ahead. From now on, I suspected that things were only going to get madder, badder and much, much hotter, and as I leant over the railings, watching the propeller churning up the calm waters of the Mediterranean, I mused over this prediction of mine. Mad, I could cope with, even enjoy. Bad, well, something's bound to happen at some point. But hot, really hot? That was still what scared me more than anything else. My ill-fated Moroccan trip had instilled a terrible fear in me, and even now, six months after the event, it continued to trouble me. I remembered how utterly dejected I had felt as I lay in that hut in the desert, vainly swatting the flies away from my face. Now, as I watched the shadows lengthen under the late afternoon sun while I moved slowly south towards Tunisia, I wondered what on earth I was letting myself in for.

TWO

A couple of things became apparent as I wandered round the interior of the ferry. First, I had the palest skin of all the passengers on the boat: the Tunisians were naturally dark and the French rally folk all had that leathery San Tropez tan thing going on. Second, I was one of only a few women on board among the handful of rally WAGs and a few veiled Tunisian wives; I was definitely the only woman on a motorcycle and, as far as I could make out, the only lone female on the ship. I stood out like a luminous white beacon and it didn't make for the most comfortable of travelling experiences.

My minority status meant that I was quickly singled out by various members of the crew and passengers to be stared at and gently prodded and questioned as if they were examining a rare species of animal. The intent was always friendly and borne out of curiosity, so it wasn't as if I felt threatened, just conspicuous. Having grown up with an adopted black brother in a mainly white part of Britain, I had witnessed at close range the reality of not fitting in, and I was reminded of the self-conscious awkwardness that goes with being the odd one out. In the end I settled on telling a useful white lie, that I was meeting my husband in Tunisia for a holiday, thus making me more respectable and, dammit, reassuringly normal! You could almost hear my interrogators breathe a sigh of relief.

A stroll round the boat revealed that there was not much to entertain hundreds of people for twenty-two hours. The duty-free shop was doing a decent trade in bulk-buy cigarettes, but unsurprisingly there was a distinct lack of booze for sale. There was, however, a 'Ramadan Special Offer' on perfumes, which also went some way to explaining why there was hardly any food on board; maybe the perfume offer was some sort of compensation – you might be starving hungry but at least you can smell nice. The Ramadan effect meant that the self-service restaurant was closed and the only sustenance available was black coffee, rock-hard croissants and some strange pizza type thing, dished up by a couple of cheeky Tunisian chappies. These two jolly stewards found me to be a highly entertaining spectacle, laughing and joking with me, or possibly, as my paranoid self suspected, at me, every time I went up for a refill.

After a few hours in my role as the on-board entertainment, I took refuge in my cabin for the rest of the evening and gave myself a strict talking-to. 'You're going to have to get used to it, Lois! You're going to be stared at and pointed at and poked and grabbed and tugged every day for the next ten thousand miles. It's time to toughen up!' But I didn't give myself too much of a hard time, as I knew that this phase of cultural acclimatisation would pass. I was still in the early days of my journey, when

24

every experience feels unbearably raw, and I knew that in a couple of weeks I would be into the swing of it.

The following morning I stood tall (if that's possible when you're five foot four), squared up my shoulders, stuck out my chest, caught sight of myself in the mirror and immediately decided against the latter, then strode out towards the seating area, looking everyone in the eye. By the time I got to the serving hatch to order my morning coffee, I was already weary of my show of false cockiness; it was tiring having to cultivate this steely exterior. I felt like Robert de Niro in *Taxi Driver* – 'You lookin' at me? You lookin' at me?' If the truth be known, what I really wanted to do was go back to my cabin and read my Ian McEwan novel in peaceful solitude. I was faltering by the duty-free shop, wondering how to spend the four hours until we docked in Tunis, when I was approached by a young, petite Frenchwoman, speaking English. She was wearing jeans and a T-shirt, had short dark hair and a friendly smile; I hadn't seen her before and she didn't look like a rally WAG.

''Allo!' she greeted me. 'I am glad I have found you! I saw you in the queue for the ferry on your motorbike with all your luggage. First I thought you were with the rally, but I think you are not, you are travelling alone, yes? When I saw you I think to myself, I must speak to her, I want to know, where is she going?' She gave me a big smile, which I returned gratefully.

'Well, I'm riding my bike to South Africa, this is the beginning of my journey. What about you?'

'I am moving to Tunisia.' She offered her hand. 'My name is Dominique.'

So I wasn't the only lone female on this boat after all. I smiled inwardly at my paranoid assessment of the situation being shown up for what it was.

'Shall we go and have a coffee?' said Dominique.

We made for the cheeky chappies at the serving hatch, who giggled hysterically at us. Over a couple of lukewarm coffees Dominique filled me in on her impending new life.

'I have fallen in love with a Tuareg!' she announced, showing me a head-and-shoulders photo of her new squeeze on her mobile phone. He was wearing the traditional *cheche*, the head-dress of the Tuareg tribe, similar to that of the Berbers I had seen in Morocco, a dark blue veil wrapped around his face and head, showing only his eyes. Although it didn't give much clue to what he actually looked like, he was certainly an exotic proposition.

'I went to Tunisia last year for a holiday, and he was the guide, we trekked through the desert on camels and . . .' She shrugged her shoulders. 'We fell in love. Now, my car is down there' – she motioned towards the vehicle deck below us – 'full of all my possessions in the world. It looks like a Tunisian's car with everything strapped on the roof! I have left my job and sold my house in France and I am going to live with him in the desert. We are going to be tour guides together.'

'Wow,' I said, impressed at this bold move. Travelling across Africa was one thing, always knowing that you would be going home eventually, but giving up everything to live in the Sahara was quite another.

'But, sometimes, you know,' she said looking me in the eye, 'I am worried and my heart does this!' She patted her chest with her right hand in a fast pounding motion. 'But I think, you must follow it, your heart I mean. I know I am doing the right thing.'

I assured her she was.

'And when I saw you on your bike, I thought that maybe you were doing something like me, I felt that you were setting off on a big adventure too.'

'You were right. And I'm the same – I'm really excited most of the time, but sometimes I have moments when I think, what the hell am I doing?'

I told her about my luckless trip to Morocco and my subsequent trepidation about returning to the Sahara. She nodded slowly, with a thoughtful look on her face.

'I think it is OK to be scared of something,' she said, 'as long as it doesn't stop you doing that thing.'

'Exactly!' I agreed with heartfelt enthusiasm, and we raised our plastic coffee cups in a toast to our impending adventures.

Dominique and I whiled away the next few hours, talking about our past lives and what our futures might hold, until the announcement came over the loudspeaker for all passengers to make their way to the car deck. At last we had arrived in Africa! Like two old friends, we bade each other a warm farewell with a hug, even though we had only met hours previously. Crikey, I thought, my British reserve is slipping away already! Dominique set off down the stairway, to her overloaded car and a new life in the Sahara, calling out, '*Bonne chance!*' as she disappeared from view.

'*Et toi aussi!*' I hollered back, pleased that I had managed to at least string a few French words together. I made my way to my bike, excited about finally rolling off the ferry on to African soil.

Tunis port was surprisingly official and organised; in fact Marseille's docks had been far more chaotic, but there was still plenty of paperwork and rubber-stamping required in order to enter the country. I was lucky enough to bump into a group of French motorcyclists who were setting off on a two-week tour of Tunisia and Libya. They were old hands at the Tunisian entry formalities and kindly took me under their wing, leading me through customs and immigration and helping me out with the form-filling. They were all riding big touring bikes and looked amused, if not a little sceptical, when I told them I was off to South Africa on my 250cc dirt bike. I rode with them out of the port, following them through the rambling outskirts of Tunis and on to the southbound autoroute, where they gallantly paid my toll before bidding me farewell and good luck as they roared off into the distance on their beefy-engined machines.

I was happy to pootle along the empty highway at my top speed of sixty miles an hour, enjoying the blue skies and dusty brown hills dotted with olive groves. I had attached great significance to having officially arrived in Africa, but the changes in scenery and climate were to be a more gradual affair and my surroundings remained resolutely Mediterranean. Despite the sight of shepherds dressed in long white gowns, tending their flocks along the scrubby motorway verges, I could have been in southern Spain or Italy. But I decided to make the most of this gentle introduction to the continent, as I knew only too well that the Sahara desert awaited me just a few hundred miles down the road, and after that lay the feral nations of Central Africa. It wouldn't be until I arrived in Namibia, many thousands of miles south, in another hemisphere, that I would be literally out of the jungle and back in a familiar world of tarmac roads, credit cards and all the other trappings of modern life. But Namibia might as well have belonged to another world at that moment, far away from where I now sat, perched at the very top of Africa, with the whole of the continent waiting for me. And the wonderful thing is, I thought to myself with a swell of excitement, that I have absolutely no idea what's going to happen over the next 10,000 miles.

After a day fuelled by nothing but ferry coffee and improvised pizzas, I was abruptly hit with hunger pangs and pulled into the next petrol station to fill up both myself and the bike. There wasn't much to sustain the hungry traveller except packets of chocolate biscuits, but the petrol station did offer a handy money-changing service for those of us fresh off the boat with a bundle of Euros. I was ushered into the manager's office, where I was greeted like visiting royalty and instructed to take a seat and drink tea while he unlocked his vault of Tunisian dinars.

'Your English is excellent,' I commented after a few minutes of grammatically correct small talk. He pointed to a photo of a platoon of American soldiers and then to a framed certificate on the wall behind his desk.

'I was trained in the US army; I lived in America for five years.'

'Oh, right! That explains it. So when did you come back?'

'Ten years ago; now I am married and I have three children.'

'So, do you prefer living in the States or in Tunisia?' I asked him, intrigued as to whether he had rejected or fallen in love with the American dream.

He looked at me, his face giving nothing away, and said, 'What do you think?'

I hoped this was a rhetorical question and that I didn't actually have to answer, so I just laughed politely. But he persisted.

'Well, what do you think?'

He was looking me in the eye and I realised I was going to have to respond one way or the other. Did I say 'America' and

29

risk being branded an infidel, a devotee of capitalism, consumerism and MTV, who assumes that all non-Westerners secretly aspire to swear allegiance to the Stars and Stripes? Or did I say 'Tunisia', in an attempt to pay tribute to his home country and possibly curry favour by dissing the evil superpower? What to do? The year was 2006, the 'War on Terror' continued apace; never before had the Muslim world and the West been more divided. I had stumbled into a social minefield! But most importantly, would my answer have some effect on the exchange rate I was about to be offered? I decided to play it safe.

'Er . . . Tunisia?' I smiled hopefully.

He just laughed and gave me a look that said, 'I don't think so.'

I scooped up my dinars and the manager wished me well for my journey with a warm smile and a sturdy US army hand-shake. With a farewell wave I was back out on the highway, heading towards the south of Tunisia and eventually the border with Algeria, where my grand traverse of the Sahara would begin, but first I had a little warm-up planned in the Tunisian fringes of the great desert.

Back in England, while preparing my bike, I had called in the services of David Lambeth, an engineer/mechanic whose stock-in-trade was preparing motorbikes for rallies. He had built me a rock-solid rack for my top-box, among other things, and I had enjoyed my visits to his workshop in a tumbledown barn in the picturesque setting of Ashdown Forest. On the phone he had sounded a little grumpy, and I had pictured a cantankerous old bloke whiling away his autumn years tinkering with bikes and moaning about the state of the world. So on my first visit I was surprised to be greeted by a young, surfer-looking dude with the cheeky smile of a naughty schoolboy. His telephone manner was, I discovered, just an unfortunate manifestation of his direct approach, which luckily is a characteristic I appreciate in people, especially people who are working on my bike. The ice had been broken on my first visit when I had asked politely to use the facilities. 'I haven't got a loo, but you can go behind that Land Rover if you want,' David had replied, pointing outside to a collection of shabby vehicles in the corner of a field.

My subsequent visits gradually revealed someone who could not only rebuild an engine or balance your wheels, but who also possessed a mischievous sense of humour, told amusing tales of his childhood ballet lessons and expressed an interest in flower-arranging. As far as someone to prep my bike went, he was OK by me. David Lambeth's other line of work was driving support trucks for motorcycle rallies, and as it turned out, he was doing just that in the Tunisian Sahara at the same time I was passing through on my way to Algeria. We arranged to meet up in the town of Douz, on the edge of the desert, where the rally and its entourage would be staying for a night.

Douz was a few days' ride away from Tunis, and as I continued southwards the autoroute petered out to become a regular two-lane highway, passing through more dusty brown hills and bustling small towns. The transformation from empty motorway into Third World traffic chaos came out of nowhere, and after my leisurely dawdle out of Tunis, I had to snap into African riding mode, sharpish. It was every man, dog, and donkey for themselves as I threaded my way through the mayhem. On the outskirts of a large town the havoc went into overdrive when I was narrowly missed by a moped which was overtaking a car which was overtaking a truck which itself had

31

started the whole overtaking furore by trying to get round a horse and cart. A bus coming the other way was forced off the road on to the verge, but it was also being overtaken by a beat-up yellow taxi which refused to get out the way of the moped/car/truck/horse/cart formation. Just as I was steeling myself for an almighty pile-up, a man shouting into his mobile phone wandered into the path of the taxi. The blasting of horns and yelling was deafening, and I was expecting to witness a spectacular crash, or at the very least, a good punch-up, but somehow everyone survived unscathed and off they all went as if nothing had happened. I had seen some loony driving in my time, but this was the best yet. As I continued on my way through the numerous small towns and villages, this scene, or similar, was repeated approximately every five minutes. I realised this was the Tunisian Highway Code in action, and I'd better get used to it.

Towards dusk the streets of the towns along the route became even busier, and soon all the pavement cafés were heaving with folk sitting around, drinking tiny cups of coffee or mint tea, smoking hookah pipes and chatting away in Arabic. The smell of barbecued meat wafted through the warm air, mopeds buzzed around like motorised insects, while sheep and goats trotted wherever they pleased. Oddly, there seemed to be a fad in this part of the country to hang fluorescent strip-lights in the trees outside the cafés, giving the whole scene a strangely avant-garde look. The only other objects hanging up outside the cafés were dead sheep, skinned and bloodstained, which when illuminated by the weird lighting gave the unpleasant sensation of riding through a huge Damien Hirst installation. But there was something else odd about the scene and it took me a few miles of watching the comings and goings of the cafés before I realised what it was. There was not a single woman in sight. Nowhere! The streets and cafés were full, but only with men. It was a very bizarre sensation and not a little unsettling.

As I moved away from the coast the following day, heading inland towards Douz, the landscape began to change, becoming drier and barren, hinting at the thousands of miles of desert that beckoned. The olive groves ebbed away, to be replaced by an eerie lunar landscape of brown undulating rock formations, providing an ideal setting for the recent *Star Wars* film that had been made here. As I approached the town of Matmata more strangeness abounded, as signs began to appear along the road advertising '*Maisons de Troglodyte*'. Here in this other-worldly setting were hundreds of tiny caves carved into the foot of the hills, home sweet home to the Troglodyte people of southern Tunisia.

Parked along the side of the road was a tour bus, which had deposited a glut of holidaying families to nose around these people's dwellings, although when I passed by they were being hawked mercilessly by a couple of Troglodytes into buying some handmade rugs and earthenware. I was quite intrigued by the idea of these cave homes, but the whole scene was vaguely depressing and I couldn't bring myself to join in. There was something uncomfortably voyeuristic about the way the tourists were poking around, laughing and taking photos of the weird-looking Troglodytes in their funny little homes, and also something grim about the Troglodytes milking the sightseers for everything they could get. It reminded me of my days of itinerant boat-dwelling, floating around the canals of London, being subjected to American tourists pressing their faces against my windows saying, 'Gee! Do you think people really live in there?' I rode on quickly, stopping a little further up the road to admire the view over the mountainous landscape and eat a sandwich.

Within seconds of unwrapping my stick of French bread and peeling open a slice of Laughing Cow cheese, two Troglodyte boys appeared from nowhere and were now standing in front of me, hands outstretched, demanding '*L'argent! Dinars, dinars!*' I gave them a couple of biscuits to get rid of them, but of course it had the opposite effect and they were now barraging me, pulling at my sleeves and attempting to rifle through my luggage. When I was at school, 'Trog' had been the ultimate insult and now I could see why. These two kids were truly the ugliest children I had ever seen, which, I'm sorry to say, did nothing to further their cause. There was no way I was going to be able to sit here in peace; my only option was to up and leave mid-sandwich. I hastily shoved everything back into my panniers while the boys tried to snatch the food out of my hand as I packed, sending chunks of bread flying and smearing processed cheese all over my luggage. Still chewing my last mouthful, I jumped on the bike and made my escape up the road with the mini-Troglodytes in hot pursuit, throwing stones and snarling, '*L'argent! L'argent!*'

I was relieved to get away from the *Maisons de Troglodyte*, and after a few miles twisting through the mountains the road descended into the scrubby fringes of the desert. Signs by the side of the road, in Arabic, French and English, warned of camels crossing, and a few miles later, much to my delight, there they were in the flesh – the ships of the desert, ambling across the dusty land and chewing lazily on clumps of yellow grass. The sight of these gracious animals raised my spirits and reminded me why I was here. At last I was in the desert, where despite my wholly unsuitable pallor I felt strangely at home.

It was late afternoon when I rolled into Douz, and I made my way through the town's ancient twisty streets and past a luscious *palmeraie* to the Hotel Tuareg, to meet up with David. I could already hear the rally as I pulled into the car park; it had taken over the grounds of the hotel and the end-of-day action was in full swing as the mechanics tinkered with the race bikes, cars and trucks to get them ready for the next day's stage. I wandered through this hive of activity, looking for David's truck, passing a German team who were changing a tyre at lightning speed to a deafening thrash metal soundtrack. Next to them the Austrian contingent were playing 'Kung Fu Fighting' almost as loudly, while working their way through a crate of beer, as they replaced a set of clutch plates. The energy of the event was palpable and infectious; it was exciting to be there.

Up in the far corner of the grounds I found David pottering around, setting up camp.

'Hey Lois, you made it!' he greeted me. 'I was going to email you the GPS coordinates but then I remembered – they wouldn't be much use to you, would they?' He grinned knowingly.

'Yes, still on the maps and compass, I'm afraid. Bit of a gadget-phobe, y'know,' I admitted sheepishly, knowing David's enthusiasm for such matters; if a gadget doesn't exist for the job, he'll invent one.

'Well, you found it OK, so make yourself at home, put up your tent anywhere. By the way, this is Reg and Jez.'

'We're the grease monkeys,' said Reg, 'although we haven't had any breakdowns or disasters yet, so we haven't had much to do, not that I'm complaining.'

If you wanted a living, breathing example of chalk and

cheese, here they were. Reg was a big, bluff Brummie, an ex-trade-union shop steward and not afraid to speak his mind on any subject. Jez, in contrast, was a mild-mannered young postman from the West Country with a quiet, gentle way about him. But they each possessed a kind heart and I was immediately made to feel part of the gang.

'Oh yes, and this is John,' added Reg, introducing me to an avuncular white-haired gentleman, reclining in a folding camp chair and sipping whisky from a tin cup.

'Are you in the support team too?'

'No, I've competed in the rally before, but this year I'm just having a holiday riding around Tunisia for a couple of weeks, so I thought I'd tag along for a few days.'

John and I were soon nattering away, as it transpired that, like me, he was a lover of all things watery and boaty (further compounding my theory that bikes and boats go together). We hatched a plan to ride together for the next few days, following David, Reg and Jez in the truck, and meeting up with the rally each night.

Our idle chit-chat was interrupted by the arrival of a small wiry middle-aged woman with frizzy hair who was running towards us across the camp, apparently most excited about her recent purchase of a sleeping bag.

'Hello, hello! Look! I found one, at the market in Douz!' she screeched to no one in particular, waving the sleeping bag around above her head.

The others made appreciative but non-committal noises, except for Reg, who groaned audibly, rolled his eyes and quickly made himself busy doing something in the back of the truck. Whoever this woman was, she settled down on a camping chair and carried on with the story of the sleeping bag purchase. Nobody made any show of an introduction, so I took it upon myself, and inquired if she was part of the rally's entourage.

'Oh no, no, not really!' she replied. 'Well, it's a bit funny, but I'm not with the rally, well, I am now, but I didn't mean to be!' She let out a shriek of laughter before offering her hand. 'I'm Lillian.'

'Hi, so how come you're here?'

'Oh my God, it's so crazy, I mean my life has just turned upside down in the last few days! I live in London and I was going to visit my aunt in Spain, I'm Spanish you see, and at the airport I met these two guys from Scotland, Andrew and Douglas, who are racing their motorbikes in the rally. I don't know why but I just started talking to them in the bar and we were having such fun, and they said, "Don't visit your aunt in Spain, come to the rally with us." So I did! Can you believe it? Sometimes you just have to do things, don't you?'

'Er, yes, I guess you do, but . . .'

'So here I am and I don't have any camping stuff, so I've been sleeping in Douglas and Andrew's tent with them, and I've just met all these lovely people on the rally, everyone's been so nice . . .'

I heard Reg splutter in the back of the truck.

'. . . And it's just amazing, I mean I don't know anything about motorbikes. I haven't been on holiday for years and I've had such a terrible time over the last few years, what with my brother and everything, but never mind about that . . . well, now I'm here in Tunisia, it's just so wacky, but sometimes you have to do something totally mad, don't you think?'

I couldn't help but admire her impulsive, if not eccentric nature, so I nodded eagerly in affirmation.

37

Towards dusk the racers began to show up, rolling into camp, tired and dusty but exhilarated from a day of desert racing. I was particularly looking forward to meeting Douglas and Andrew, two men who could change a strange woman's holiday plans at a moment's notice and get her to share a tent with them. They turned out to be another case of chalk and cheese, with Andrew being the easygoing friendly one and Douglas making a bid for the title of World's Angriest Scotsman, appearing to be in a state of permanent black rage for no apparent reason. He spent a lot of time banging around in the back of David's truck, rifling through boxes of tools and shouting and swearing, but as nobody could understand what he was saying due to his thick Glaswegian accent his ranting went largely ignored. Occasionally Lillian would glance in his direction with a worried look and whisper to me, 'He's in the Marines, you know. I think something awful has happened to him.'

Fortunately there was one female rider in the team to balance out the testosterone overload, something which David was also grateful for.

'Lois, Tamsin. Tamsin, Lois,' he said, pointing to a girl lying flat on her back on the ground, covered in dust and groaning cheerfully about her aching muscles, but still managing to offer me a friendly greeting. 'It's always good when there are girls on the rally,' David added, 'it makes things a bit more civilised.'

'What? You mean like her?' Reg grunted under his breath, jerking a thumb in Lillian's direction, to which David responded with diplomatic silence and a slight lifting of the eyebrows.

Douglas and Andrew went off to get drunk at the hotel bar, and Reg and Jez got busy tinkering with the rally bikes, making sure they'd be ready to race the next morning. The rest of us sat around on upturned crates, whiling away the evening in the time-honoured fashion of yakking, eating and drinking. After the awkwardness of the ferry journey and the run-in with the junior Troglodytes, it felt good to be among sociable, like-minded folk. I decided to make the most of my few days with these affable companions before I once again set off to tackle the mean streets of North Africa alone. As I wriggled into my sleeping bag that night, I had to admit that my cultural acclimatisation still had some way to go.

I was dimly aware of the racers roaring off at some ungodly hour the following morning, and when I crawled out of my tent most of the camp followers and support crews had already packed up and gone. Fortunately David took a more relaxed approach to such matters: after a couple of leisurely coffees we loaded up the truck and with me and John on our bikes and the others in the truck, we prepared to set off to the next campsite.

'We're going to a place called Ksar Ghilane.' John showed me on my map. 'It's a little oasis and there's a Roman fort there too. It's only about sixty miles away but about half of it's on dirt tracks. How are you in the sand?'

'Er, well, I've only ever ridden in sand a couple of times, so, I . . . um . . . it's . . .' I petered out, feeling rather foolish that here I was, supposedly about to ride across the Sahara and ultimately the length of Africa, when in fact I had virtually no experience of sand riding, and on the occasion that I had attempted it in Morocco, when I wasn't fainting or throwing up, my performance had been anything but adept.

'Well, I'll have a go, but I won't be winning any races,' I summed up.

John made a good show of hiding his misgivings, but I could see his face clouding over with doubt, which only added to my concerns. Now, as well as my usual fears of getting heatstroke or falling off in the sand, I was worrying about spoiling his fun too.

The top speed of David's truck only touched forty-five miles an hour, so John and I decided to make our own way and meet them at the campsite. Our route took us back along the highway that I had ridden the previous day, before turning down the Pipeline Road, a dead straight gravel track that led south into the desert. The going was easy enough, like any well-maintained dirt road, but occasionally we encountered stretches of deep, soft sand that had been blown across the track, and my back wheel slithered around as I gripped the handlebars and hoped for the best. I was following along behind John, trying to keep up with his huge 950cc machine as he blasted through these sand drifts, but a couple of times I came a cropper when my bike slid out from under me as it lost traction in the soft sand. On both occasions John turned round to help me pick up my heavily laden bike, which just added to my feelings of incompetence.

'The only way to ride this stuff is to stand up and give it some throttle,' he told me with saintly patience. 'If you feel your bike wobbling around, that's the only way to save it – by using power to get through. It goes against the grain, because of course if you're wobbling around your instinct is to slow down, but that's the worst thing you can do.'

I listened and nodded, feeling like a total idiot, and trying not to think about the 2,000 miles of desert that lay ahead of me. What on earth had I been thinking? I was ridiculously inexperienced to be attempting such a journey. Then I remembered Austin's sage words and I applied them to my current situation: the only way to prepare for a ride across the Sahara is to ride across the Sahara!

With that thought in my mind, I made the last few miles to Ksar Ghilane with no more falls, and we were duly rewarded for our labours. It was a serene little beauty spot on the edge of the Grand Erg Oriental, the sea of dunes that spills over from Algeria into southern Tunisia. Surrounded by palm trees and a couple of shacks selling ice-cold Cokes was a natural pool of warm water, in which the early arrivals from the rally were already whiling away the afternoon under a cloudless sky. Clusters of fresh dates hung tantalisingly from the palm trees, and camels could be seen striding across the sand against a backdrop of rolling orange dunes, with the crumbling ruins of the ancient fort in the distance. I was in desert bliss.

Lillian was equally thrilled by the postcard location and came running towards us in her swimsuit, waving a towel.

'Oh hello, hello! Come along, let's go for a dip before dinner!'

John sloped off to set up his tent, and Tamsin and I were rounded up for pool detail. The three of us sank into the heavenly warm water, accompanied by Lillian's shrieks of delight and a running commentary on her day's adventures spent hitching a ride in the Swedish team's support truck. Through the palm trees I saw David's truck trundling into camp in a cloud of dust and a while later he came to round us up for dinner.

'Where are we going to get dinner round here?' I asked Tamsin as we dried off.

'There's a catering truck that travels along with the rally.'

'Oh my God, have you not seen it?' yelped Lillian. 'The

41

food's terrible! And the people running it are really weird. They're German!' she added in an unsuccessful attempt at a whisper.

Lillian's assessment of the catering unit was correct on all counts. Parked in the far corner of the camp was a colossal black Tatra lorry with steam belching out from a greasy chimney and the steady rumble of a generator powering the industrial cooking equipment. There was something oddly sinister about the truck; maybe it was the way its ugliness jarred against the natural beauty of the surrounding desert, or how it loomed over the gathering of brightly coloured race vehicles with its oppressive Soviet styling. But it was probably more to do with the terrifying army of hard-faced women that stood behind the serving counter with their arms folded over their surgically enhanced breasts and a look on their faces that would put you off your food, if indeed it had been edible in the first place. Complete with bleached blonde hair, facial piercings and diamond-studded teeth, they looked to me as if they'd been pensioned off by the German porn industry some years ago and were now bitterly resigned to slopping cabbage and *Bratwürst* into tin bowls for the rest of their days. The entire operation was ruled over by their diminutive ringmaster, who was straight out of a 70s skin flick with his greying mullet and gold jewellery. Together they ran the operation with an iron (or possibly latex) fist, doling out the meagre portions of tasteless food with Teutonic accuracy and turning hardcore desert racers who dared to ask for second helpings into quivering nervous wrecks.

Over our unpalatable dinner we shared stories of our day's events and plotted tomorrow's journey.

'Next stop is a place called Bir Aouine,' said David, checking his itinerary. 'It's about a hundred miles away in the middle of nowhere, there's nothing there at all, just an airstrip and a hole where water comes out of the ground.'

I looked at the map and it took a while to locate the tiny blue dot that marked the availability of water amid a huge expanse of yellow.

'And it's off-road all the way,' added John.

'Yeah, it's piste to start with, then across the dunes.'

I gulped inwardly at this news and made a mental note to go easy on the German lager; a hangover was the last thing I would need tomorrow morning.

Unfortunately a good night's sleep was not on the cards for any of us. As if having been served raw sausages and over-boiled vegetables by a poor man's Pamela Anderson in the Sahara wasn't bizarre enough, we were entertained into the small hours by the Polish rally team, who started up their welding and grinding equipment around dusk, and wound up their evening of toil with a rousing sing-along of Polski folk songs. As I zipped up my tent I caught a glimpse of one of their mechanics striding along in his greasy overalls, singing heartily with an enormous axle slung over his shoulder, like something from a Soviet propaganda poster. When I did finally manage to doze off, it was only until around 4.30 a.m., when the catering team cranked their generator into life, no doubt to start boiling the vegetables in time for that night's dinner.

'You two had better stick with us today,' said David to me and John the next morning. 'We have to go through a military area and I've got a permit for the rally.' To make us appear more legit, David handed us each an official rally sticker, bearing the legend 'Off-Road Pro', which only succeeded in making me feel like a complete fraud. But nevertheless I peeled off the backing and applied it to the front of my bike, and off we went, deeper into the desert.

I don't know what happened that day – maybe that sticker had some magic effect, or maybe it was a simple case of sink or swim. But I swum like I had never swum before. It was as if a switch had been flicked and suddenly it all came together; I was flying along across the sand, keeping up with John and loving every moment of it. But more importantly, I wasn't wilting in the desert heat, or even feeling in the least bit weary; if anything it was quite the opposite. Any nervousness had completely disappeared, to be replaced with utter exhilaration, and as we roared across the desert I relished every dune, every rock, every grain of sand! I knew I was experiencing a significant turning point, and for the first time since leaving home I felt nothing but pure excitement about the Saharan adventure that lay ahead. It dawned on me that I had spent the last few months chewed up and dragged down with fears about this trip, but now here I was, completely free of any anxiety. The sensation was almost like an artificial high, and I realised how easily desert riding could become a serious addiction. Even if it only lasted today, I knew I had experienced an epiphany.

'Wow!' said John, when we stopped at a track junction to wait for the truck. 'You seem to have got into the swing of it!' I was riding on air.

Bir Aouine was a strange place, although David was right, it wasn't really a place at all, just a cracked, sun-baked landing strip in an endless expanse of empty desert. There wasn't even so much as a dune or a palm tree on which to focus one's eye, so I was quite surprised to find out that the rally would be having a rest day here and staying for two nights. The following day the bleakness of our surroundings was further exacerbated by the most unlikely occurrence – a rainstorm. Cries of, 'Rain! In the Sahara! I don't believe it!' echoed around the camp in various European languages as everybody rushed into their tents or trucks. The downpour was accompanied by furious winds that lashed through the camp, tugging at guy ropes and sending people chasing across the sand in pursuit of airborne clothes, runaway race cards and wisps of errant toilet paper. Then a rumour swept through the camp: 'The Germans have got Mars Bars!' And all attempts at rescuing windswept personal belongings were abandoned as a swell of wet, weary sugar-deficient rallyists stormed the catering truck to fork out one Euro per Mars Bar to the sour Krauts, who were clearly relishing their hold over their captive market.

By the end of the day the rain had subsided but the winds had now whipped up a vicious sandstorm, which resulted in the oddly entertaining sight of hundreds of people queuing for their dinner wearing motorcycle goggles. We all awoke the next morning relieved to be moving on and cheered to find that the Sahara had made a return to form with a dazzling display of blue skies and scorching sun. The day's stage took us back to the relative civilisation of Ksar Ghilane, but after a dip in the pool and an ice-cold Coke, John and I decided the time had come to get going; I on my way to Algeria and him back home to England. We bade fond farewells to everyone, with promises to stay in touch, and with cries of 'Go for it!' and 'Ride dangerously!' we were sent on our way.

John and I rode together back up the Pipeline Road before reaching the tarmac, where we would each go our separate ways. After we had shaken hands, wished each other good luck, and I had thanked him for his gallant companionship, he disappeared into the evening and I took the opportunity to nip behind a large rock by the side of the road to answer the call of nature. But I barely had time to get into position before an old Tunisian man bearing a silver tray complete with teapot and tiny cups appeared out of nowhere, hobbling towards me and calling out, 'Tea! Tea! You like to drink tea, Madame?'

I wanted to explain that, as he might be able to ascertain from my current position, the intake of liquid was the last thing I had in mind at this present moment, but as usual, my French failed me. As I made my ungainly retreat and hopped back on the bike, I suddenly realised what it was the rally provided – protection. You got all the fun of riding in the desert and travelling in exotic lands, but without any of the hassle and the hawkers. I had effectively been sealed from the outside world for the last few days. I could certainly see the appeal, and I liked to think I would have a go at a desert rally one day, but I knew it wasn't what I had come to Africa for this time. My few days travelling with the rally had been a great experience, but for better or for worse – I was out on my own again now, back on the road with the Troglodytes and the tea-sellers, and only my wits to protect me.

THREE

After my desert-riding epiphany in Tunisia, I was now bursting with enthusiasm for the Algerian leg of my journey which would take me deep into the heart of the Sahara. However, there was one element that was slightly dampening my zeal. In 2003, after thirty-two European tourists had been kidnapped in the Algerian Sahara by an Islamic militant group, the authorities had effectively banned all independent travel. A visit to the embassy in London had confirmed that I wouldn't be allowed even to set foot in the country without being accompanied by an official Algerian guide. No guide, no visa. End of story.

As someone who shudders at the thought of 'guided' anything, I had hummed and hawed over this conundrum as I pored over my maps, plotting my African itinerary. I was desperately keen to see Algeria and to take this classic route straight across the Sahara, the same route that Theresa Wallach and Florence Blenkiron had travelled all those years before, but the idea of travelling for several weeks with a paid chaperone was not only an unappealing prospect, but also out of my league money-wise. However, after a bit of digging around and cold calling, I was put in touch with Jacques, a Belgian guy who was driving his Toyota Land Cruiser along the same route in mid-November, along with his girlfriend Josianne and their English cousin, the unlikely named Angel. They were hiring a guide through an Algerian travel agency and were more than happy for me to ride along with them and share the fee.

After leaving the rally I headed west to the border town of Nefta, where I would meet my new travelling companions. These final miles in Tunisia took me on an otherworldly ride across the Chott el Jerid, a vast, dry salt lake that glittered in ethereal shades of pink and purple as the sunlight glinted off the salt crystals. Far away in the distance, in the middle of the lake bed, I could just make out the bleached metal carcass of a 1960s bus that had been driven across the Chott and abandoned where it now stood, its paintwork long since stripped by decades of sun and salt.

I was a little wary about hanging around one of the border towns, which are so often shifty places, full of black marketeers and pushy money-changers, but I was relieved to arrive in Nefta to find a quiet, dusty little place. There were a few hotels, restaurants and the usual collection of white-robed men squatting on their haunches in the shade, drinking tea and passing the time of day. I was in the unenviable position of having to find a hotel for three people I didn't know and of whose budget I had no idea. I made a couple of laps of the main drag checking out the local hostelries, but they were either unfeasibly pricey or unbearably squalid. I couldn't decide which was worse: booking three strangers into some swanky place that was way beyond their means, or consigning them to a night in a flea-infested bunk-house. In the end I decided to go for the latter option; if they're intending on driving and camping across the Sahara they must be pretty tough cookies, I reasoned, and I felt sure they could handle a night of roughing it.

I called Jacques with directions to the Hotel Medina and settled in to wait for them, giving me plenty of time to inspect my insalubrious surroundings. Every wall, floor and surface in the hotel was coated with a veneer of griminess, which along with the cracked windowpanes and stained mattresses gave the whole place the air of a crime scene. The shower was a trickling lead pipe sticking out of the wall and a visit to the communal toilets required Wellington boots, not to mention a brave heart. The other occupants of the hotel were gangs of manual workers, who were sleeping like sardines, ten to a room. The only reason I knew this was because I caught a glimpse of them through a half-broken door, snoozing among piles of tools and battered leather boots. After a couple of hours I saw the Belgian Land Cruiser pull up outside and ran downstairs to meet my new travelling companions, trying not to touch the sticky banisters as I clattered down the steps.

'Lois, hi!' said a voice from the cab.

'Hello! You must be Jacques – glad you found it all right.'

Jacques stepped outside and shook my hand in an oddly formal manner. I guessed him to be about my age, maybe a bit older, but he looked quite serious. He was short, dark and wore old-fashioned horn-rimmed spectacles, which along with his khaki trousers and photographer's jacket lent him the air of a learned explorer from the colonial era. Josianne, his girlfriend greeted me with the standard Euro double kiss. She was dark-haired, petite and smiley, not to mention a dead ringer for Catherine Deneuve. Thankfully they both spoke excellent English, and as their cousin, Angel, was also English, from Basingstoke, it was decided there and then that it would be the team language.

'Yeah, whatever, it doesn't bother me either way,' said Angel, sliding out of the car and stretching. 'I can speak French and English. Anyway, hi, I'm Angel,' she said, choosing neither the handshake nor the double kiss, but instead a little wave of her right hand. I would never have guessed she was Jacques's cousin. She was blonde, pretty and a little on the plump side, but in a cute, baby fat kind of way, rather than having eaten too many Big Macs. She was wearing a pair of zip-off trousers, white Birkenstocks and a tight pink T-shirt with the word 'Babe' emblazoned in silver glitter across her chest. Her wrists were swathed in various charity rubber bands, declaring her allegiance to making poverty history, curing breast cancer and fighting AIDS.

The four of us set about unloading the car, and the general mood was cheerful and light-hearted, all of us animated about our imminent desert adventure, but as we climbed the stairs to our rooms I could see the smile on Josianne's face slipping away as she registered the awfulness of their surroundings.

'Um, er, sorry about the hotel, I know it's not exactly luxurious, but the decent ones were really expensive, and I didn't want to make you have to spend loads of money,' I apologised awkwardly.

'Oh, it's OK, it's only for one night, and we'll be out of here first thing in the morning,' said Jacques with resolute practicality.

I could see Josianne looking around with a mixture of disgust and dismay, and to be honest, I felt pretty much the

50

same way. Angel hadn't said anything yet, but she didn't look exactly overjoyed.

'I'm sorry, I wasn't sure what . . .' I trailed off, knowing that I had made the wrong decision in checking into the Hotel Medina, and kicking myself for getting off to a bad start with my new travelling companions.

'Oh well! Never mind, it's all part of the African experience!' said Josianne, forcing a reassuring smile and lighting a morale-boosting cigarette.

'Yeah, don't worry about it,' said Angel. 'I'm sure we're gonna see much worse than this over the next few weeks. This is nothing compared to some of the places I stayed in Mali. After all, TIA,' she said with a knowing look.

I wasn't quite sure what she meant, or if I had heard her correctly.

'Sorry, TIA?'

'This Is Africa,' she said with a laugh.

I was relieved the situation had been saved with good humour, and after unloading the car we went into town for dinner, putting off our return to the Hotel Medina for as long as possible.

'Have you been to Africa before, Lois?' Jacques asked as we tucked into our distinctly un-Tunisian meal of margherita pizzas.

'Only to Morocco for a couple of weeks,' I replied, deciding not to dwell on that story too much, 'so this is all new to me. What about you three?'

'Yeah, I've been to Morocco too, on a cycling holiday, years ago, when I was at university. Ever since then I've wanted to drive across the Sahara.'

'I travelled overland to Timbuktu,' said Angel.

51

'That must have been fun – were you on your own, or . . .'

'It was on an overland truck, there were, like, fifteen of us, it was really cool, but like really humbling at the same time, y'know, seeing how people live in poverty and everything.'

'I've never been to Africa,' said Josianne. 'This is my first time.'

'Don't worry, it's not as scary as it seems,' Angel reassured her. 'You'll get used to it.'

'I'm not worried, Angel,' said Josianne. 'Do I look worried?' she asked me, sparking up a Marlboro Light.

'Er, no, you all seem like extremely well-adjusted, unworried people!' I said, trying to smooth over any ruffled feathers.

'So, Lois, you're going all the way to Cape Town?' Jacques said, quickly changing the subject. 'Are you going through Cameroon?'

'Yes, after Algeria I'm going to Niger, then Nigeria, and then I'll enter Cameroon in the north.'

'That's what I thought; we're going to Cameroon too, that's the route that we'll be taking . . .'

'We're visiting a friend of mine, a guy I met in Mali, he's doing some aid work out there,' interrupted Angel. 'He's really cool.'

'Er, yes,' Jacques continued, 'so you can travel with us until Cameroon if you want.'

'Oh right, thanks, yeah, well, that would be nice,' I said vaguely. I wasn't sure what I wanted to do yet, and I was reluctant to make too many concrete plans, but they seemed like pleasant enough people.

'I think it would be good to travel together in Nigeria; it's only a couple of days but I've heard very bad things about it,' said Josianne.

'Yeah, me too,' I agreed. 'My dad's wife is Nigerian, and even she thinks I shouldn't go there!'

'Guys, chill out!' said Angel. 'When I was travelling on the overland truck, everyone was getting, like, so stressed about . . .'

'OK, let's get going, shall we?' interrupted Josianne, stubbing out her cigarette on her plate next to her rejected pizza crusts. 'We've got an early start in the morning.'

'Yes, let's cross the Sahara first, before we start worrying about Nigeria,' added Jacques.

He was right; it seemed like tempting fate to make any post-Sahara plans at this stage and we all fell silent for a moment, remembering the enormity of our imminent venture, all except for Angel who continued with her tales of humbling derring-do.

The 5 a.m. call to prayer from the nearby mosque woke me the next morning before my alarm and I lay in the dark in my sleeping bag, listening to the repetitive chanting and ruminating over the forthcoming leg of my journey. This was the big push, across the Sahara desert. Tunisia had been a good warm-up, but as far as Muslim North Africa went, it was an easy, relaxed country to travel in, on a par with Morocco, and similarly geared up to the European tourists who treated both countries as their desert playgrounds, taking camel treks or tearing across the dunes in their 4 × 4s. Algeria would be a whole different ball game: the riding would be tougher, covering hundreds of miles on sandy pistes and rocky tracks. The temperature would rise as we travelled ever deeper into the Sahara, and as a white woman riding her own motorcycle, I wondered how I would be received by the strict Islamic

Algerians. All this unknown territory was both a thrilling and a daunting prospect.

Dawn washed gently over the black sky as we crawled out of our beds and made our way out into the street. There were already a few men up and about, packing crates of dates into a cart pulled by a somnolent donkey. A couple of mopeds flitted past as we loaded our respective vehicles while cramming in a caffeine- and sugar-heavy breakfast of coffee and sickly almond pastries from the tiny grocery store next door. Jacques was making some final adjustments to his roof-rack while the girls arranged the luggage in the back of the vehicle in an impressively orderly fashion. I performed my routine checks of oil, chain and tyre pressure, and then my favourite act that signifies the new phase of a journey: I re-folded my map to show Algeria, just a big empty space with a couple of wiggly lines across it.

'OK, are you ready?' said Jacques, as he climbed behind the wheel. I gulped down the dregs of my coffee, jumped on the bike and followed them out of town towards the Algerian border.

The morning was pale and cool, and as we travelled east the first glimpses of sunlight broke out from the overcast sky to illuminate the vast expanse of the *chott* in the distance. To our left, on the outskirts of the town, was a huge *palmeraie*, the green of the fronds muted by a cloud of mist and sand that hung above the trees, and as I rode along behind the car, taking in the still beauty of the desert morning, I revelled in the unpredictable nature of my journey, wondering how the next few weeks would work out for us all.

I must admit I was glad to discover that these new travelling companions of mine were no hard-bitten, desert tough guys, but were about as green as me when it came to Saharan travel.

54

Jacques, a cartographer for the Belgian Institut Géographique Nationale, was the oldest of the party at thirty-five, and this expedition had been his idea, fulfilling his long-held desire to drive across the Sahara. Josianne was younger than him at twenty-nine and had taken a sabbatical from her job as a translator to make this journey. As for Angel, she had just left university and had some vague ideas that she had shared with me over dinner about working in eco-tourism and setting up a yoga retreat in India. At twenty-three, she was the youngest of the group and appeared to have very little in common with the other two except for the fact that she was Jacques's cousin. We made for a curious set of travelling companions and I hoped that we would surmount the challenges and strains that a journey across the Sahara would inevitably bring.

Like border posts the world over, the Algerian entry point of Taleb Larbi was a bleak, uninspiring place, comprising nothing more than a row of squat concrete buildings and a barrier across the road. We parked by the side of the road and hung about, waiting to be approached by someone claiming to be our guide, and discussed the few pros and many cons of travelling with an enforced escort.

'Well, you never know,' I said, trying to come up with something positive, 'he might be some wise old nomad of the desert who'll share the ancient secrets of the Sahara with us, or something . . .'

'I wonder if he'll speak English.'

'No, probably not, just French and Arabic, but then at least we can talk about him in English,' said Josianne with a grin.

'Josie! That's not very nice,' said Angel. 'We must treat him with respect. Just because his culture is different from ours doesn't make him an inferior person.'

'I didn't say that it did, Angel,' she said, and I could tell she was trying to keep the snappiness out of her voice.

'How's your Arabic?' I asked everyone, moving on to a new subject.

'*Salaam aleikum, wa aleikum as-salaam, shukran . . .*' Angel began reeling off a list of useful phrases before anyone else had a chance to answer. I had written out a similar list but my attempts to memorise them over the last few weeks had been stymied by the traditional English malady that strikes every time I try to learn a foreign language. Angel obviously had no such trouble.

'Very impressive!' I said when she had finished, but I noticed Josianne rolling her eyes at Jacques, whose own facial expression remained resolutely blank.

'Yeah, well, when I was in Mauritania, on the overland trip, I made an effort to speak Arabic to the people, but no one else bothered, and I thought that was really rude, y'know. I think you've got to at least try, don't you agree? English people are so arrogant about their language, they just expect everyone to speak it . . .'

Her lecture was interrupted as we caught sight of a tall, lanky young man dressed head to toe in Adidas bounding towards us, speaking loud, rapid Arabic into a mobile phone that made my old Nokia look like an ancient relic. He came to a halt in front of us, flipping the phone shut and flashing a grin as white and shiny as his trainers.

'Hello! Hello! You are Jacques! Are you Jacques? I am Hamid! I am your guide! Welcome! Welcome to Algeria!' he cried, in heavily accented English.

'*Salaam aleikum,*' we said, although Angel said it loudest and in an unintentional comedy accent which failed to disguise her

56

Home Counties origins and just served to make her sound like an Arabic Sloane Ranger. But our greeting was instantly silenced as Hamid's phone burst back into life with a display of flashing lights and the distinctly un-Islamic ring tone of Céline Dion wailing the theme from *Titanic*.

'Oh, please, sorry, please, excuse me,' he apologised, before silencing Céline to launch into another rapid-fire exchange in his mother tongue. The rest of us shot each other surprised and amused glances at the arrival of our most unlikely Saharan guide, who from first impressions owed more to Ali G than to the ancient Tuareg nomads of the desert.

'I am very sorry, please come with me now,' apologised Hamid, terminating his phone call.

We duly followed him to the immigration office, where we joined a slow-moving queue of robed Arab men carrying sacks of onions. The wait provided us with an opportunity to make our introductions.

'So, Lois, it is you who ride this big bike, yes?'

'Yes, it is.'

'You do not get tired?'

'Um, well, not really . . . well, sometimes, I suppose, but it's not really that big.'

The day was warming up now and the temperature in the windowless room was already stifling. I took off my jacket and Hamid looked at me surprised.

'Ah, under your big jacket you look like real woman!' he exclaimed.

I forced a polite smile but inwardly groaned at the quality of banter that was clearly going to accompany my ride across Algeria.

'Hamid, would you prefer to speak French instead of

57

English?' asked Josianne. 'We can all speak a bit of French.'

For the first time since arriving, Hamid's face clouded over.

'No. I like to try speak English. Not French. The Algerians, they do not like to speak French.'

'Er, OK, fine,' we replied. Recalling a few details of the Battle of Algiers and the bloody divorce between Algeria and its former rulers, I wasn't surprised he didn't like speaking French. We had only been here a few minutes and had already made our first cultural clanger, much to the dismay of Angel.

'Josie, he's hardly going to want to speak the language of his oppressors, is he?' she reprimanded her.

Warming up with the heat of the day, Angel shrugged off her fleece to reveal a different T-shirt from yesterday, this time bearing the unlikely slogan 'Porn Star' in pink diamanté. A more unsuitable item of clothing to accompany her entry into Algeria I could not imagine, and I wondered if she was wearing it on purpose, in some sort of ironic post-feminist, anti-Islam stance. But she was too guileless to make such a conscious statement; in her eyes it was just a clean T-shirt. I could only hope that Hamid's English vocabulary didn't stretch to such subject matters.

'Yes, I want to speak English,' Hamid was saying to the others. 'I want to study in the USA. I am student now in Algiers, I study chemical engineering, but I must do more study when I finish.'

'Oh, so you're not a full-time guide?'

Hamid faltered slightly, maybe realising that his allegiance to the world of chemical engineering was not exactly inspiring his clients with much confidence about his ability to lead them across the Sahara.

'I live in Algiers at my university, but my home, my family, is in Tamanrasset, in the desert. My father has friend who is owner of guide agency, so sometimes I work for him too.'

While we waited for our passports to be stamped, I probed Hamid gently for any amusing tales of hapless-tourists-in-desert-drama type situations. I wasn't trying to catch him out, just make friendly conversation, but his apparent lack of any amusing, or even not so amusing yarns caused me to wonder if he had indeed *ever* guided any hapless tourists in the desert at all. Well, the good news was that his chance had finally arrived, and by the time he waved us goodbye at the Niger border, 1,600 miles away, I feared he would have tales a plenty.

'Here is your passports,' said Hamid, handing them back to us.

'Oh, I think I've got yours, Angel,' I said as I opened it up to find a picture of a coy-looking Angel pouting at me. I also noticed that her real name was Angela, but I thought better of mentioning this. In my limited experience of such matters, I have found that people who make up names for themselves rarely like to make light of it.

The Algerian entry procedures dragged on and on, taking us in and out of the baking, cell-like offices. After the tedious checking of our visas by immigration, there followed the even lengthier customs declaration, helped along by Hamid whispering in our ears, 'You must say no GPS, no binoculars, you must say no, it is illegal in Algeria.' Fortunately this didn't require any acting skills from me, as my luggage contained neither. Then there was the declaration of our finances, where Hamid encouraged us to claim that the collective amount of cash in our wallets totalled fifty Euros.

'We change more money in next town,' he muttered. 'I know man there, he give good rate.'

59

This plan was met with approval from Angel, who assured us that the exchange rates at borders were always a rip-off.

The next concrete building contained a very jovial doctor, whose little room was actually quite homely, strewn with ancient manila files, dog-eared pictures of his many children and scaremongering posters warning us of the gruesome diseases that awaited us in Algeria. He inspected our yellow fever certificates, scribbled something in a leather-bound book and sent us on our way to our final halt, the police station, where Hamid was required to have every inch of our route approved by the chief of police. The only trouble was that the chief was on a very long lunch break. The heat of the midday sun was now quite unbearable, so we waited for him in the relative cool of the police station lobby, where a collection of 'Wanted' posters stared out at us with dark, empty eyes.

A couple of hours later the screeching of tyres and barking of dogs marked the return of the chief of police and we snapped out of our heat-dazed reverie. We staggered to our feet as he marched past us in a self-important flurry of gold braid, clanking medals and pomade. Hamid rushed after him, almost begging and scraping, and it was painful to see the pecking order being acted out so publicly. A junior officer appeared from behind a closed door and the three of them launched into what sounded to my ignorant ears to be a blazing argument. Their tones of voice seemed aggressive and there was a fair bit of shouting and gesticulating, but throughout the entire exchange all three men routinely touched each other; sometimes just putting a hand on the other's arm but often holding hands for long periods of time while they yelled at one another. It was quite bewildering and I wondered what those 'body language experts' who cod-analyse photos of celebrity couples in gossip magazines would have made of it.

Eventually, five long hours after we had arrived at the border, we were fully legit, and free to go. Hamid seemed relieved, but still flustered, as he left the police station clutching a pile of paperwork.

'Everything OK?' I asked him as he climbed into the passenger seat of Jacques's Land Cruiser.

'Yes, yes, all OK, it is good. No problem.'

We bumped our way across the dirt courtyard and out on to the road. I was too busy getting excited about finally being given the run of Algeria to notice Jacques's sudden erratic driving.

'Lois! Come here! This way, this way!' Hamid was shouting out of the passenger window, waving his arms urgently. Jacques made a sharp swing to the left and as I followed suit I saw why. A welcome party of stone-throwing children awaited us on the verge of the road. I shielded myself on the other side of the Land Cruiser as a couple of their better-aimed missiles clunked against the side of the car.

'Three years ago, a tourist, he hits five children here, he kill them,' explained Hamid later when we stopped to fill up with petrol in the nearby town of El Oued. 'So now they throw stones at the foreign cars.'

We kept up a brisk pace from El Oued, passing through the grimy, industrialised towns of northern Algeria. Our route took us south along a road running parallel with the Libyan border, following an oil pipeline and a row of pylons that stalked the highway, marching across the dusty plains and dominating the landscape. It wasn't an attractive part of the country, and I longed for the wild, open spaces and endless sand seas of the real Sahara that awaited us a few hundred miles away. We were heading for the town of Djanet, six days' ride away in the south-east corner of the country, along a road that was marked as tarmac on my Michelin map. But it was after Djanet that the real action would begin, when we would cut west across the desert to the ancient oasis town of Tamanrasset. It was a 300-mile journey on tracks marked as enticing dotted lines on the map. Their crooked scrawl crossed vast swathes of empty sand, depicted as tantalising patches of bright yellow, before winding their way over the Hoggar Mountains, whose 6,000-feet peaks burst out from the yellow flatness in an incongruous blot of brown, the only high ground for hundreds of miles in any direction. It was going to be an exciting ride.

Dusk was almost upon us and Jacques pulled over at the side of the road. We'd travelled about 150 miles and had managed to break away from the urban north into wild open country, although the electricity line still dogged the road.

'We will stop now and make our camp,' said Hamid. 'I think I must drive for you on sand,' he said to Jacques. 'You do not have experience of drive in desert, no?'

Jacques looked more than taken aback and I could see him struggling to stay calm.

'No, Hamid, I haven't driven in the desert, you're right, but that's what I've come here to do, to drive across the Sahara.'

'But it is late and almost night, I think it is best if I drive now, I show you and then maybe tomorrow you try.'

'I think I can manage.'

'Oh, Jacques, just let him do it,' said Josianne from the back seat. 'We don't want anything to go wrong.'

Jacques responded by accelerating away in silence, peeling off the tarmac and zooming across the empty plain. I followed in hot pursuit, until he came to a halt out of sight of the road and out of earshot of the buzzing pylons.

'I think this will do for tonight,' he said coolly, stepping out of the car.

Hamid was giggling. 'I think Jacques he wants to be rally driver!' he tittered, but no one made any response.

'OK, we will make camp here,' said Hamid, 'but first we make fire. Which way is the wind?'

I wet my right index finger in my mouth and held it up in the air, using the method of figuring out wind direction that my parents had shown me as a kid on camping holidays. Hamid burst out laughing.

'What is this you do with your hand?' he asked, looking at me as if I was a simpleton.

'I'm testing the wind direction.'

'Ha ha! No, no, no!' He reached down to the ground and took a pinch of sand which he released into the warm evening air. It was instantly whisked away in the gentle breeze, disappearing in an easterly direction. 'That is how we do it in the Sahara.'

We got busy gathering up dead branches of the straggly bushes that were dotted around the sand, then made our campfire, set up our tents and prepared a meal of vegetables and pasta.

'Who does this land belong to?' Angel asked Hamid, as we waited for the pan of water to come to the boil.

'Uh . . . I am sorry. Please, I do not understand?'

'Who does this land belong to, who owns this land?'

'Y'know, does it belong to the Algerian government?' I

chipped in. 'Or the oil company? Who is the owner of this land here, where we are now?'

Hamid looked confused by the question, and it wasn't only due to linguistic difficulties.

'This place here? It is just the desert, it does not belong . . .'

'Someone must own it,' Angel persisted, but the conversation had already reached stalemate due to Hamid's complete lack of understanding of our European fixation with property, ownership and boundaries.

'In England, every single inch of land is owned by someone, or some company or organisation,' I explained to him, but he just looked at me nonplussed.

'It is just . . . the desert,' he said with a shrug.

After dinner Hamid shared his first secret of the Sahara with us.

'I show you how we wash dishes in the desert,' he announced. 'First, you take the sand,' he said, scooping up a small handful, 'then you take little water, but just a little, and you do this.'

He mixed the two ingredients together on the plate to form a paste and rubbed away until the sand had become a dry lump, absorbing all traces of the food.

'Then you throw away and take new sand, just sand, no water this time, and do it again.'

He rubbed the dry sand around the plate a few times before brushing it off and showing us the final result. The dry sand had acted like the rinse cycle, leaving the plastic plate sparklingly clean and dry, with not a morsel of food or grain of sand left behind.

'Amazing!' I exclaimed, and the four of us set about washing up the pans, plates and cutlery with more enthusiasm than is usually associated with the task.

'Now, I make tea,' announced Hamid, and from his

backpack he produced two tiny blue enamel teapots, four shot glasses, a bag of tea leaves and a massive amount of sugar. 'Tea, very important, I drink tea every morning and every night. You will drink tea with me.'

We watched his ritual begin as he boiled one pot of water on the embers of the fire, before adding the leaves and then pouring the brew from one teapot to the other several times. Then the sugar was added and each glass filled with the amber-coloured liquid. It was a bitter shot, but made palatable by its teeth-rotting sweetness.

'Now, you have second tea,' Hamid said when we had each downed our first round. 'Second tea stronger.'

He poured another four glasses of the heavily steeped tea, which had now taken on a darker brown colour. We dutifully gulped it down, and I could see Josianne and Angel wincing slightly. I noticed that Hamid sipped his at a very leisurely pace before making his next announcement.

'Now, we have third tea. First tea not strong. Second tea, strong. Third tea . . . very strong.'

I swallowed the final mouthful in one hit. It was like drinking tar.

'Aah, it is good, yes, the Algerian tea?'

'Mmm, lovely,' I agreed, not wanting to hurt his feelings.

'I drink coffee usually,' said Josianne, looking at her little glass of brown liquid with foreboding.

'I never drink coffee,' declared Angel. 'I don't drink anything with caffeine in it, it's so bad for you, and I don't want to get addicted to it.'

I couldn't help but laugh. I had never heard anything so absurdly unadventurous from the mouth of a twenty-three-year-old. Watching her sitting there with her pink porn-star T-shirt, lecturing the grown-ups on the dangers of caffeine, I suddenly felt very old and slightly depressed at the hopelessly un-rock 'n' roll youth of today. Forget the speed cameras and the immigrants; it was the likes of Angel that were the real threat to our country.

It was dark now and the fire had died down to its last orange embers. Bedtime called, and as we unzipped our tents it became apparent that nobody had thought about where Hamid was planning on sleeping.

'Have you got a tent?' Jacques asked him.

'No, no, I not need tent, I sleep here,' he motioned to the ground next to the fire. 'It is good.'

'Do you have a sleeping bag?'

'No, I just sleep here, it is OK.'

I realised that Hamid had arrived at the border carrying nothing but his rucksack, which as far as I could work out contained mainly tea-making apparatus.

'We have a spare tent you can use if you want, or you can sleep in the car,' insisted Jacques, but Hamid would have no truck with our wimpy ways and stayed put, cross-legged, staring into the dwindling fire as the rest of us crawled into our tents.

When I awoke next morning I was shocked at how cold it was; I could see my breath in the air, even inside the tent, and to think that I had been worrying about over-heating in the Sahara! I pulled on all my clothes and emerged to find Hamid sitting by a newly made fire, already in the throes of his morning tea ritual. Angel was next to him, wrapped in a woven blanket of ethnic design, hunched over the flames and weaving her hair into small plaits. Not long after, Josianne and Jacques appeared from their tent bleary-eyed.

66

'Oh God! I don't think I slept at all,' Josianne said wearily, lighting her first fag of the day. 'I don't know why.'

'Oh no, you poor thing. I slept really well, but I always do in the desert,' said Angel. She was now busy attaching little coloured wooden beads to the end of her plaits.

Soon we were on the move again, still heading towards Djanet, and already the day was warming up, suggesting ferocious temperatures to come. The road finally split away from the pylons and we found ourselves travelling through true Saharan scenery as we crossed the Grand Erg Oriental, with its enormous orange dunes rolling away in every direction. In the town of Hassi Messaoud we stopped to stock up with supplies for the journey ahead.

'There is big market here,' Hamid told us. 'We buy food, there is no other market now until Djanet.'

The marketplace was a rambling, colourful affair, selling everything from piles of vegetables and heaps of spices laid out on the ground to mobile phones and fake designer sunglasses. Our arrival caused quite a stir, and we were soon surrounded by inquisitive kids who flocked around the bike, while the menfolk gaped at us from a distance with a little more wariness. There were only a few women around, covered from head to toe while shopping together for vegetables. I wanted to buy a pair of sunglasses, so Hamid instructed the others to wait with the car and bike while the two of us went off together. After weaving our way through the maze-like alleys of the market, we found a place selling sunglasses and Hamid entered into a conversation with the stallholder. It sounded like a lively exchange but I was too busy trying on the shades to take much notice. Then Hamid suddenly grabbed my arm and pulled me out of the stall, while the proprietor continued to shout after us in a torrent of Arabic.

'Come, come, we must go,' Hamid was saying as he pulled me along.

'What's wrong?' I asked.

'This man, he is crazy,' muttered Hamid, looking quite distressed. 'Come on, come on, we find more sunglasses, another place.'

But the man had left his stall unattended and was following us, still shouting at Hamid.

'What's going on?' I asked.

'Nothing, nothing, it is OK, he is just crazy.' Hamid twirled his index finger next to his head, in the universal sign language for lunacy.

The stallholder was clearly enraged about something; he had caught up with us now and was yelling at Hamid and tugging at his sleeve. Hamid turned round and shouted something in his face. The man backed Hamid into a corner next to a pile of rotting vegetables and launched into a furious tirade. I only understood one word, but it was enough to explain everything: 'American'. He was clearly angry with Hamid for fraternising with what he assumed was the enemy – me.

Hamid and the stallholder kept up their lively dialogue for some time, and just as I had seen in the police station, while they ranted and raved they constantly touched each other and at times even held hands. Eventually they seemed to come to some sort of understanding, but Hamid was clearly shaken by the incident, and we hurried back to the others after picking up a pair of sunglasses from another, more friendly vendor. Hamid went off with Jacques and Josianne to help them shop for our supplies, while Angel and I waited behind with the vehicles, trying to ignore the stares of the men, who continued to gawp unashamedly, despite our attempts to cover up with long sleeves, trousers and headscarves.

'*Salaam aleikum,*' Angel kept saying to the staring men in her posh Arabic voice, but they didn't respond.

When the others arrived back with our provisions Hamid was obviously in a state of extreme stress. His normally cheerful face was visibly pale and stricken with anxiety.

'Come, come, we must leave. Now!'

He jumped in the car, started the engine while the other three clambered in as fast as possible, and set off down the road. Unfortunately the donning of helmet and gloves somewhat hampers a quick motorcycle getaway, and by the time the others had disappeared from view I was already attracting a large and curious crowd. There was nothing else to do but ride out of the throng and follow the Land Cruiser's dust. I found the car parked outside a stall, where Jacques was buying bottles of water while Hamid hopped around nervously, fending off his fellow countrymen.

'Hurry! Please, come, we go now, hurry, hurry,' he kept saying to Jacques, as he shoved the dozens of water bottles into the boot of the car with little regard for the Belgians' fastidiously ordered packing system. Josianne and Angel were safely behind the glass of the Land Cruiser rear windows, and it occurred to me that the exposure of travelling by motorcycle is both its appeal and its downfall. Here I was, laid bare to everyone and everything, to the hawkers and the gawping men, the persistent children and the burning sun. There was no door to lock between us, no button to press that would roll up a window and remove me from their world. I was a sitting duck. But there was also the smell of the spices that drifted out from the market, the occasional gentle breeze that brought such relief from the heat, the sound of a hundred Arabic conversations competing with the warbling *Rai* music that pumped out of a little café. Despite the awkward situation that we currently found ourselves in, I wouldn't have swapped the saddle of my bike for the confines of a seat in the back of a car.

'Now we go for petrol!' Hamid called out to me as he chucked the last bottle of water in the boot, and I followed them out of the marketplace on to a potholed main road, lined with auto repair shops. We drove around looking for a petrol station that sold unleaded petrol for my bike, but there was none to be found.

'There is no unleaded now, only in big cities and in the north of Algeria,' Hamid explained. 'From now on, you have only super.'

I had no idea what effect leaded petrol would have on my bike, but I had two choices: fill it up and see what happened, or go home. We pulled into a petrol station in the centre of the town and I rolled up at a vacant pump.

'*Salaam aleikum,*' I greeted the attendant. He wore the white robes and full beard of a devout Muslim, and as soon as our eyes met he quickly looked away without responding to my greeting. I stayed sitting on my bike and unscrewed the filler cap as he lifted the nozzle from the pump. His eyes flicked back towards the bike, just momentarily, so as to put the nozzle into the tank. Once it was in position he turned his entire body away so his back was facing me. He kept his arm outstretched behind him, squeezing the trigger as he pumped the fuel into my tank while looking in the opposite direction.

'OK, OK, thank you. OK, you can stop now!' I hollered as, somewhat inevitably, the petrol overflowed all over the tank, on to my sheepskin saddle and down my legs. I paid him, received my change and concluded our transaction without him speaking a word or even looking at me.

As we left town and broke out into more flat, scrubby desert, I felt rather depressed by my encounters in Hassi Messaoud. I had of course realised that travelling through Muslim countries would bring its fair shares of challenges, and as a great believer in the concept of 'when in Rome' I had entered willingly, and I hoped, tolerantly, into their world, covering up with long-sleeved clothes and scarves and attempting to learn a few words of Arabic. But I had failed to grasp fully just how little I would be able to mingle with the locals – and this was even with Hamid at my side! I was immensely grateful for the company of the Belgian crew, as I could hardly begin to imagine how lonely a solo journey through Algeria would be. The only people we came into contact with on a day-to-day basis were men, and they either gawped at me as if I was an alien, or worse, refused to even look at me. I now realised how difficult it would be to make any connection with the local women, as except for the occasional sight of a veiled wife shopping in the market they were nowhere to be seen, hidden away in the home, looking after the kids. They certainly weren't whizzing around town on motorcycles, that was for sure. It was a classic case of culture shock: I wasn't really ready for Algeria, and Algeria certainly wasn't ready for me. Fortunately, I had another 1,000 miles to get used to it.

FOUR

We settled into something of a routine after a few days: rising early to chilly dawn starts, pushing on south towards Djanet, and, when the midday heat became insufferable, pulling off the road for our standard lunch of Laughing Cow cheese on French bread. This wasn't our first choice of sustenance, but they were pretty much the only picnic ingredients to be found at the small towns that cropped up every couple of hundred miles. And the dreaded Laughing Cow had a stranglehold on the market, being so highly processed and crammed with salt that it could survive unrefrigerated even in extreme heat, which admittedly is not really a selling point for a cheese unless you happen to be in the Sahara. Each evening, as dusk began to fall, we would drive off the main highway, racing across the sand for a mile or so, to transform a previously innocuous patch of desert into our temporary home. By the time we had set up camp, made a fire and cooked our evening meal, the night would be pitch black and utterly silent, with just a crystalline sprinkling of stars above us. Jacques and Josianne would head off to bed, I would settle into my tent to write my diary by torchlight, leaving Angel and Hamid sitting by the dwindling fire, whiling away the night discussing whatever it is that earnest twenty-three-year-olds discuss in the middle of the Sahara desert.

I enjoyed this repetitive rhythm of our journey, slowly making our way across the Sahara, but Josianne was starting to show the signs of someone who clearly did not relish the quotidian plod of overland travel. She had barely slept since we had arrived in Algeria, and the novelty of the grand adventure was wearing off fast. Our route had risen out of the great undulating dunes of the Grand Erg Oriental and was now crossing the rocky Tinrhert plateau, with its towering slabs of black stone and rock-strewn ground. It was a harsh environment, like riding through a giant quarry, with none of the exotic charm of the golden sand dunes we had passed through previously. There was no way to avoid spending a night in this hostile terrain, and we drove around, bouncing over rocks and dipping in and out of dry gullies, looking for flat ground to pitch our tents. But when it came to setting up camp, Josianne stayed put in the back of the car, smoking and looking miserable.

'Are you OK?' I asked, while the others were busy making the fire and preparing dinner but she just shook her head in response. She had been so upbeat when we set out from Tunisia that I was surprised at her being the first to crack.

'Oh, I don't know, I'm just being silly,' she said eventually. 'It's just that being stuck in the car all day with . . .' She tailed off, holding her tongue, but I knew what she had meant to say.

'It's driving me crazy! I guess I didn't realise how much we'd be just sitting in there, but I don't want to spoil it for Jacques, he's loving every minute of it. I'm not really crazy about camping anyway, I'm a city girl at heart, and now, after what Hamid said about the snakes, I don't even want to get out of the car!'

'What snakes?' This was the first I'd heard of snakes; being on the bike meant I missed out on the group conversations that took place in the Land Cruiser.

'He said we shouldn't camp near rocks because snakes live under them, and now look where we are, nothing but bloody rocks everywhere!'

'I'm sure there won't be any snakes,' I lied hopefully.

'Oh, I'm sorry,' Josianne said. 'Just ignore me, I'm being silly.'

She stared at the ground, thoroughly dejected.

'Well, look, I've got an idea – there's an airport at Tamanrasset. We should be there in about a week or so. Maybe you could fly from there to Cameroon somehow, or to somewhere else, and we could meet you after we've crossed the desert?'

Josianne looked at me apologetically and shook her head.

'No, I can't do that.'

'Why not? I'm sure Jacques would understand.'

'No, it's not that,' she hesitated, 'it's just that, well, it sounds silly, but I'm scared of flying.'

'As well as snakes?'

She nodded, and managed a small smile. I wanted to ask her if she'd seen *Snakes on a Plane* but I managed to resist.

'Look,' she said with a glimmer of resilience, 'I'm here now and I've just got to get on with it.'

Thankfully, a snake-free night was had by all, and although Josianne was still subdued in the morning, she was making a brave show of getting on with it. But it wasn't just Josianne

74

whose mood was darkening as we headed deeper into the desert; Hamid was becoming increasingly anxious too. Each town we passed through was flanked by *barrages* – police and military checkpoints where I was invariably greeted as a man until I removed my helmet, and the welcome was rescinded in awkward surprise. Now that we had officially entered the supposedly dangerous desert region of Algeria, we also had to register our arrival and exit with both the gendarmes and the police in every town, involving tedious sessions of form-filling that required a baffling amount of minutiae including the names and addresses of our parents.

'Is this really necessary?' I asked Hamid as we rolled into the town of Illizi for the night. We were all hot, weary and hungry, but as usual, the bureaucracy had to come first.

'Yes, yes, is very important,' insisted Hamid. 'I make promise!'

'What do you mean, you make promise?'

'I make promise! I make big promise, for all of you!' He waved an official piece of paper in front of me with his signature at the bottom.

'In the police station at the border, Hamid had to sign this statement to say that we were his responsibility, and that no harm would come to us,' explained Jacques.

'He's taking it very seriously.'

'All the Algerian authorities are totally paranoid now, after the kidnappings that happened a few years ago, so that's probably why. He said that if anything happens to us he'll be in serious trouble.'

'Oh, that explains why he's been so nervous.'

We left Illizi the following morning, but only after Hamid had made fifteen copies of each of our passports in preparation for the many checkpoints that awaited us. We'd only gone a few miles when he pulled off the road and wound down the window to call me over.

'Everything OK?' I asked.

'Lois, in ten kilometres there is very dangerous hill, very steep, please you must be very, very careful.'

'Oh, right, thanks for the warning,' I replied and we continued on our way.

After another four kilometres, Hamid once again pulled over to talk to me.

'It is six kilometres now, the hill, very steep, very dangerous.'

'Er, yes, OK, thanks.'

A few kilometres later the scene repeated itself.

'It is coming now, the steep hill, after this corner.'

By this point I had worked myself into quite a state about this hill of doom. I started fretting over what on earth it was awaiting me round the corner that required three separate warnings, imagining some boulder-strewn descent or a steep rocky staircase. I went into the corner slowly, and as I rounded the bend the road descended from the plateau down a reasonably steep gradient with another sharp bend halfway along it. The road surface was a little potholed and gravelly, but nothing out of the ordinary for this part of the world, and the view over the vast emptiness of the desert was thrilling. At the bottom, I waited for the others.

'Oh, Lois! I am so happy you are OK!' Hamid announced entirely seriously when they pulled up next to me. His face, which had been all furrowed brows and anxiety at the top of the hill, was now beaming with relief.

'Well, it wasn't that bad after all.'

'But it is very dangerous, I think, on the moto. I must tell you because nothing bad must happen. I have made the promise,

76

the promise I show you before. It is very important.'

I realised then that Hamid saw his role in our journey not as a desert guide or even as an escort, but as a nanny. Sure enough, when we stopped for lunch he had found something new to fret about, and as I unbuckled my helmet I could see him and Jacques in the cab, looking at the map, in the midst of what appeared to be a serious discussion.

'Lois . . .' Jacques beckoned to me out of the window.

'Everything all right?'

'There is a bit of a problem about the next part of the journey, to Tamanrasset.'

'Oh dear, what?'

Hamid's face had taken on its all too familiar worried expression again.

'Er, it seems Hamid is concerned about the route, he thinks it is dangerous.'

'Well, I'm sure it'll be OK, didn't we get all that approved at the border?'

'Er, well that's the thing . . .'

By now Josianne and Angel had joined us, bearing slabs of bread slathered with Laughing Cow.

'What's the thing?' asked Josianne.

'Well, it looks like Hamid only got our route approved up to Djanet. After that we need another permit or something . . .'

'Is this true?' I asked him. I couldn't believe this had only come out now.

'It is OK! It is OK, please! Maybe I get permit in Djanet,' Hamid protested.

'But if he can't get the permit, he is saying we must join a convoy or hire a truck for the bike, in case something happens,' Jacques explained.

77

'Please, please! It is OK for car, but if something happen to you and moto . . . I make promise!' Hamid looked as if he was close to tears; buckling under the responsibility of keeping us safe and sound. I decided it was time to square up with him.

'Hamid, look. I know you are very worried about our safety, but I have come to Algeria to ride my motorcycle across the Sahara. After Algeria I am going all the way down through Africa.'

'Yes, yes, I know this, but I think it is dangerous, I try to help. After Djanet, we go Tamanrasset. No road, you understand, no . . . *goudron,* what is the English word . . .?' he asked Jacques.

'Tarmac.'

'Ah yes, tarmac. No tarmac. It is five hundred kilometres, just desert, it is very hard for you on moto.'

'I know, I know, but the thing is, Hamid, this is what I do for fun. The worse the road is, the more fun it is. Do you see what I mean? So please don't worry so much.'

'I think it is very dangerous on moto.'

I sighed inwardly. It was cultural stalemate. He just didn't get it.

'Well, maybe it is dangerous, but . . .'

'What about your husband?' he wailed, 'What does he say about you ride moto in desert?'

'Well, he thinks it's a good idea. He's ridden his motorcycle all over the world.'

Hamid shook his twenty-three-year-old head.

'I would not let my wife ride motorcycle.'

'Well,' I replied with the painfully obvious response, 'it's lucky I'm not married to you then.'

I knew Hamid was well-meaning, so I couldn't get properly

annoyed with him, but his constant fretting was somewhat dampening my enthusiasm. With him and Jacques in the car, making the decisions about where we were going, when we would stop, where we would sleep, I was beginning to feel that my grand adventure was ebbing away from me and that I was merely tagging along on their journey. Hamid was a good Muslim boy, which meant he didn't drink, he prayed five times a day and he didn't think women should get involved in any decision-making. Although Jacques made an effort to include me, it was usually the case that any plan had already been hatched between the two of them, and my involvement was more a token gesture than an active part in the plotting.

Now we had settled into something of a routine, the dynamics of the group were finding their natural order, but Hamid was obviously not happy with his role as Jacques's assistant and was still insisting that he should drive the car when it came to our 300-mile off-road leg from Djanet to Tamanrasset, as according to Hamid it was going to be 'very difficult'. Jacques was a mild-mannered fellow, but when it came to this subject he dug his heels into the sand and refused to budge. I didn't blame him – after all, this was what he had come all this way for. Occasionally Josianne was allowed a stint behind the wheel to break up the monotony of her passenger status, but Angel was consigned to the back seat permanently, despite dishing out endless advice about the techniques of desert driving, gleaned from her fabled jaunt to Timbuktu on the overland truck tour.

'So did you all take it in turns to drive the truck, then?' I asked her one evening after she had monopolised the conversation with talk of reduced tyre pressures, engaging freewheeling hubs and using sand ladders.

'Well, no, but y'know, I just picked these things up from talking to the guys,' she said airily.

'So, Jacques, are you going to let Angel have a go behind the wheel?' I asked him, but when he didn't respond Josianne stepped in.

'Angel can't actually drive, unfortunately,' she said.

'Actually, Josianne, that's not true. I can drive, I just don't have a licence,' she pointed out, visibly smarting.

'Yes, and possession of a driving licence is the standard measure of whether someone can drive or not,' said Josianne in a sarcastic tone. Until now she had managed to keep her irritation under wraps, but it looked like the temperature of the Land Cruiser was as icy inside as it was hot outside.

Knowing how impressed Hamid was by Jacques's Land Cruiser, I wondered if his motives were a little less honourable than merely wanting to offer assistance in the sticky sections. Boy racer syndrome is a worldwide phenomenon, and Hamid was certainly not immune to the pleasures of showing off behind the wheel of a desirable car. And he wanted to look the part of the Tuareg guide. Since we had arrived in the south of the country, he had made a sartorial shift towards this image too: his Adidas attire was now packed away, replaced with the Algerian traditional dress of jellaba and sandals.

'These clothes are for the north,' he explained as he folded up his tracksuit and stowed his trainers in his backpack. 'Now I am in the south, in the desert, I wear my jellaba.'

We had been on the road for a week and at last Djanet was in sight, just a day's ride away now, and we were all spurred on by the trappings of relative civilisation that awaited us. Hotels, showers and restaurants were calling, but Hamid had other ideas, and insisted that first we must visit some prehistoric rock paintings near Ihiri, a little oasis village on the way. To be honest, I could have lived without this excursion, but Josianne and Angel were quite keen, mainly to make a break from sitting in the back of the car. The paintings were located in a remote spot two hours' walk away from Ihiri in a beautiful river gorge, thick with palm trees, and although we set off at seven thirty in the morning, by the time we arrived, the heat was draining the energy from us; but still, it was good to be walking for a change, and in such spectacular surroundings.

'Here we are!' announced Hamid at last, pointing proudly at a faint, childish picture of an unidentifiable four-legged creature scrawled on the side of a rock. There was a feeling of the emperor's new clothes as we all oohed and aahed to order. An exhausting clamber over some rocks and through the river took us to another similar work of 'art' and more appreciative noises were made.

'These pictures are a bit rubbish,' I whispered to Josianne, who nodded in silent agreement.

'Now we must go here, there is more picture over here,' Hamid told us, pointing in the direction of a giant mound of boulders.

'I think I'll just stay here,' I said. Not only did I have little desire to see any more of these rock paintings, but the heat was becoming too much to bear and for the first time on this journey I was beginning to feel the worrying signs of heat exhaustion that I remembered from my Morocco trip. My head and neck felt like one of the boulders we'd been climbing over and even the tiniest movement sapped me of energy.

'Me too,' added Josianne, and we both sheltered under a rock until the others returned half an hour later.

'What was it like?' Josianne asked Angel.

'Oh, it was amazing! It was really beautiful, you should have seen it!'

'It was much the same as the others,' said Jacques.

Two hours later we traipsed back into the village, by which time I was feeling quite ill and thoroughly weakened by the heat. I gulped down water and oranges and got ready to ride the last 150 miles to Djanet. Fortunately this final stretch passed through the most spectacular desert scenery we had encountered so far, making for a grand finale to the first leg of our journey and raising my weary spirits. The road cut across an expanse of primrose-yellow sand, from which monolithic rock formations and volcanic plugs burst forth into the sky. From a distance these great rock towers appeared in silhouette, and their jagged summits looked like fantasy citadels, perched on the top of fairytale mountains.

The temperature in this desert heartland remained overwhelming, hovering around thirty-five degrees Celsius, but we ploughed on without stopping and rolled into Djanet by late afternoon. Whether it was because I knew we were due a rest day, or just the culmination of the heat and the anxious excitement of the last week's travel, by the time we pulled into the hotel courtyard I was exhausted beyond measure, and as I dismounted the bike I could feel my aching limbs crying out for respite. The hotel was by no means the luxurious pad of our fantasies, but as far as we could make out, it was the only one in town. Angel and I dumped our bags in another crime-scene bedroom and staggered into the restaurant, where Hamid was hanging out, chatting to the cook and watching surprisingly saucy music videos on the Egyptian equivalent of MTV.

'Oh Lordy! I ache all over and I am starving!' I announced as

I plonked myself down at the table opposite Hamid.

'Where is Jacques and Josianne?'

'They're coming,' said Angel. 'They said to order them some food.'

'OK, I order food for all of us.' Hamid made his way over to the counter as I slumped on to the table.

'Maybe you're dehydrated,' Angel said. 'Try drinking some Coke, it'll put some sugar back in you.'

'Good idea,' I groaned. 'Can you order me a Coke, please, Hamid?' I called after him.

He turned round and shook his head.

'No, no Coke, it is not good for you now.'

'What d'you mean?'

'Coke, very bad to drink before food. Lot of gas, make you full.' He patted his stomach by way of illustration.

'Don't worry, I'm really hungry, nothing will stop me eating my dinner, I can assure you of that!'

'No. No Coke. It is bad for you drink Coke now.'

'Please, Hamid, can you just order me a Coke?'

'No, no. You do not drink Coke now.'

'Hamid, I have walked for four hours in the desert and ridden non-stop for a hundred and fifty miles, all in forty degree heat, I am totally knackered and I fancy a cold Coke at the end of the day.'

'No. You will not eat after drink Coke. It is bad to drink Coke before food. No Coke.'

Hamid turned back to the counter and ordered our Coke-free meal.

I didn't have the energy to argue, or the bolshiness to challenge Hamid's dictate and stride up there and order it myself, but as I laid my head on the table I wondered how on earth I had arrived in this bizarre situation: overcome with exhaustion in a grotty restaurant in the middle of the Sahara with a twenty-three-year-old Algerian man dictating my nutritional needs while watching scantily clad Egyptian women gyrating in widescreen.

Hamid slipped off that evening, claiming he had to 'see a nomad about a camel' and promised us that he would return with the necessary permit for us to continue our journey to Tamanrasset. He was as good as his word, and the following morning we found him at breakfast in fine spirits, having succeeded in his mission. The rest of us were not quite as chirpy. Josianne was feeling ill, and I had spent the night discovering that our bedroom was not only a crime scene but home to a lively flea circus too, and had woken up covered in bites. Hamid borrowed the car, claiming he had errands to run, and once the midday heat had passed, the rest of us took a stroll around the town.

Djanet was lively place, built on the edge of a *palmeraie* and buzzing with the activities of everyday life in this part of the world. Veiled Tuareg men razzed around the streets in 'desert-ready' 4 × 4s with rows of jerrycans strapped to the roof and *guerbas,* water carriers made from goatskins, slung on the side. As we made our way along the main drag to the market we spied a familiar car parked up in a prominent position. Sure enough, Hamid was leaning out of the driver's window wearing his shades, surrounded by a group of admiring men who were giving Jacques's car the once-over. Rather than spoil Hamid's moment of glory, we took a detour behind a row of palm trees and let him continue his Land Cruiser fantasy in peace.

The following morning Josianne and I set off on a ridiculous, fear-induced shopping trip for supplies for the next leg of the journey. We were expecting to make the 300-mile journey to Tamanrasset in three days and we knew we would be travelling across the wilderness, where there would be no shops or petrol stations along the way. While Hamid and Jacques got busy filling up the jerrycans with fuel and water, we wrote a shopping list that would have kept an Algerian village in food for a year. Our method was roughly to work out what we had eaten over the last few days, then double it because we would be expending more energy riding and driving on the dirt, double it again in case we got lost or stranded, and then double it again because, well . . . you never know. We traipsed in the scorching heat from the bread shop, to the fruit and veg shop, to the grocery store, each time laden down with more and more provisions. The morning sun was already beating down and I was regretting our decision to do the shopping on foot.

We returned to the hotel to find the others packed and ready to go.

'Oh my God!' exclaimed Jacques as we piled the food into the back of the car. 'Where are we going to put it all?'

He insisted on keeping the interior of the car in impeccable order at all times. All food preparation was to be done outside and nobody was allowed to eat their sandwiches inside the car in case they dropped any crumbs.

'Don't worry, we'll squeeze it in somewhere,' said Josianne. 'Forty loaves of bread, fifty oranges, ten boxes of Laughing Cow, five kilos of onions . . . Oh yeah, and a hundred Marlboro, I'm not going to risk running out of them . . .' She gave a running commentary as she transferred the shopping into the car.

'This is like, totally obscene,' said Angel. 'People are starving here and we're just buying all this food that we don't need.'

'People aren't starving in Algeria,' said Josianne briskly, 'and anyway, even if they were, does that mean we have to starve too? Think how much we're contributing to the economy – trade not aid, isn't that what you're always going on about?'

'It's not that simple, Josianne,' Angel said, exasperated, and launched into a woolly lecture on the greed of the West and something tedious about the manipulation of the world agricultural economy with tarrif barriers and farming subsidies.

'Hamid!' Josianne called out while Angel was still blathering on. 'Are people starving in Algeria?'

He was on the roof of the Land Cruiser, strapping down the jerrycans to the roof-rack, and looked confused at the question, which he answered with a shrug of his shoulders and the smile of a simpleton.

'No, they're not,' said Josianne to Angel. 'OK?'

'There's no need to be like that about it,' Angel whimpered, and for the first time she showed a chink in her suit of smug armour. 'I just think it's important to understand . . .'

'Well, I tell you what,' said Josianne, butting in, no longer trying to hold back, 'you don't have to eat any of this food, OK? There you go, that'll help you to empathise with the non-existent starving Algerians.'

'Oh, oh . . . fuck off, Josie!' she said and burst into tears, stomping off to the café, her Birkenstocks slapping against her feet as she stormed away across the dusty car park.

I stayed out of the way for a while, leaving Jacques to broker a ceasefire between his girlfriend and his cousin. I felt sorry for him, having his meticulously planned Saharan adventure hijacked by emotionally charged female outbursts that he didn't really understand. All he wanted to do was study his maps, of which he had many, and make notes about fuel consumption and daily average temperatures in his leather-bound notebook. I finished loading up the food with the help of Hamid, who was kind enough not to mock our panic buying. He ate very little, and seemed happy enough as long as he had his twice daily tea ceremony.

'Very good, very good,' he kept saying as he went around the car, checking bolts and making adjustments to the roof-rack.

After a while the others returned, with the two girls in a sombre mood. Angel's face was still red and puffy from crying and Josianne barely spoke a word but just smoked incessantly. Feeling distinctly awkward, I acted as if nothing had happened and went about my business with a false cheeriness, which only succeeded in making everyone feel even more uncomfortable.

'So, are we ready to hit the desert?' I said, itching to fire up the bike and get going, away from this claustrophobic grumpiness. I was excited about the next few days; this is what I had come for, a proper off-road adventure in the Sahara. The ride from the border to Djanet had been pleasant enough, but as far as I was concerned the real action started when the tarmac ended.

'Ah, yes, well, there is one more thing I do,' announced Hamid. 'I need more permit, just one more.'

We all groaned in unison and our mutual response encouraged a few smiles between us, thawing out the iciness at last.

'It is OK, please, it is just one permit for travel in desert, is very easy. I get from gendarmerie at Bordj el Haouas.'

I looked on my map. Bordj el Haouas was a little town on the main highway that we had driven through previously on our way into Djanet.

'Oh, it's OK,' Jacques said, looking over my shoulder. 'It's on our way.'

'Yes, yes, we go to Bordj, then across desert to Tamanrasset, it is no problem,' Hamid assured us, and at last we set off on our Saharan odyssey.

We retraced our steps out of Djanet, back along the road past the towers of volcanic rock, and arrived in Bordj el Haouas, a small, quiet settlement made up of a few houses lining a wide main street. The gendarmerie was the only building of significance and easily identified by the Algerian flag flapping around in the breeze. Hamid pulled up outside, gathered his pile of papers and ran up the steps. A few minutes later he returned with a surly young officer, who greeted us with a brusque nod and circled our vehicles with the air of a vulture about to go in for the kill before addressing Hamid in Arabic.

'Your papers, Lois, he need your papers, for the moto, and you Jacques, for the car,' Hamid translated in a nervous whisper. He was clearly uncomfortable in the presence of authority and within five minutes of arriving was already visibly quaking in his sandals.

The officer marched back into the building, with Hamid trotting along behind him. The door slammed shut and the rest of us sat at the side of the road in the shade and waited. Bordj el Haouas felt like a ghost town: the streets were deserted except for a soldier manning a *barrage* and a few elderly men pottering about who stopped to stare at the bike and exchange greetings. It was eerily quiet, but it was already late morning and most people were inside, out of the already unbearably harsh sun. We sipped water and tried not to move too much in a bid to conserve energy, but after twenty minutes Hamid had still not reappeared from the building.

'I wonder what he's up to?' Josianne said.

'Oh, he's probably just filling in forms as usual, it always takes ages.'

'Yeah, but not normally this long.'

'Shall we go and find him?'

'No,' said Jacques, 'I'm sure he'll be out soon, we're not in a hurry.'

But another twenty minutes passed and there was still no sign of Hamid. The heat was becoming overwhelming, but there was no café or restaurant where we could take cover; all we could do was sit still in the shade and keep drinking water.

'Something must be going on,' Josianne said when he still did not emerge. But as soon as she'd uttered the words, the door of the gendarmerie flew open and Hamid came pegging it down the steps. He was still clutching his ever-increasing pile of paperwork, but his face was almost the same colour as mine and his expression told us immediately that Josianne was right. Something was definitely going on.

'Big problem, big problem!' he wailed. I had never seen him so obviously upset.

'What's wrong?'

'It is you!' he cried, pointing at me. 'The police will not give you permit to ride in desert, they say they never see woman on motorcycle before, and no woman can ride motorcycle in desert – they say it is impossible!'

'Oh, for crying out loud!' I exclaimed, with a mixture of disbelief, anger and frustration. I had known my presence might be controversial, but I'd been trying to keep a low profile, and apart from the odd whinge with Josianne, I had kept my opinions on the Islamic attitude to women to myself for fear of upsetting Hamid. But it wasn't just the obvious sexism that annoyed me about this situation; it was the sheer stupidity, the utter lack of logic. Here I was in Algeria on an English-registered motorcycle that I had ridden from England;

surely it was pretty evident that I had some idea of what I was doing. I thought about trying to explain this to Hamid to use as a counter-argument, but I knew that using logic and reason to deal with this state of affairs would be of no use. Common sense, even in Arabic, was clearly a foreign language to the Algerian authorities.

'Lois, just chill. It's a different culture,' Angel started saying. 'It doesn't mean it's wrong or right, but we're in their country now. You might not agree with the teachings of Islam but . . .'

Give it a rest! I wanted to say. I didn't know how much more of her gap-year philosophising I could stand, and I was about to tell her as much when Jacques stepped in.

'Right. So what happens next?' he asked, bringing his calm approach to the proceedings in the nick of time.

'I have idea!' declared Hamid. 'They say man must ride moto, not woman. So I say – I will ride moto!'

There was a slight problem with this scheme, not least that I actually wanted to ride my bike across the Sahara, but also a more practical issue.

'But Hamid, you don't know how to ride a motorcycle,' I pointed out.

'I ride moto once when I was little boy. I fall off and hurt my leg. My father he is very angry and I never ride moto again!'

'Right. So what are we going to do?' I asked.

'I think we should all just chill out,' Angel suggested, while Hamid sat on the ground, looking thoroughly weary of the whole affair, with his head in his hands.

'Don't worry, be happy,' spouted Angel, stroking Hamid's arm, which seemed to cheer him up slightly as he stared up at her with big sad brown eyes.

I tried to put myself in his shoes for a moment, and I

90

couldn't help but feel sorry for him. He was in a difficult position, forced into the role of unofficial mediator between two hugely disparate cultures. He wanted to look after and please his clients, and he was very tolerant of what must seem to him to be our decadent Western ways. But he also felt enormous pressure to do the right thing according to the law and customs of his country. It was the equivalent of me taking a group of Islamic fundamentalists on a tour around the drinking dens of Soho and wondering why they were having trouble enjoying themselves.

'OK, I know what we do. I *tell* police I will ride moto now, but Lois, you must go now, quick, out of the town. But please, listen, there is one more *barrage* ahead and they must not see you. We will make different route.'

He showed me on the map. We would avoid the final checkpoint by riding off-piste across the desert, and then pick up the track to Tamanrasset about thirty-five miles along its course, successfully avoiding any further chauvinist policemen. This detour was entirely cross-country, no tracks, no signs, nothing. On the map it was just a patch of yellow emptiness. We would have to take bearings as we went along and hope that we could connect up with the track without too much difficulty.

'OK, as long as you're sure we can get away with it. I don't want to get you into trouble.'

'It is the only thing we can do,' he said, sounding aggravated. 'But please, Lois, please, any more *barrage*, you must not let police see you are woman, please, you must wear helmet and jacket and cover your face.' He walked back up the steps into the gendarmerie with the demeanour of a naughty schoolboy called in to see the headmaster.

FIVE

Although I felt bad that I had caused Hamid so much grief, I couldn't help but feel a sneaky thrill at being on the run as we made our escape from Bordj el Haouas. Hamid had told me to look out for the wreck of a burned-out car at the side of the road; this was the marker for where our cross-country detour would begin. When the charred, twisted chassis came into view I made a quick check over my shoulder for the Algerian fuzz before veering off the road and cutting across the wide open plain. Unusually Hamid was behind the wheel of the Land Cruiser and was giving it some serious welly, while the others sat in the back looking a little worried by this new turn of events. The terrain was hard-packed sand, and flat as an ice-rink, which made for fast easy riding. Hamid overtook me to lead the way and I opened up the throttle to keep up with him until I was riding flat out, as fast as my loaded bike could carry me. There was nothing in sight but a few distant escarpments far away on the horizon, and the sun glared out of a clear sky. Hot air blasted my face as I flew across this wild emptiness, the illicit nature of our flight only adding to the heady sensation of total freedom. It was everything I had hoped riding in the Sahara would be.

We had left the tarmac road around mid-afternoon, leaving us a few hours of daylight to find the piste to Tamanrasset. There were no tracks or tyre marks on this virgin sand and I relished the thought that we were blazing a trail across this untouched patch of the desert. Hamid had seemed confident about taking this detour and I blindly accepted that he knew where we should be going. I had foolishly succumbed to the woolly notion that his Tuareg blood somehow endowed him with a sixth sense when it came to matters of Saharan navigation. But by the time dusk began creeping over the sky, it became apparent that his nomadic pedigree had failed to cut the mustard and Hamid wasn't as certain about our off-piste adventure as he had made out. We were supposed to be heading in a roughly westerly direction, but as the sun began its nightly descent it was sinking away to our left, then behind us, then to our right. Hamid was driving round in a huge circle, and the track was nowhere to be seen. To make matters even trickier, we were now in an area littered with boulders and piles of rock, making it harder to keep on a straight course.

'Is everything all right?' I asked Jacques as I rode alongside the driver's window.

'Yeah, just trying to locate the track.'

'Are we lost?'

'Well, I wouldn't say that exactly.'

'We seem to be heading south, judging by the sun.'

93

'Well, I think Hamid's just trying to find a route, it's difficult to drive in a straight line over this sort of ground.' But I knew he was being polite. Hamid was meant to be navigating, but I could tell that Jacques the cartographer was not going to be able to stand this display of incompetence for much longer.

Not for the first time I felt somewhat left on the sidelines, and although I had my own maps and compass, the task of navigation was squarely in the hands of the boys, with me following along in their tyre tracks. I wasn't entirely happy with this arrangement, albeit unofficial, but I consoled myself with the thought that I was probably just a control freak, and that I should enjoy the experience of carefree riding without the added responsibility of navigating too. The truth was, though, that I actually enjoyed map-reading, but with the two men battling it out for supremacy in the front of the car, I thought it best to leave them to it.

In the back the girls weren't saying anything, even Angel was quiet, but I could see from Josianne's expression that the atmosphere in the Land Cruiser was a little tense. In the passenger seat Hamid's brows were so furrowed they had almost merged into one, as he floundered with Jacques's many maps, trying to fold and unfold them and getting into quite a muddle.

'It is OK, Lois, everything OK,' he said with a hint of irritation when I asked if he was all right.

He was obviously out of his depth, and as far as he was concerned, it was all my fault. If I hadn't come up with the foolish idea of riding across Algeria none of this would have happened. They could have stuck safely to the marked tracks in their car, without the need to launch the covert operations associated with smuggling a girl on a motorcycle across the desert.

94

I realised it was time for me to back off and leave the decisions to the blokes. *Must be more submissive, must be more submissive*, I scolded myself, but the truth of the matter was that for the first time on this trip I was genuinely concerned for our safety. Here we were, essentially a bunch of strangers in the middle of the Sahara with a twenty-three-year-old student masquerading as a guide. No one in the world had a clue where we were, not least the Algerian authorities whom we had deliberately thrown off our scent. It wouldn't take long for this adventure to turn into an emergency situation, and I was thankful suddenly for our excessive shopping trip this morning; in the darkening gloom, forty loaves of bread and ten boxes of Laughing Cow didn't seem so ridiculous after all.

After some more blundering around, it became too dark to continue and our only option was to make camp for the night. We settled on a flat rocky plain sheltered by a small escarpment, and as I pitched my tent by the light of my head torch, I noticed that the small rocks underfoot were in fact lumps of pastel-coloured marble ranging from pinkish white to mauve and pale blue. I picked up a small but particularly attractive pink chunk and stowed it away in my luggage with the sanguine thought that one day, when I was safely back home in London, it would remind me of this uncertain night in the Sahara desert.

We went through our usual motions of making a fire and cooking our standard meal of pasta and vegetables, but darkness plays havoc with rational thought and the general mood was one of awkward unease. We talked in light tones of treating ourselves to a hotel when we reached Tamanrasset, of the improvements Jacques wanted to make to the Land Cruiser and the cold beer he had promised himself at the end of the journey. But nobody mentioned the unmentionable. We were all toeing the party line: we weren't lost, we just hadn't found the track yet. This purposeful avoidance of the subject was crucial if we were going to keep our spirits up, but Angel, who had been unusually quiet throughout the meal, breached the unspoken agreement and began sobbing into her plastic plate, first gently, then in loud gulping gasps.

'Oh God! What are we going to do?' she blubbed through her tears. 'We're lost, lost in the Sahara! Oh God, Jacques, what are we going to do?'

She clung on to her cousin's arm and buried her head in his shoulder, crying more noisily than ever.

I got the impression that this wasn't the kind of relationship Jacques had with his cousin, and he looked extremely embarrassed, verging on alarmed, at this new turn of events. This wasn't part of his plan: there was nothing in his Sahara Handbook about dealing with hysterical twenty-three-year-old girls, and he floundered in obvious discomfort until Josianne and I stepped in.

'Don't worry, Angel, it'll be fine,' I said.

'We're not lost, we just haven't reached the track yet,' said Josianne, reeling off our mantra and putting a consoling arm around her.

'It'll be better in the morning; everything always seems worse at night.'

We trotted out these lines while Angel continued to wail about dying of exposure and dehydration.

'Please, Angel,' said Hamid, and I had never seen him so upset, his face contorted with desperation, 'please, please don't cry, I make promise to you. Everything will be all right!'

With dinner over, Hamid and Jacques, finding themselves

96

torn between comforting a sobbing girl or washing the dishes, chose the least onerous of these traditionally female tasks and set about scrubbing the plates with great vigour while Josianne and I eventually persuaded Angel to go to bed. But despite the rest of us putting on a brave show of confidence, sleep didn't come easily to any of us that night, and at three in the morning I woke myself up with a scream as my tormented motorcycling dreams culminated in a spectacular crash. Startled, I sat bolt upright, gasping for breath with my heart pounding, and it took me a good few seconds to realise it had been a figment of my troubled imagination.

I thrashed around in my sleeping bag for a couple of hours, but I had to admit defeat and eventually I dragged myself out of my tent. It was getting light and with the new dawn came a fresh surge of optimism, although Hamid was still subdued and his worried expression was now permanently etched on to his face in a caricature of anxiety. The morning was cool and dewy, and the marble-strewn ground twinkled in the pale light, but we were all aware that within a couple of hours the sun would be beating down on us once again, as fierce as ever, and we packed up quickly, eager to get going and seek out the elusive piste before the heat of the day sapped our flagging reserves of energy and hope.

For the first couple of hours we ploughed on as before, along soft sandy riverbeds, winding around clumps of camel grass and gunning it up steep rocky scarps. But Hamid's navigation was as vague as ever, and often he would instruct Jacques to swing the car round for no apparent reason and take off in the opposite direction. All I could do was keep following them and hope that Hamid had at least some idea of where he was going. By late morning we were still no nearer finding the track, the sun was approaching its insufferable position high in the sky, and an air of helplessness was taking root. I was beginning to conjure up survival plans when the car came to an abrupt halt ahead of me. I pulled up alongside to see what had happened, as Jacques stepped out of the driver's door holding his IGN map, a prismatic compass, a ruler and a pencil.

'I'm going to find out exactly where we are, *finalement!*' he said to no one in particular. '*C'est stupide!*'

He stalked off in a purposeful manner, laid down his kit about twenty yards from the car and took a sighting on to a craggy summit. Hamid, meanwhile, remained sitting in the passenger seat in silence, pretending to study another of Jacques's maps.

Thankfully for all of us, Jacques's survival instinct and cartographer's sensibilities had overruled his politeness, and while he checked and rechecked his sightings in diligent silence, the rest of us took the opportunity for a break. Josianne, Angel and I got busy spreading excessive amounts of Laughing Cow on to big hunks of bread. Eventually Jacques returned to the car with the beginnings of a smile showing on his previously clenched teeth.

'I know where we are,' he announced. 'Hamid, you will drive while I navigate us to the track, it is about twenty kilometres this way.' He pointed in a roughly north-westerly direction and Hamid nodded in silence. With Jacques's new-found leadership and our continued existence now looking more hopeful, team morale skyrocketed and our forty loaves of bread once again seemed excessive and slightly foolish.

We set off with more speed and purpose than before, flying along, in and out of dry riverbeds and across rocky fields of black basalt, before finally, off in the distance we spied a definite grey scar across the landscape. Jacques leaned out of the car window, pointing towards it.

'That's it, Lois, that's the track!' he shouted in an excitable tone that I had never heard him use before.

As we raced towards it we could see a couple of cairns along its edge and then, to our utmost joy, there stood an ancient, rusting sign by the side of the trail. Scratched into the rust and barely legible were the words we had all hoped to see: 'TAM 440'. At last we had found the piste to Tamanrasset. Josianne, Angel and I literally jumped for joy and ran around the sign in circles before whisking out our cameras to capture this precious moment. Although lacking any obvious photogenic qualities, this piece of rusty metal seemed more beautiful than all the golden dunes and Saharan sunsets put together; it meant we weren't lost. As we danced around, whooping and laughing, Josianne nudged us gently and pointed towards Hamid. He was slumped in the driver's seat of the car, almost crying with relief.

The change in everyone's mood was immediate but most notable in Hamid, who, after the initial wave of relief, became strangely bullish now he was back on old ground, despite the fact that he had been no way involved in the turnaround in our fortunes. Jacques had allowed him to drive this stretch, maybe to compensate for his crushing vote of no-confidence as a navigator, and now he was blasting along and waxing lyrical at every opportunity about his spiritual connection with the Sahara.

'I am home, the desert is my home! I can never be happy in the north, in Algiers. Now I am home again, this is where I belong. We go to Tamanrasset, I am with my people, my family, you meet my father, my brother . . .'

The Adidas-clad chemical engineering student with the Céline Dion ring-tone was just a distant memory. Now, Hamid was a noble prince of the Sahara, a fearless Tuareg guide.

Fortunately most of this tourist-brochure-inspired gushing took place in the car, so I only got the odd snippet when we stopped for the night. And histrionic as it was, it did nothing to diminish the thrill of our spectacular journey to Tamanrasset. However, what constitutes off-road fun to a motorcyclist equates to gruelling misery for a passenger in the back of a car, and it was obvious that Josianne and Angel were not relishing the experience of bumping over rocks and ploughing through sand all day long. But Angel, since her outburst, had been altogether less vocal and more bearable, and had struck up some sort of friendship with Hamid. Each night when the rest of us had retired into our tents, they continued their routine of sitting by the fire, conducting meaningful conversations. I overheard her trying to initiate a serious discussion about animism, which I considered to be quite ambitious considering Hamid's limited English and utter devotion to what he referred to as 'my Koran'.

For me, this incredible ride across the heart of the desert was everything I had dreamed of back home as I had pored over my maps of Africa, marvelling at the sheer size and might of the Sahara. All my fears and anxiety about the heat had proved to be unfounded, and although it was indeed blisteringly hot, and the riding was physically gruelling at times, it was still a magical experience to be riding my motorcycle across the sands to Tamanrasset, a place that had been in my dreams for so long that it had taken on almost mythical status. The last day's ride that took us into the town was the grandest finale a motorcyclist could hope for, through the foothills of the

Hoggar Mountains and along the most exhilarating rocky trails I had ever ridden. The track had all but washed away, and there was nothing else to do but hang on tight and go for it, flying and bouncing over huge rocks, in and out of steep-sided gullies, making accidental jumps and wincing as the rear suspension bottomed out again and again. But the bike never failed me, and even with the luggage, the heat and the brutal terrain, its 250ccs of power were plenty to keep me whizzing along at a fine pace. It was exactly what I had come here for. As we descended from the mountains the track snaked through an area of thorn trees before turning into a mass of tyre tracks in the flat, sandy ground, and it was obvious that civilisation was not far away.

'Yes, yes, we have made it, here is the good road, proper road!' Hamid announced as a strip of blacktop loomed up in front of us.

Our 325-mile ride across the wilderness was over. This was the Trans-Saharan Highway, the main road that runs south from the Mediterranean coast through the middle of Algeria to Tamanrasset. The others were all glad to be back on a relatively smooth tarmac road, but I felt a strange sense of anticlimax at our return to the real world. We hadn't seen another vehicle since leaving Djanet and now here we were, sharing this busy highway with cars, trucks and tankers all heading into Tamanrasset, the nearest thing to a bustling metropolis in the Sahara. The last three days had been a high-octane experience where moods were lifted and slammed on an almost hourly basis. The whole spectrum of emotions had coursed through each day; the exhilaration and sheer joy of blasting across the sand, the serenity of the silent moonlit nights, the inevitable fear and frustration of getting lost or injured or breaking down.

In the desert, one's survival lay on a knife edge and every experience and emotion was heightened accordingly. Riding in the Sahara was a tough but truly life-affirming experience, and all I knew was that I wanted more.

'Don't worry, Lois, we're only halfway across the Sahara,' Jacques pointed out when I expressed my sadness that it was all over. 'There's still hundreds of miles of sand to go after Tamanrasset.'

As we drove through the town the streets were busy with folk going about their business, and I was surprised to see several women walking around in Western clothes, although still with their hair and face veiled or covered with a headscarf. Taxis beetled around all over the place and there was even a traffic jam and a roundabout. The noise and activity was a shock to the system after days in the empty desert and our peaceful nights under the stars. But the town had a relaxed, friendly atmosphere and I warmed to the place immediately.

'I am home! Tamanrasset! My home!' Hamid cried over and over again as we pulled in to fill up with fuel on the outskirts of town, his face radiating joy and relief. He seemed to know everybody and was constantly stopping to embrace or shake hands with yet another long-lost friend or relative.

I had unconsciously kept the adrenalin switched on since arriving in Algeria, and only now that we had successfully completed this first leg did I realise how utterly exhausted I was. Hamid deposited us at a quiet *auberge* made up of little whitewashed buildings set around a sandy courtyard, where bright pink flowers limped up the walls, clinging on for dear life in the dry heat. We all felt pretty much the same way as these struggling plants; tired, caked in dust and in varying states of ill health. Josianne continued to be tormented by lack of sleep, Angel was complaining of feeling feverish and Jacques looked pale and tired, and although I was in decent health, every bone in my body ached from the last few days of riding and my legs were bruised and scraped from flying rocks. I was also looking forward to washing my hair, which was matted together with sweat and dust; this would be its first battle with shampoo for over three weeks. We stumbled zombie-like into our rooms and it wasn't long before we were all tucked up in bed, leaving Hamid to go home to his family at last.

'Tomorrow, I come find you here, and we go to my brother's house for dinner,' he informed us, before borrowing the Land Cruiser to skedaddle off home in style, claiming he needed to make a few adjustments to the roof-rack.

Sure enough, twenty-four hours later Hamid pulled into the courtyard and we piled into the car to be driven across town along unlit streets to our dinner date. Down a dark alley Hamid pulled up outside a squat concrete house where we were greeted by Faisal, the elder brother and a shorter, more portly version of Hamid.

'My brother does not speak English very good, but he is saying to you "Welcome to his home",' Hamid explained.

'*Shukran*,' we chorused in response, before removing our shoes and padding our way into the main living room. It was almost completely bare, with just a row of cushions against the far wall, a rug on the floor and a stereo system in the corner.

'Please, please,' said Faisal, motioning to us to sit down, and we lowered ourselves obediently on to the cushions. There were appetising aromas coming from the kitchen, the entrance to which was covered by a heavy tapestry curtain in the doorway.

'Faisal he has just married and the house it is new, he live here just three month.'

'Oh! Congratulations!'

'His wife from Algiers, now she come to live in the desert with him.'

Behind the curtain we could hear the pattering of feet and the clanking of pots and pans. Every now and then Faisal would get up and slip behind the curtain, returning with dish after dish of mouth-watering food.

'This is salad. This is . . . how you say?'

'Beetroot?'

'Ah yes, beetroot.'

'This is couscous, you know couscous yes. With vegetable.'

'Aah! This very good, this is camel meat.'

Our collective eyes lit up with genuine excitement; after weeks of Laughing Cow cheese, it was wonderful to even smell such delicious food. There were no plates, just cutlery, so we all piled in together, picking bits out of each dish. The meal was a treat for our flavour-starved tastebuds, but our appreciative noises were now competing with the clinking and sloshing sounds of washing-up that emanated from the kitchen. Hamid obviously knew what we were thinking and answered our unspoken question.

'In Algeria, the wife make food and she stay in kitchen, she does not eat with the guests,' he told us in a matter-of-fact way.

There wasn't much to say to that, so we just nodded in polite comprehension and carried on eating. But I couldn't help but feel slightly uncomfortable with the situation.

'Yesterday I noticed that there were quite a few girls walking around the town wearing jeans and T-shirts, and some were not wearing veils,' Angel said to Hamid.

'Yes, this you see sometimes and in Algiers it also happen very much.'

104

'Is this allowed, I mean is it disapproved of?' I asked.

'In Algiers I think it is OK.'

'I guess it's the capital, so it's probably more cosmopolitan,' said Josianne.

'And there's probably still a lot of French influence there,' I suggested.

'So, not all women have to wear the veil?' Angel persisted.

'The Koran, it says woman must cover hair and all of her to the feet and how you say this?' Hamid pointed to the end of his sleeve.

'The wrist.'

'Yes, yes, to the wrist and to the feet. But if woman is very beautiful she must show only the eyes.'

'Right, so the more beautiful she is, the more she has to cover herself up?'

'Yes, yes, this is right.'

He said it so acceptingly; the thought that this might even be open for discussion had clearly never entered his head.

'But what about that Egyptian TV channel we saw in the hotel in Djanet, the one with all the girls dancing in bikinis? It was just like MTV. How come that's allowed?'

'Ah, yes, Egypt is different.'

'How come?'

'In Egypt, you know, there is more woman than men.'

I didn't quite see how this was relevant, but Hamid continued with his theme.

'Yes, there are many many woman, not many men in Egypt.'

'So why is that?' asked Jacques.

I thought Hamid was about to enlighten us with some current demographic about the male to female ratio in Egypt, maybe due to some employment law or the effects of mass migration, but I had grasped the wrong end of the stick completely.

'There are more women in Egypt,' he was saying, 'because many, many years ago all the baby boys were killed, but the baby Moses, he was put in a basket in the reeds and he was found by the daughter of the Pharaoh . . .'

I wanted to laugh, because I had so obviously misjudged the conversation, but I managed to keep a straight face and kept nodding, trying not to look at the others. But Hamid must have picked up on the wave of scepticism that washed over his heathen clients.

'What? What? Why you laugh . . .?'

'No, no, sorry, Hamid, it's just that I wasn't expecting you to . . .'

He interrupted me, looking hurt. 'Why you laugh? It is true, I tell you! It is true! It is in my Koran!' he protested, outraged.

Luckily the awkward moment was interrupted by Faisal appearing from the kitchen with an invitation to Josianne and Angel and myself to slip behind the curtain and meet his wife.

I have to admit that I was expecting to find a seriously grumpy, resentful, miserable woman behind the curtain. This assumption was based purely on the fact that if I was banished to the kitchen to make a meal that I wasn't allowed to join in, for a load of guests that I had never met, I would be a seriously grumpy, resentful, miserable woman. So I was more than surprised when we stepped into the kitchen to find a young, slim, very pretty woman greeting us with a warm smile. She was already getting ready for bed and was wearing her nightdress, but she greeted us warmly, kissed us all in turn and sprayed our hands with her perfume.

'Thank you for the meal, it was lovely,' we said politely.

She replied graciously in French and then English.

'You speak English too?' I asked.

'Yes, a little, I speak Arabic of course, but also French and some English. I studied in Algiers before I married Faisal.'

'Oh yes, of course, congratulations on your marriage!'

'Thank you.'

'What did you study?' asked Angel.

'I did a degree in finance at the University of Algiers.'

I gulped. This woman was trilingual and better qualified than me.

'And now you have moved to Tamanrasset. Do you like it here?' asked Josianne, obviously as fascinated as I was by this tale of ambition and potential slain by tradition and religion.

Her face gave nothing away as she smiled and nodded, responding positively about her new life in the desert with Faisal.

I wanted to ask her so much: do you really like it here in the middle of nowhere, away from your family and friends? Why did you go to university when you knew that your adult life would be spent hidden away from the world? Do you ever think it strange that your husband's brother will never see your face? Don't you mind that your skills and education are wasted, that all those years of study were for nothing? Do you mind making all this food and then not being able to join in the meal? Do you want to climb out of the kitchen window and come on the road with us? See the world, have an adventure?

But of course I said none of these things, and after more small talk we parted ways with further kisses and warm smiles and gratitude for her fine cooking.

'What a shame,' whispered Josianne as we climbed into the car to make our way back to the *auberge*, and even Angel

107

managed to restrain herself from launching into one of her politically correct lectures on diversity and religious tolerance.

After a couple of days of resting, recuperating and tinkering with our respective vehicles, we were ready to continue our journey south. It was 200 miles of sandy piste to I-n-Guezzam, the Algerian exit at the border with Niger. This was where we would finally bid farewell to Hamid. Despite our cultural disparity and our few rocky moments, we had each formed some sort of a relationship with him over the last two weeks and although we were looking forward to travelling independently again, there was a sneaking fondness for him. Once we had stopped expecting him to act like a guide, and accepted him as a fellow travelling companion, we had discovered a warm, kind individual with all the usual exuberance one would expect to find in a twenty-three-year-old male. His youthful enthusiasm and the way his face showed every trace of emotion, along with his gangly appearance, reminded me of an eager-to-please puppy, and I couldn't help but warm to him, despite our differences.

Although the tarmac road gave way to a sea of rutted sand a few miles south of Tamanrasset, the route to the border was surprisingly busy, with heavily loaded trucks and convoys of cars blasting along in clouds of dust. There was a line of painted oil drums placed every kilometre to show the route, but even with these markers it was easy to stray off the piste, becoming disorientated by the criss-crossed tracks and identical scenery in every direction. The relative cool of the Hoggar Mountains was behind us and now we were back at sea level, wilting in the oppressive heat. This was how I had imagined the Sahara when I used to pore over my maps at home; dead flat, baking hot and nothing but sand in every direction. It was a disconcerting sensation and I was grateful to have the others to follow. But occasionally I would be forced to take a different path to avoid some deep ruts, or I would lose sight of the Land Cruiser in a dust cloud, and sometimes find myself following another white car by mistake. These brief moments of disorientation quickly turned to panic in my mind, and within a few seconds my imagination was rushing through the disaster unfolding before me. Lost in the desert, stranded, alone, running out of water, food, petrol . . . eventually dehydration, heatstroke, delirium, and finally, death. It's a standard sequence that every traveller in the Sahara considers at some point, but it made me all the more appreciative of my companions. And although Hamid hadn't turned out to be much of a guide, there was still a sensation, albeit illogical, that his mere presence ensured us some sort of security. But from tomorrow we would be on our own, four rookie desert travellers with half of the Sahara under their belts, and another half to go.

We spent our last night with Hamid camped behind a rocky outcrop, far away from the main piste.

'We must go further,' Hamid had urged us when we suggested setting up our tents a few yards from the track. 'The trucks drive all night and sometimes the driver, he will fall asleep and maybe drive into our tents.'

Being mown down in my sleep by an Algerian truck driver was not how I wanted my African adventure to end, so we made sure we were safely out of the way and lit a big fire to alert any dozing truckers of our presence. As we prepared dinner there was a sensation of an era coming to a close, and under a magnificent streaky pink sunset we talked and laughed over the adventures of the last few weeks. Although unspoken, it seemed important to make light of past petty squabbles, and instances of bad temper now seemed trivial and vaguely silly. Soon sleep was calling, and in time-honoured tradition, if such a thing can be formed in the space of three weeks, Jacques, Josianne and I crawled into our tents, leaving Angel and Hamid to set the world to rights one last time. I fell asleep to the sound of their earnest, whispered tones over the crackling of the fire.

We reached the town of I-n-Guezzam at the Algerian exit by late morning the next day. It felt like a strangely impermanent place, as if its few narrow streets and mud-brick houses had been thrown together with little thought, giving it a neglected, squalid air. Litter and sand drifts were piled up against the walls, and for the first time in Algeria I sensed an undercurrent of lawlessness and danger. Although in the other towns along our way we had been met with a certain coolness, verging on suspicion, there had always been a sensation of order and cleanliness. But border towns seem to bring out the worst in people, and at the rundown petrol station we happened upon a scene of near anarchy where a huge crowd of men were shouting, bartering, pushing and generally creating mayhem for no apparent reason. Hamid looked more scared than the rest of us, and when I pulled up next to the pump he began shouting after me to get away. Out of the car window Angel snapped a few pictures of me filling up my bike among the mob, but an eagle-eyed policeman swooped on the camera and forced her to delete the pictures under his glare. Hamid was now white with fear and making a fast getaway, shouting at me to follow. We left the town, heading towards the lone buildings of the customs and immigration.

It was only a mile or so to the exit post, but there was no obvious track and the only route was straight across a sea of perilously soft deep yellow sand. It was beautiful to the eye but I could tell that this short stretch was trickier than anything I had ridden so far. The sun was blazing hotter than ever, sapping my energy and turning every movement into a test of endurance. The lack of shadows on the ground made it difficult to pick a good route in the powdery, rutted sand and my bike felt unbearably heavy. The raging heat was already weakening me, making me light-headed and nauseous, and for the first time since arriving in Algeria I felt the wave of sickly fear that I had not felt since that awful day in Morocco. I knew I had to keep the power on and keep going, but under the glare of the midday sun I misjudged a deep rut; my front wheel slammed into it with a jolt, bottomed out and I went flying over the handlebars for my first Saharan spill.

'Lois! Are you OK, Lois?' Hamid was calling. He had spied my supine form in the rear-view mirror and was now heading towards me, the Land Cruiser bumping and swaying over the rolling dunes. I was unharmed but feeling thoroughly drained. I recalled the words of the Algerian gendarme: '*A woman cannot ride a motorcycle in the desert. It is impossible.*' Maybe he had a point, I thought grimly. Then my other side fought back. I'll show him, I declared silently as I struggled to my feet. We righted the bike and fired it up, but the deep, soft sand sapped every cc of power, and the engine was struggling to get it moving again.

'We need to lighten the bike,' I said to Hamid.

'Yes, yes, we take everything off.'

'Let us take your luggage,' said Jacques.

We unloaded as much weight as possible from my panniers

and bundled it into the back of the car. With these few less pounds I picked enough speed to get moving again and garnered all my energy to stand up on the foot-pegs and gun it as fast as I could towards the buildings. But almost as soon as I'd got going, I plunged into another unseen rut and performed the same dramatic somersault over the bars. I lay there on the baking ground, cursing out loud, swearing at the sand, the sun, the bike, Algeria and of course, the real culprit, myself. What a nightmare for such a short distance!

'Maybe the Algerian authorities really don't want me to leave,' I suggested to Hamid, but he didn't appear to understand my facetiousness.

Jacques and the girls waded through the sand with water, more offers of assistance and sympathy. I felt bad for wasting their time on such a stupid little stretch of sand.

'I will let the tyres down,' Hamid said with an authoritative air. 'It will help, how you say, the . . .?'

'Yeah, the grip, the traction . . .' I nodded weakly as he unscrewed the valves, letting the air hiss out.

This was all we could do to help matters, and once again I was back in the saddle, revving like mad, with Hamid behind the bike, pushing with all his might to get me going. The rear wheel spun furiously, flinging plumes of sand into the air, but eventually I was moving again, and finally, utterly exhausted, I careered my way into the parking lot of the Algerian customs building. A pair of clipboard-wielding customs officer came out of the front door to inspect our vehicles. Hamid and the others were milling about by the car but I was still wearing my crash helmet and pushing my bike into the shade.

'It is you who ride this big moto?' asked the customs officer, with an expression of confusion.

'No, no,' said his colleagues dismissively, 'this moto is for a man.'

They stood next to me arguing about whether or not I had been riding it. I couldn't be bothered to set them straight, so I left them to it and followed the others into the immigration office to have our passports stamped.

For once I was glad of the slow-moving bureaucracy; it gave me a chance to get my breath back and collapse on a chair in the cool confines of the building, with its high ceilings and concrete floor. Outside, the intensity of sun scared me; it was fiercer than I had ever known and I dreaded what the next 1,000 miles across the Nigerien Sahara would bring. I was shocked at how just those two slow-speed tumbles had sapped me of so much strength. My face was drained of colour and I still felt exhausted. Hamid's paranoid warnings about the horrors of his neighbouring country weren't doing much to raise my morale either.

'It is deep, deep sand all the way, big dunes, soft sand,' he kept telling us. 'Very hard, very difficult. And you must not tell the people where you go, not the police, no one. Tell no one where you going. Do not trust anyone.'

He turned to Josianne and Angel.

'You have bread, yes?'

'Yes, we still have some bread left, why?'

'There is no bread in Niger.'

With passports and vehicle papers all stamped out, the time had come to say goodbye to Algeria and to Hamid. We took it in turns to shake hands, hug and offer words of thanks, although for what, none of us were really sure. Angel was the last to bid him farewell and there was a slightly uncomfortable air about their parting, with some half-hearted promises about

113

keeping in touch. We watched Hamid walk away, a lone figure lolloping across the sand back towards I-n-Guezzam, where he would catch an overnight bus all the way to Algiers, arriving in time to change back into his tracksuit and trainers and continue with his chemical engineering studies the following morning.

'Well, it's just us now,' said Josianne, lighting a cigarette.

I wasn't sure from her tone of voice whether she considered this to be a good or a bad thing, but Angel certainly looked relieved.

'Oh my God!' she exclaimed. 'That was like, so embarrassing!'

'What?'

'Just now, saying goodbye to Hamid.'

'I thought you two were new best friends.'

'Oh God, I have to tell you. Last night, when we were sitting by the fire, after you all went to bed, Hamid proposed to me!'

'What!' we screamed, our eyes lighting up with the salacious hunger of a gossip columnist. After all, scandalous tittle-tattle is a rare commodity in the middle of the Sahara.

'Yeah, he had it all worked out; we would spend half the year in Belgium and the other half in Algeria. He even said he would let me have a job.'

We all burst out laughing.

'Wow! How radical!'

'So were you two getting it on then, all that time sitting around the fire?' I asked.

'NO!' squealed Angel in protest. 'We were just talking, or I thought we were. I like talking to people, I'm interested in different cultures and things, that's why I like travelling. I didn't think he'd take it like that. God, I feel really stupid, I was just being friendly.'

114

'Oh, the innocence of the young!' I teased her.

'Yeah, yeah, so are you saying that if you talk to a guy, he'll think you want to sleep with him, right?'

'Yep, pretty much.'

We all laughed some more, until Jacques interrupted our girly cackling.

'Come on, ladies, let's get going. We've got a border to cross. How are you feeling, Lois? You're looking a bit better than earlier.'

'Ready as I'll ever be.'

'OK. Let's go. Niger, here we come!'

SIX

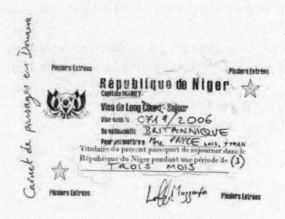

Hamid's fear-laden warnings turned out to be founded on nothing but good old-fashioned neighbourly distrust, and our passage across the ten miles of no man's land between Algeria and Niger was uneventful. Nevertheless, once the reassuring sight of the Algerian exit buildings disappeared from view there was nothing on the horizon at all, in any direction, and it was a disconcerting sensation to be in the midst of such a colossal, empty sea of sand. Eventually, far away in the distance, small shapes appeared, marking the Nigerien entry post of Assamaka. As we made our approach we could see it was a tiny village of shacks made from mud-bricks, tree branches and sticks, with flattened cardboard boxes for roofs. The surrounding desert scenery remained identical to that of Algeria just a few miles behind us, but when we rolled into Assamaka we stepped into another world. Now we were in Black Africa.

After the frosty detachment of the Algerian officials, here the gendarmes were sitting around barefoot in the shade with radios blasting out the uplifting sound of Afrobeat, making my heart soar. It was also a refreshing sight to see women walking around unveiled, taking part in everyday life. Soon quite a crowd had gathered, and everyone was shaking our hands while the smiling, camouflage-clad soldiers were giving us hi-fives at every opportunity. A couple of the women saw me arrive on the bike and came running over, punching the air, making whooping exclamations of surprise. They were speaking in Hausa, one of the many languages of Niger, but it was translated roughly as the local equivalent of Oprah Winfrey's favourite expression, 'You go, girl!'

Out of the crowd, a tall man, dressed almost formally in a black shirt and trousers, took control of the situation and shooed away the crowd.

'Please, come with me. Bring your passports and papers.'

This was Abba, the village chief. He had a certain nobility about him, but this was almost disguised by his humble manner and I found his air of gentle authority to be reassuring in our state of heat-stricken culture shock.

Abba was very keen to dispel the stereotype of the corrupt African official, and he made a big show of demonstrating that the bureaucracy involved in entering his country was above board. We were issued with receipts and shown official documentation to prove that our payments were kosher. It felt strange to be going through such an organised process in surroundings that were teetering on the brink of meltdown. Even the offices of the police, customs and immigration were nothing more than tumbledown shacks held together with twine, and the battle against the shifting sand had long since

117

been abandoned by the residents of Assamaka. At the insurance office, a sand drift had piled up against the door, allowing it to open only wide enough for each of us to squeeze through, one at a time, holding our breath.

Abba took us on a stroll through the village, where we bought a bowl of mealy stew from a group of women who were busy stirring away at huge iron cauldrons over a fire while men passed to and fro carrying pails of water on ancient wooden yokes. Some enterprising villager had set up one of the shacks as a grocery shop, selling OMO washing powder, tomato purée and cold Cokes from a fridge running off a rattly petrol generator. Recalling Hamid's parting warning, I was also amused to see a bountiful supply of bread for sale. The goats and chickens of Assamaka outnumbered humans by about five to one, and the livestock had the run of the place, bleating and clucking under our feet wherever we went. By the time we had completed our tour it was dusk and a sliver of a crescent moon was making its appearance in the darkening sky. We were all utterly exhausted, mainly from the heat but also from the incessant nature of our journey. The mental strain of keeping up with constantly new surroundings is a fact of life on the road, but we didn't feel we could reward ourselves with a rest day until we had crossed the Sahara, and that was still a long way off.

'Border crossings wear me out,' I said wearily to Jacques as I began unpacking my tent. We were setting up camp on a patch of flat sand outside Abba's hut in the centre of the village.

'Mmm,' he said in an absent-minded way, and I noticed he was scribbling in his notebook.

'Are you writing a diary?'

'No no, just recording a few details,' he muttered.

'He makes a note of where we spend each night, what

distance we've covered, how much fuel we've used, the average daily and nightly temperature . . .' Josianne said, teasing him in a gentle way. 'Don't you, *mon cher*?' She ruffled his hair, but he ignored her.

'Oh, Jacques! You're such a nerd!' giggled Angel. 'Mum said you were always like that, even when you were little! She said you might be autistic.'

'Well, Angel, if it wasn't for Jacques and his "nerdiness" we would still be stuck in the desert with Hamid, driving round and round in circles,' I pointed out, always keen to stick up for the geeks of the world, but Jacques ignored all of us, continuing to log his precious facts and figures in his notebook. I don't think he had heard a word of what were saying.

'I'm knackered,' I announced. 'I'm off to bed.'

'Well, you should get a good sleep tonight, there's not much to disturb us here in the middle of nowhere.' Josianne said, looking around at the sleepy village in the fading light.

'I hope so. We'd better get an early start tomorrow, before it gets too hot.'

We bade each other goodnight and collapsed exhausted into our respective tents.

But as night fell, the formerly peaceful Assamaka erupted into life as a steady stream of Toyota pick-ups began to arrive, loaded with contraband Marlboro. Out of our tent doors we watched the furtive comings and goings of the cigarette smugglers with wary interest, but they left us alone, and when they disappeared off again into the anonymous night we finally laid down our weary heads, able to sleep at last. We savoured about five minutes of peace before it was snatched away from us again as the village generator powered up. Like the roar of a river or a motorway, we could probably have tuned it out and slept through its steady rumble, but around midnight its drone was accompanied by a terrible screaming, like a madman rhythmically yelling the same unintelligible word over and over again. I could hear the others in their tent next to me, groaning in despair, all of us desperate for sleep.

'What the hell is that?' I called out.

'I don't know!' came back the reply from Josianne, muffled by layers of canvas and lack of sleep.

'I don't like it!' came Angel's tremulous voice from the other side.

None of us wanted to get out of our tents to investigate who or what was making such a disturbing noise, so instead we lay there tossing and turning until five in the morning, when the screams were drowned out by the call to prayer from the village mosque.

'Oh my God, I am so tired,' groaned Josianne as we crawled forth at dawn. We all mumbled in agreement.

'What the hell was that noise?'

'I dunno.'

'I don't want to know.'

'That was officially the worst night's sleep of the trip so far, even worse than when we were lost with Hamid,' I declared.

There didn't seem to be much point in trying to go back to bed, and we wanted to get going before the heat of the day kicked in.

We were heading for Arlit, a uranium mining town on the edge of the Sahara and the first settlement we would reach. It was 120 miles away, on a long lonely piste across more vast emptiness. But there was something to look forward to on our arrival: Angel's legendary overland truck tour had resulted in her meeting some aid workers in Mali, and through one of them she had managed to set up some vague contacts in Niger. In Arlit she had the phone number of a Frenchwoman called Marian who was going to put us up for the night, and in Agadez she had been given the contact details of a man who worked for the mayor and apparently would arrange for us to stay at the mayoral residence.

'The mayor? We're going to stay with the mayor of Agadez? Are you sure?' I said, amazed at this news.

'Would I lie to you?' she said, looking extremely pleased with herself. 'It's not what you know, it's who you know! It's all about contacts!' she added, tapping the side of her nose with her index finger in what she hoped was a mysterious fashion.

By the time we got ourselves into action the entire village was already up and about, busy making food or tending the animals. Abba came over as we were packing up.

'So, you leave now – did you sleep well?'

We all nodded dishonestly, but I had to ask.

'What was the noise in the night, the screaming?'

'Oh, that? It is just a goat,' he replied.

'A goat?' said Jacques, with a raised eyebrow.

'Well, I suppose a man can get pretty lonely in the middle of the Sahara,' said Josianne, and Angel giggled.

'Well, *bon voyage*,' Abba said with a smile. 'I hope you enjoy Niger.'

We all thanked him for his help and for making our entry into his country as painless as possible.

'I wonder if you could maybe make some donation to the village?' he asked Jacques quietly. 'Not money, I do not mean money,' he insisted. 'Maybe food, or something useful?'

We rifled through the car and rounded up the excess provisions that we had bought in Djanet.

'This is what travelling's all about it, giving something back,' said Angel as she watched the rest of us pack the food into plastic bags.

The residents of Assamaka waved us off and within a few minutes the village had disappeared from view and we were alone in the Saharan emptiness, blasting across a flat plain of brown sand, moving ever southwards. The morning was still cool and a layer of dew had settled overnight on the ground, creating a thin crust on the sand which made a firm surface for fast, effortless riding. The exhilaration of travelling at speed across this landscape without the menace of the midday sun or the perils of deep sand was just what I needed to conquer the demons that had resurfaced during the previous day's trials. After a few hours our route took us through an area of giant orange dunes, which the bike climbed and crested effortlessly, reaffirming my love affair with desert riding. As far as motorcycling goes, this was as pure a thrill as I had ever known, and I put yesterday's traumas down to a blip. I was back in the game.

But the heat was intense, and when we stopped for lunch it became apparent that Josianne and particularly Angel were suffering badly in the car: the air-conditioning was rendered useless by this intense heat. The only way I could deal with the extreme temperature was to drink water constantly and to keep riding. The minute I stopped it felt as though I would shrivel up and die, as if every drop of fluid in my body was being distilled with each second I spent under the sun's rays. By the time we arrived in Arlit, we were all utterly worn out and craving nothing but sleep and shelter. Strange as it was for us northern Europeans, the sun was no longer something to celebrate, but our direst enemy.

On any long, arduous road trip there's always the clinging hope that the day's destination will turn out be a Shangri-La, a dream paradise that will make all the slog, the dirt and the exhaustion worthwhile. Arlit wasn't it. It was a dirty, rundown mining town in the middle of nowhere. The sandy streets were strewn with litter and rubble and a layer of brown dust covered the entire town. Once we'd accepted the fact that Arlit itself was not the beauty spot of which we had all been secretly dreaming, we transferred our fantasies to Marian and her undoubtedly big house, with its foaming bath, fluffy towels and crisp cotton sheets.

'Maybe she'll even have a washing machine,' Josianne suggested dreamily.

We stopped at a phone kiosk and Angel called the contact number that her friend had given her. A conversation in French ensued but Angel came out of the booth looking confused.

'Uh, not exactly sure who that was, it was some guy. He said Marian's out of town.'

'Oh no!' Josianne and I cried in unison, and even the ever stoic Jacques looked a little disappointed.

'Chill, guys, it's OK, I've got it all under control!' said Angel. 'He said he's going to come and meet us here and I think he said we can stay with him or someone else, or something like that.'

About fifteen minutes later a ramshackle pick-up pulled up with a couple of men in the cab, who instructed us to follow them. We drove through the bumpy dirt streets past rows of run-down shacks and stalls selling food cooked on little fires at the side of the road. The wood smoke mingled with the dust and traffic fumes, lingering in the still air and coating my face with a layer of grime as I rode along behind the truck. We stopped in front of a house where we were introduced to another man in a similarly shabby pick-up truck. He nodded a greeting and told us to follow him. None of us had much of a clue what was going on, but I for one was secretly relieved to be operating on autopilot. The thought of having to make decisions or use any initiative was too much for my fried brain at this point.

We were eventually deposited at a one-storey breezeblock house surrounded by a high wall. This was where we would be staying tonight, and it belonged to the driver of the second pick-up, a big imposing man of Tuareg descent who introduced himself merely as O.B.. His eyes suggested a lifetime of struggle and his serious manner made him quite an intimidating host. We had no idea who he was or how he related to Marian, and I sensed that he had no idea who we were either, but he didn't seem to object to taking us in and, although gruff, made an effort to make us feel at home.

'Welcome, please come in.'

'Hello, *bonjour*.' We shook hands in turn as we stepped into his two-roomed house. It was a simple dwelling, but compared with the other homes I had seen in Arlit, I guessed that this basic dwelling with its walled compound and steel gate represented a certain status in the community. The walls and ceiling of the main room were decorated with ornate fabrics complete with tassels and fringes, and although there was no mention of a wife, I guessed that this décor was the result of a woman's hand. I couldn't imagine O.B., with his battered pick-up truck and defiant eyes, concerning himself with upholstery decisions at the local market.

'What would you like to do? Do you need to eat? Would you

like to wash?' he asked us as we slumped on to the sofa. 'You must want to wash, you have been travelling all day. Then maybe later you would like to see Arlit – we can go out to dinner.'

We were in that awkward position of the transient guest: grateful for the hospitality of a stranger and keen to show our appreciation, but all we really wanted to do was lie down in the dark and sleep. The idea of having to make polite conversation in a foreign language was tantamount to torture. Even the thought of washing was too much effort, especially once we discovered it involved filling up a bucket of cold water and pouring it over ourselves in the outhouse. Nobody mentioned our clean linen and bubble bath fantasy at the mythical palace of Marian. Even remembering it made me feel a touch foolish; here we were in one of the poorest countries in the world in the middle of the Sahara desert. Radox and fluffy towels? What on earth had we been thinking? It made me realise how much I relied on the stuff of fantasy when the going got tough. Our morale was boosted by the most insignificant things; being able to buy a cold Coke, or eat something other than a Laughing Cow sandwich; and the basic elements we took for granted at home, such as running water or washing machines, had become our objects of desire.

Josianne had been feeling steadily worse over the course of the day and was now shivering and throwing up, almost certainly suffering with sunstroke. Angel was not much better and was complaining of a headache and feeling sick. Jacques was putting a brave face on it, but he too looked wan and weary, and although I had somehow escaped lightly this time, I was thoroughly exhausted. Fortunately O.B. realised that the greatest gift he could give his house guests was sleep, and he

125

suggested we reconvene later that evening for dinner. He slipped out, closing the door behind him, and within a few minutes we were all dead to the world on his living-room floor, the only sound being the whirring and clattering of the ceiling fan, interrupted occasionally by Josianne's feverish groans.

O.B. returned at dusk to a more civilised state of affairs. Josianne was still too ill to join us, but the rest of us clambered into the back of O.B.'s pick-up and we bumped our way through Arlit until we pulled up at an incongruous complex of 1960s buildings, complete with tennis courts, on the outskirts of town.

'What is this place?' I asked O.B. as we parked up and made our way down a space-age corridor that looked like a set from Kubrick's *Space Odyssey*, albeit one that had not seen the benefit of a feather duster since 1969.

'It belongs to the mining company. It is a restaurant and bar for the workers.'

'What? For the miners?'

He laughed without mirth.

'No, no, for the French, for the white men.'

The building's groovy architecture suggested it had been built in the late 60s, but forty years in the Sahara had taken its toll, and although the funky plastic fixtures and fittings and the futuristic orange trill phone in its clear perspex bubble had taken on a faded weariness, the place still exuded a Carnaby Street air. Anywhere else, the textured white polystyrene wall tiles would have been ripped out as a potential fire risk, not to mention their lack of aesthetic value, but here in a dusty mining town on the edge of the Sahara they were still hanging on in there, four decades later.

O.B. was almost right about the clientele; it was mostly white

European men, although he wasn't the only black face in the restaurant. At the table next to us sat an impeccably groomed Nigerien man and his three very sweet small sons, who were dressed identically in starched collar and tie, grey suit, and polished black shoes. They were each perched on one of the adult-sized, moulded acrylic seats, with their shiny little feet dangling six inches above the floor. Although the silver cutlery looked incongruously big in their tiny hands, their table manners were straight out of a 1950s etiquette guide and it occurred to me that they were the best-behaved children I'd seen for a long time, and not just on this trip.

O.B. seemed to know everyone in the place and was treated with great respect by the waiting staff and punters alike.

'Do you have to be a member to come here?' Angel asked him.

He nodded.

'So, do you work for the mining company?'

'No, no,' he replied, shaking his head.

'Oh. So what do you do for a living?' asked Jacques.

O.B. muttered something in French that I didn't catch.

'Driving,' translated Angel.

Jacques, for the sake of polite conversation, asked a few more questions, but it was obvious that O.B. didn't want to discuss the details of his employment and was being deliberately evasive. In the end he muttered something to Angel that I didn't catch.

'I think he said he's a cigarette smuggler,' whispered Angel with wide eyes when O.B. went off to the loo.

We never found out for sure whether O.B. was one of Niger's shady Marlboro Men, but what we did discover over dinner was that he was a mover and shaker in the Tuareg rebel movement. He had fought in the uprising in the 1990s, when the Tuareg had launched an armed struggle for autonomy after years of persecution by the governments of Niger and Mali. Now it all made sense; his status in Arlit, his worldly-weariness, and the eyes that had seen it all. When we arrived back at his house O.B. reached up to the wall and took down a large framed photo.

'Look,' he said with a hint of pride, and actually smiling for once. 'This is me, shaking hands with the leader of the Tuareg rebels.'

It was the only time I saw him truly animated.

By the next morning Josianne was feeling ready to move on, and after a lengthy tea-drinking ceremony with O.B. and his various friends, who kept popping in and out, we bade farewell to our mysterious host and began to make our way towards Agadez. I was excited about arriving in this fabled city, harbouring romantic notions of the ancient Saharan trading-post, with its famous landmark, the great sixteenth-century mud mosque, towering above the maze of narrow streets in the old town. To boot, we had the added excitement of staying with the mayor of Agadez. Angel had made the necessary phone call and had managed to speak to someone, she wasn't sure who, that would meet us at the police checkpoint on the edge of the city.

It was a long and swelteringly hot ride of 150 miles from Arlit to Agadez, although after the first twenty miles or so the dusty track became a tarmac road, known as the Uranium Highway, which had been built to speed up the trucks that carted thousands of kilos of uranium from Arlit to the nearest seaport, hundreds of miles away in Benin. The mine's boom years were over, and now the road was neglected and scattered with potholes. But still, it was a relief to be able to indulge in some relatively mindless riding for a change, allowing me to relax in the saddle and take in my surroundings. We had left the rolling dunes and lunar emptiness of the previous few weeks behind us, and as we headed further south, although the days were hotter than ever, there were definite signs of life in the dusty ground. The dry earth was becoming dotted with vegetation; scrawny trees and shrubs were cropping up, patches of anaemic yellow grass lined the road, camels were making way for donkeys, cows and horses. We had entered the Sahel, the semi-arid strip of the continent that lies below the Sahara.

'Below the Sahara!' I said out loud to myself as I processed this information. Suddenly, the significance of all this greenery dawned on me. I've done it, I thought, I've really done it – I've ridden across the Sahara! I took a dreamy moment for this truth to sink in before I was blasted out of my reverie by a ramshackle truck, crammed full of people and animals, overtaking me at full speed with inches to spare. The driver blasted his horn and the human cargo waved as they roared past in a storm of dust, reminding me that I was still in Africa and that I still had a long way to go.

As promised, when we rolled up at the city limits of Agadez, our man from the mayoral office was waiting for us astride a little motorbike. He introduced himself as Mohammed, and seemed most jolly, smiling non-stop as we introduced ourselves. After exchanging pleasantries in French, he instructed us to follow him into town.

'So who's he?' I whispered to Angel as I put on my crash helmet and got ready to set off again. I was more than slightly confused about who was who and where we were going, due to my lack of French comprehension.

'Um, he's one of the mayor's aides,' she said in a vague manner, which suggested she was as mystified as I was.

'So is he taking us to the mayor's place?' asked Josianne.

'Yeah, yeah, he's cool,' said Angel. 'Look, just chill out, guys, TIA, remember?'

'I am *chilled out*,' said Josianne, mimicking Angel's English-posh-student voice. 'I'm just asking where we're going. Is that allowed?'

I noticed Jacques tensing up at the signs of another catfight in the making, and he began busying himself with the task of picking minuscule scraps of dirt from the car floor.

'OK.' I shrugged my shoulders and climbed on to the bike. 'Let's just see what happens.'

We followed the mysterious Mohammed through the rough and ready streets of Agadez. The town was far from my romantic image of an ancient desert trading post; more a standard model of African poverty. The streets were choked with rickety cars and bicycles, ploughing through the dust with unfeasible loads. No person or vehicle went unladen; whether it was just a couple of inner tubes strapped to the back of a bicycle or a twenty-kilo sack of grain perched on a moped. Street vendors, protected from the sun by tatty golfing umbrellas, sold black bananas and yellow oranges alongside stalls doing a roaring trade in mobile phone cards, Africa's new booming industry.

We eventually arrived at a modest house in the back streets. It was similar to O.B.'s place in that it was a one-storey breezeblock building contained in a walled compound with a solid steel gate, but it boasted several rooms and even, to our delight, an outhouse with an improvised shower and a real loo, albeit lacking a seat. Although these were indeed luxurious trappings, the house didn't strike me as being quite in the league of a mayoral residence. It looked like a regular family home. There were a couple of battered bicycles in the yard, a few kids' toys knocking around and some sheets drying on the washing line. Maybe we were just stopping off here first, before we went to the mayor's pad, I thought. But then Mohammed ushered us in, offering to carry our bags and introducing us to his sister and her children who also lived there.

'So, is this the mayor's place?' Josianne asked Angel as she unpacked the car.

'Look, I don't know!' she said, blushing with shame at the collapse of her grand announcements.

'I see, so maybe Mohammed is the mayor of Agadez? Maybe this is his palace?' asked Josianne, just a little facetiously.

'Look, I don't know, maybe he bloody is. Just because we think that mayors live in palaces doesn't mean that they do in Niger. You've got to stop judging everything by Western European standards . . .'

I skipped out of the way into the house before they kicked off again.

'Does anyone know who this man is?' Jacques asked me while we laid out our sleeping kit on the floor of an empty room. There was just enough space for the four us in there if we squashed together tightly, sardine style, and I feared it was going to be an uncomfortable night in more ways than one.

'No, I don't think so.'

'Oh well,' was all he said and he laid out his mat and sleeping bag before unpacking his belongings. Once he had arranged his notebook, pen, glasses case, head-torch and guidebook in a neat arrangement in which everything was laid out in size order and at ninety degrees to the wall, he seemed to relax, and went outside to lock the car, but the girls were still bickering and he fled back into the house to make polite conversation with our host.

Through the bedroom window I could hear the row picking up steam.

'Look, why does it matter if he's not the mayor?' Angel protested to Josianne.

'It doesn't matter, except that you've been going on and on about your "friend the mayor of Agadez" all day. "It's not what you know, it's who you know," blah blah blah. You go to Africa for three weeks on some student bus trip and now you think you're Kofi Annan.'

I heard a strange laugh behind me that I didn't recognise. Jacques was standing in the door and had heard the argument through the window too. I realised that it was the first time I had heard him laugh.

'One nil to Josianne,' was all he said, with a hint of a smile.

None of us wanted to ask Mohammed if he was in anyway connected with the mayor but he unwittingly cleared up the confusion by telling us about his work with the UN and showing us his UN identity card. He spoke highly of Angel's aid-worker friend Françoise, calling her a very bold woman, and I assumed they had worked on a charity project together. One thing was certain: he was definitely not the mayor of Agadez. We didn't press him on the subject of his mayoral connection or how we had ended up here at his house; it was easier just to go with the flow, and Mohammed was a most agreeable host. Later that evening his sister served us a meal of gazelle meat, a highly prized dish in Niger due to the gazelles being nearly extinct from years of illegal hunting. But this wasn't the moment to start quoting statistics from the World Wildlife Fund, so we all tucked in, acutely aware that politeness comes before principles every time.

Later on, when we piled into our room, Angel sneaked outside, leaving the rest of us lying on top of our sleeping bags, trying to cool down under the noisy ceiling fan. Ten minutes later she crept back in.

'I just borrowed Mohammed's mobile and called Françoise,' she whispered.

'Oh yeah? Everything all right?' I asked.

'Yes, but she says she's never heard of Mohammed. She doesn't know who he is!'

'What! That's a bit strange. I thought he said he knew her.'

'Yes, he did, but she says she doesn't know anyone called Mohammed in Niger!'

'Hmmm, very strange.'

'Well, we're here now, so we might as well get on with it,' said Josianne and switched off the light, leaving just Jacques's head-torch illuminating his notebook and attracting the bugs.

At last we had a day off, and as we were in Agadez, home to the Great Mosque, one of only a few genuinely ancient buildings in Africa, it would have been churlish not to pay it a visit. So, temporarily putting aside our godless souls and my aversion to sightseeing in general, we headed off into the old town with Mohammed as our guide. We arrived in an ancient courtyard at the foot of the mosque, where a group of robed men were lolling about on the floor, chatting and drinking tea under an awning made of palm leaves.

'First we must see the Sultan,' said Mohammed in a

reverential whisper. 'You cannot enter the mosque if you do not greet the Sultan first.'

'OK, where do we find him?'

'This is him, here.' He pointed to one of the men under the awning. 'He is, like, how do I say' – he paused for a moment to think of the words – 'your Queen.'

'Ah, OK, I see.'

I couldn't remember the last time I had seen Elizabeth Regina II hanging out with her mates in the town square, barefoot and drinking a cuppa, but the point had been made. This was a big deal.

'And you must take off your shoes before you shake the hand of the Sultan.'

I felt as if I was being set up for a practical joke, but we followed Mohammed's orders and removed our shoes before stepping under the awning.

The Sultan was a young man, clothed in white robes and sitting on a wooden chair, while his cronies sat around him on the floor. We approached quietly in turn, padding up to him with our bare feet, and offering our right hand.

'*Salaam aleikum.*'

'*Wa aleikum as-salaam,*' he responded politely, although I got the impression that he found it slightly bothersome having his conversation with his friends interrupted by all these strangers coming up to say hello.

We turned round, picked up our shoes and walked back to Mohammed, who was looking a little aggravated. He was shaking his head and waving his hands in a circular motion as if trying to direct us somewhere.

'No! No! You should not turn your back on the Sultan!' he said, looking vexed. 'You must walk away from him backwards.' He did a quick demonstration which looked suspiciously like Michael Jackson's moonwalk. 'Oh well, never mind,' he said, returning to his normal cheery self, as if none of this really mattered after all. 'Now we shall go into the mosque.'

We dodged the hawkers flogging silver jewellery and other tourist tat, and entered the mosque through a tiny archway where we handed over our shoes and the necessary fee to a tiny, wrinkled old man who looked about 200 years old. We ducked under another low arch and made our ascent up the ninety-nine steps that spiralled to the top of the tower. The higher we got, the tighter the staircase became, until we were bumping our heads crawling through ever tinier arches, before finally reaching the summit for a spectacular bird's-eye view of Agadez. The city spread out into the distance like a giant mud version of Hampton Court maze.

'It is the oldest mud mosque in the world!' declared Mohammed, patting the perimeter wall proudly and surveying his home town.

Angel and I split off from the others on the way home to buy our provisions for the next leg of the journey and something for Mohammed and his family by way of thanks for his hospitality. There was, perhaps unsurprisingly, a lack of the usual presents one would buy for children, and in the end Angel decided on a couple of exercise books for them. I didn't want to intervene but it seemed like a spectacularly dreary gift. As we made our way back to Mohammed's house our status as two apparently single foreign women attracted a lot of attention, not from the men, but from the masses of ragged children who spilled out of every house and shack on to the streets. They came running over to us with their hands outstretched, shouting, '*Nasara! Nasara!*' – white person. They weren't particularly intimidating and we did our best to brush them off gently, but soon a group had formed and they were following us down the dusty street, demanding that we give them a gift.

'*Nasara! Nasara! Donnez-moi un cadeau!*' they yelled after us over and over again.

I looked over my shoulder to see that the initial count of four or five children had swelled to about fifteen and they were picking up more recruits as they went along.

'*Nasara! Nasara! Donnez-moi un cadeau! Nasara! Nasara! Donnez-moi un cadeau!*'

They were close behind us now and their numbers had increased to such a size that the crowd took up the width of the street. They were gaining on us like a child army, filling the air with their shrill chanting.

'*Nasara! Nasara! Donnez-moi un cadeau!*'

'It's so sweet, isn't it? Like being the Pied Piper,' said Angel.

'More like a witch-hunt.'

'They're only babies, Lois,' said Angel, all wide-eyed and hurt on behalf of Africa's children.

'Yes, I know, but let's get out of here or take a different route back, or something.'

But it was too late. Angel yelped as a handful of stones hit her back. She turned round to face the kids, sending a few of them running off in fear, but there were still plenty more who were obviously enjoying the thrill of the chase.

'Children, children, please, please stop, we having nothing to fear from each other. We are all the same. It doesn't matter what colour our skin is.' She spoke in French, but it failed to disguise her primary-school-teacher tone. The kids took no notice of her plea and continued pelting her with gravel.

'Come on, let's get out of here!' I said, grabbing her arm and yelling a few choice words at the kids as I pulled her away. Thankfully a child's world is a small one, and once we picked up speed and made a few detours out of their immediate neighbourhood we managed to shake them off and make fast tracks back to the safety of Mohammed's walled, gated refuge.

Angel retold the story to Jacques and Josianne in hysterical hyperbole, painting my role as someone who had single-handedly scuppered her negotiations for world peace. I couldn't be bothered to argue, and I did agree with her that it was a depressing experience, but as ever on a road trip, the consolation came from the fact that we could leave it all behind; we were always moving on. The evening was spent with Mohammed and his family, and we left early the following morning, bidding them a grateful farewell.

'Please, give my regards to Françoise,' he said to Angel as he opened the gate to let us out. There didn't seem much point in telling him the truth at this stage, so we just smiled and nodded in assurance as we waved goodbye.

We were back on the road again, and although the Sahara was now officially behind us, and we were jubilant that this huge hurdle had been surmounted, a new spectre now loomed, one that had certainly been troubling me since I started planning this trip – Nigeria.

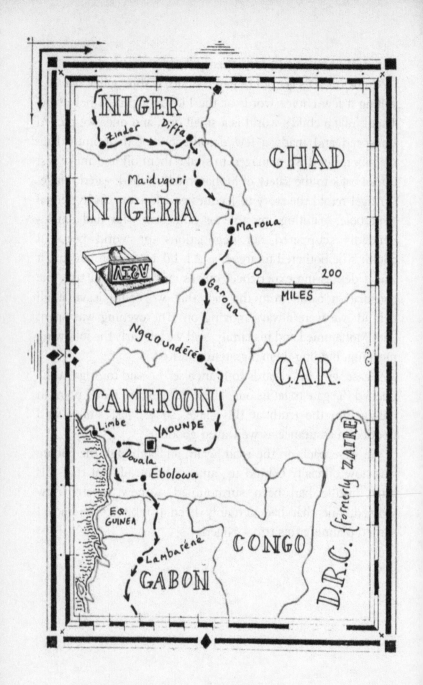

SEVEN

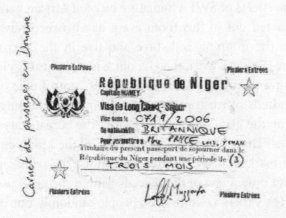

If the job of a foreign embassy is to represent its country abroad, then my visit to Nigeria House in London to apply for a visa had only helped to reinforce its country's reputation as the epitome of African chaos.

Situated in Northumberland Avenue, among the austere buildings of Whitehall, and built in the same sombre Portland stone, Nigeria House almost manages to look stately. But as you make your approach it soon becomes apparent that its glory days are long gone. The windows are grimy, and behind the streaky glass the posters, showing enticing scenes of Nigerian life, appear to date from the early 70s, and have faded accordingly. A handwritten sign sellotaped to the main door directs visa-hunters and passport-chasers down a side street to an unmarked fire door. Any attempts at pomp and circumstance are abandoned here as you make your way down a dingy staircase into the basement, in an entrance more suited to an illegal drinking club than an official government building.

At the bottom of the stairs a final door opens on to anarchy. Under the streets of SW1 a miniature piece of African mayhem is being acted out in this room every day between nine and eleven in the morning and three and five in the afternoon, except on Tuesdays when the visa office is inexplicably closed. The waiting room has the air of an out-of-control dole office, with hundreds of frustrated punters yelling and pushing and banging on the glass screens that protect the bureaucrats from the masses. There is a ticketing machine, of the kind you find at a supermarket cheese counter, to organise the rabble into a queue, but only a few of the officials behind the glass use the system. The others seem to pick people randomly out of the crowd.

On the day I went to apply for my visa the place was heaving with discontent. The majority of the people in the room were Nigerian, either native or British-born, renewing second passports or applying for a visa to visit the folks back home. Many of the elder generation wore the traditional outfits of brightly patterned tunics, or gowns and matching headdresses for the women. The younger cohort, though, were almost all fully anglicised, sporting either smart city suits or the de rigueur trainers and sportswear. Dotted among the sea of black faces were the harried expressions of a few middle-aged white businessmen and the bushy-tailed bright eyes of young, earnest aid-workers.

There was no apparent order to the system, and queues were cropping up and splitting off all over the place. I took a ticket and a seat and immediately received a telling-off for sitting in the wrong place from a do-gooder type woman with greying hair and dangly ethnic earrings made out of feathers and beads. It soon became obvious that there were old-timers here who understood the system, and I was showing myself up as a new kid on the block. I found a less controversial position next to an agitated middle-aged white chap who fiddled with the lock of his briefcase incessantly.

'Bloody shambles, eh? Bloody Nigerians,' he muttered to me out of the corner of his mouth without making eye contact.

'Mmmm,' I replied in a bid to still his attempts at conversation.

'Africa, eh? Eh? Only want a bloody visa. But oh no! That would be too simple, wouldn't it?'

'Mmmm.' I tried to concentrate on my book about the music scene of the LA Canyons in the late 60s.

'Huh! Well, *inshallah*, eh? *Inshallah!* That's all you can say isn't it? *Inshallah.* Huh!'

I was just about to say 'Mmmm' again when our non-conversation was interrupted by louder than usual shouting down the front. A weasely white man in a shabby brown suit, whom I had seen arriving just minutes before, was trying to shoulder his way up to the counter in front of everyone else. But a giant Nigerian man in a more expensive suit was having none of it.

'Hey you! Get to de back of de queue,' he boomed.

The weasely man just ignored him and continued pushing his way towards the glass screens.

'You! Man! Go to de back of de queue!' he roared again, advancing towards him. 'You come in here like you own de place. You queue like everybody else!'

Everyone was watching now, and there was an air of nervous

141

excitement buzzing around the room, but the weasel was studiously ignoring the Nigerian, despite the fact that he was now yelling just inches away from his face. Suddenly there was a guttural roar from the Nigerian and a collective gasp from the crowd as he launched himself at the weasel and rugby-tackled him to the floor. A proper old-school punch-up began, with everyone piling in, trying to pull the Nigerian off. During the entire incident the bureaucrats behind the glass had barely raised their eyes; they just continued with their form-filling and rubber-stamping as if this sort of thing was a regular and unremarkable occurrence.

Relative order was eventually restored and the weasel's humiliation was complete as he was forced to pull off a ticket and scurry to the back of the room, dusting down his scruffy suit. Thankfully I was saved any more insightful commentary from my neighbour, as my ticket number was called out by the severe-looking woman at booth number three. Two and a half hours after I had arrived I was walking out the door with a scrawled slip of paper and instructions to return three days later to do it all again when my visa would be ready to collect.

Lordy! If this is what the embassy's like, what on earth is the country going to be like? I wondered as I walked back up the staircase. I was leaving at the same time as a young Nigerian man who was wearing the full traditional dress. His tunic and trousers were of a bright yellow and orange print and he wore a matching round hat embroidered with gold braid. He was tall and slender, with a graceful walk and the air of an African prince about him. At the top of the stairs he moved aside and held the door open for me. As I stepped out into the street I thanked him and flashed a grateful smile. He jerked his head back down the stairs and rolled his eyes.

'What a bleedin' palaver, eh?' he said in pure cockney and sauntered off towards the Embankment.

Thus, my introduction to Nigeria did not inspire me with much optimism. Most people's contact with Nigeria goes only as far as deleting emails from implausibly named African businessmen who want to pay large sums of money into their bank account, but I have a slightly closer link because my father is married to a Nigerian woman. However, she did little to put my mind at ease about her home country and after listening to her tales of corruption, bribery and general skulduggery I decided to plot my trans-African route with the minimum amount of Nigerian miles and to seek out the country's back roads, far away from the sizzling fleshpots of Lagos and the notoriously volatile Delta region, where white oil-workers are kidnapped on a regular basis.

As it turned out, Nigeriaphobia isn't solely the preserve of its old colonial masters; my Belgian companions felt exactly the same way about the next country on our itinerary, although Angel claimed that we were all making a fuss over nothing and kept telling us to chill out.

'I think we should avoid the main roads and the big border crossings,' Jacques suggested as we studied the Michelin map of North and West Africa. We had stopped on the outskirts of Agadez for fuel and to decide how to tackle the next ominous leg of our journey.

'Yeah, I agree. Let's find the smallest out-of-the-way crossing in the bush somewhere; they'll be less used to tourists and hopefully not as wised-up about bribes.'

'It looks like here then.'

Jacques was pointing to the south-east corner of Niger and

the small town of Diffa, where the Komadougou River forms the border with Nigeria. Although the map didn't indicate any sort of route across the river, it did show the red and yellow flag symbols that mark an official border post. There were a few dirt tracks shown on the Nigerian side, so we figured there must be some way of crossing the river. But most crucially, it was in a remote part of the country, and therefore less travelled than the other border crossings that connected the big cities. It looked like our best bet if we wanted to keep a low profile.

'And if we go this way it means we can probably get across Nigeria in a day and cross the border into Cameroon by the evening,' added Jacques.

'Really? How many miles is it to Cameroon?'

'Two hundred.'

'Crikey! Two hundred miles, some of it on dirt tracks, and two African border crossings in one day? You're pretty optimistic!' I said.

'I think we can do it; the less time we spend in Nigeria the better.'

'I think it's going to be pushing it, but let's have a go.'

We left Agadez and began our journey to Diffa, 600 miles away through the hot, dusty lands of the Sahel. The Sahara was now definitely behind us, but still its sandy menace continued to edge into this part of Africa, bringing threats of drought and desolation further south each year due to the slash-and-burn farming employed by the ever-increasing population of the fragile Sahel. The ongoing struggle against the encroaching desert was evident in the shape of the scrawny crops planted in the villages, struggling to grow in the dusty ground. After a couple of days riding through this sun-baked, arid land, it became obvious that it wasn't just the crops that were scrawny in Niger, it was everything: the plants, the trees, the donkeys, the goats, the people. Water was scarce, and therefore food also.

There was little evidence of the world as I knew it in this faraway corner of the country. Women transported unfeasibly large bundles of firewood on their heads, children collected sticks along the side of the road or dragged stubborn donkeys through the dusty villages, while hordes of men buzzed around on smoky little two-stroke bikes carrying loads several times heavier than themselves. Life in Niger was an endless grind of hard work, and not helped by the marauding Arabs, according to one truck driver who was more than happy to have a good moan in the ear of a stranger. He had stopped next to us at a roadside stall, where we were buying the standard fare of anaemic oranges and white bread. His truck was crammed full of cows with huge comedy horns, straight out of one of Desperate Dan's cow pies. He saw me looking at them and struck up a conversation, but he seemed unhappy with the state of his bovine cargo and when I asked where he was going with them, he launched into an angry tirade.

'I take them to the market near Zinder but these cows are not good, they do not have enough to eat. It is the Arabs, they come here with their camels, from Chad, from Libya, with many, many camels. You see the camels, yes?'

I confirmed that I had indeed seen a few camels along the way, nibbling at the yellowy grass by the side of the road, and I must admit I had been surprised to see the ships of the desert so far off course.

'Yes, yes! Exactly! Eating the grass!' he said, becoming animated as he warmed to his subject. 'The grass that is meant for *our* animals, our goats, our donkeys, our cows. And you see the number, here, on the camels?' He pointed to his hip.

'Oh yes, I did see that,' I said, remembering that some of the camels had had a number branded on their haunches in various different colours.

'Sometimes the number it is just forty, fifty, but sometimes four hundred, five hundred! This is the number of camels that belong to the Arabs. They keep coming with more camels, more and more. Soon there will nothing left for us.'

I made a few sympathetic noises, and I was genuinely intrigued, not just by the subject matter, but also by the snippet of classic jingoism I had just witnessed. Change a few words and it could have been lifted straight out of the *Daily Mail* . . . 'They come over here, taking all our——' (fill in the blank to suit your own situation). But for some reason I found his xenophobic grumbling strangely reassuring: was it because here in this poor, parched African country, surrounded by unfamiliar people, customs and climate, I had latched on to something I recognised as universal to the human condition? Something in this Nigerien cattle farmer that made him the same as everybody else? I wasn't even sure myself, but our brief conversation stayed with me and from then on I looked out for the immigrant camels along the road and noted the digits scorched into their flanks.

As we headed east towards Diffa, the scrub turned to lightly wooded grassland and I hoped that at last, down here in the far south of the country, there would be enough greenery for all Niger's animals, indigenous or not. We were deep inland now, and the temperature remained steady in the high thirties. Niger was turning out to be a fascinating but testing country in which to travel. Our days were long, hot and dusty, and for me, physically demanding on the bike, riding all day on the broken-up roads with their long stretches of sandy ruts and huge potholes. We could no longer rely on the traditional morale boosters of food and lodging, as there was little in the way of either to look forward to at the end of each day's travel. Our diet was limited and basic: Laughing Cow cheese was still troubling our palates on a daily basis, and a night in one of the few hotels along the way was more likely to cause a plummet in morale than the boost we so desperately craved.

The strain was beginning to show, and we were all struggling to keep positive. Angel hadn't said 'TIA' for at least three days, and was rapidly failing to take her own advice and 'chill out'. She was beginning to moan about the heat, the lack of decent food and not being able to wash her clothes; she had been wearing the T-shirt that said 'Same shit, different day' for at least a week now.

'Same shit T-shirt, different day,' Josianne commented after Angel had complained non-stop for twenty minutes about the lack of laundry facilities.

'Very funny, Josianne – fashion queen,' Angel spat back at her, sulking for the rest of the day. Even the normally cool Jacques seemed irritated by every little thing and was becoming more and more finicky as a result. He had read somewhere that this road to Diffa was dangerous and insisted on us registering with the police in every town, even though when we turned up at the station they greeted us with bemused expressions and only at Jacques's prompting wrote down our names and passport numbers on a scrap of paper.

I wasn't feeling much better: being permanently hot, filthy and exhausted was taking its toll on my spirits too. Although we all made a pretty good job of not taking our grumpiness out on each other, with the exception of the occasional spat between Josianne and Angel, our general mood was a world away from the optimism and excitement that had launched us into Algeria a few weeks earlier. But I suspected that it was nothing more serious than good old travel weariness, and all we needed was a change in our routine, or a day's rest, to reboot our enthusiasm.

We arrived in the small town of Gouré, a couple of hundred miles from Diffa, in our customary state of fatigue. It was late afternoon and we were seeking out a Catholic mission we had heard about where we hoped we could stay the night, or at least camp in their grounds. We had no idea where it was, or even its name, so we lapped the sandy streets of the town a few times, but to no avail. I was so tired and worn down by the heat that even turning the bike round to double back on ourselves required a Herculean effort. In the end we got the locals involved in our search and were soon following a couple of eager young men on mopeds who, misunderstanding our request, delivered us to a Lutheran church on the edge of town.

'Non,' I tried to explain. 'Mission Catholique, pour dormir.'

'Ah, oui, oui!' they said, taking us on another bumpy ride across town and in and out of a few ditches before coming to a halt outside the church of the Seventh Day Adventists, also vying for the souls of the residents of Goure.

'Er . . . non, non. Catholique, mission Catholique,' we repeated, shaking our heads.

By now we had picked up quite a few helpers on our quest, which was predictably dubbed 'Mission Impossible'. One of the older boys who had joined the gang instructed us to follow him on his bicycle. We rode back down the main drag, slithering about in the deep sand, past the ramshackle market and then alongside a makeshift football pitch, before pulling up at a plain metal gate set in a high wall. There was no sign on the gate and nothing to suggest what lay behind the wall, but at least it didn't appear to be the headquarters of yet another marginal religious sect.

The boy was pointing at the gate, telling us to go in.

'Is this the mission?' I asked the others, who, being natural French speakers, had more of a grasp on what was going on.

'I don't know, I don't know what it is.' Josianne shrugged.

'*Entréz, entréz,*' the boy was saying.

Jacques was looking sceptical, as if he suspected we were being led into a trap.

'Well, let's have a look,' I suggested.

The boy pushed open the gate and we stepped inside. I could hardly believe my eyes. We were standing in a tended garden, with flowerbeds and potted geraniums and even an attempt at a lawn. From the gate there was a path leading up to two houses, yes, real houses with doors, windows, porches and steps. It felt like a long time since I had witnessed such a scene of Western domesticity, and it was an almost surreal sensation, as if I had entered a secret world, a magic garden that could vanish in a puff of smoke or at the wave of a wand. Was my lack of decent sustenance, showers and clean clothes driving me to domestic hallucinations? At that moment there was the sound of movement from one of the houses and out of the front door stepped a rosy-cheeked family: Mum, Dad, two daughters and a son. Somehow we had been delivered into the wholesome bosom of the Waltons.

'Hi guys,' said Dad, as if he'd been expecting us. 'Welcome.'

He was tall and lean and spoke in an American accent. His open, friendly face was tanned, although the rest of the family

149

had managed to dodge the sun's rays and remained translucently white-skinned, with blond hair and blue eyes. They were an Aryan dream.

We trotted up the garden path towards them and the outside world of dirt streets, traffic fumes, dust, and mud huts melted away behind us.

'I'm Tim Kusserow, this is my wife Barbie, and this is David, Beth and Hannah.'

We shook hands and made our introductions. The children smiled shyly, except for the eldest, David, who gave us each a firm handshake and a winning smile.

'Um, we were looking for the Catholic Mission . . .' Jacques started explaining.

'Oh, that's over the other side of town. But if you guys are just looking for somewhere to stay the night you're welcome to sleep here if you all don't mind squeezing into the lounge,' Tim offered.

'Oh, right, well . . .' We all nodded in agreement. 'Yes, that'd be great, thank you very much.'

'OK! Always good to have some visitors,' he said with a big smile.

'Do you live here?' I asked him.

'Well, we actually live near Diffa, but we've been house-sitting here for a while for some friends while they're away; we're missionaries, from North Carolina.'

'Oh, right.' I wasn't quite sure how to respond to this news. I had never met a missionary before, so I was intrigued, but slightly unnerved too, wary of a night-long session of fire and brimstone.

'We're actually leaving tomorrow morning to go back to our place, so I'm afraid we can only offer you one night here.'

'Oh, that's OK, we're heading for Diffa too as it happens. We're going to cross into Nigeria there.'

'Hey! Maybe we can all travel together in convoy?' Tim suggested, looking genuinely excited by this prospect.

We all agreed that this sounded like a fine idea, and we set about unpacking our kit and settling in for a spot of temporary domestic bliss.

The house would have been considered basic by American standards, but it was the height of luxury compared to the other dwellings we had seen in Niger. To me it was a haven. I missed my cosy houseboat and my life with Austin so much that it warmed my heart to be taken into a happy family home, even for just one night. But Jacques, Josianne and even Angel had become very subdued, and I wasn't sure if it was down to tiredness or the fact that they felt uncomfortable around such overtly religious people.

'I'm going to the market to get some onions for tonight's dinner,' announced Barbie. 'Does anyone want to come?'

After sitting on the bike all day I fancied a stroll. The others opted to stay put, so Barbie and I set off in the late afternoon sun, back to Gouré's main street. She wore a long dress and headscarf as worn by the local women, in an attempt, she explained, to blend in with and appease the locals, who were mainly Muslim.

'So, do you mind me asking, do you actually try to convert them to Christianity? I imagine it must be quite difficult.'

Fortunately Barbie was an open and engaging conversationalist and more than happy to give me the scoop on missionary life in the twenty-first century.

'We don't really try to convert them, no. Our main task here is translating the Bible into their language.'

'And are they receptive to that?'

'Well, yes, to some degree. Jesus is mentioned in the Koran, so they already know about him. But we also help with other things, medical projects, that kind of thing.'

'They're not hostile towards you?'

'Oh no, we've been here for years, they know who we are. The children have grown up here, David is fourteen now. We go back to the States occasionally, but most of our time is spent in Niger.'

We arrived at the market to a rather sorry array of fruit and veg. Little wrinkled women sat behind improvised tables displaying their wares, which often consisted of just three tomatoes or a bag of rice. Fortunately one woman had the onions that Barbie required, but by buying just two she cleared out fifty per cent of the woman's stock. At a nearby stall, next to some squashed guavas, I found a pile of coconuts, which after so many weeks of dietary monotony was a cause for celebration. I bought a couple for dessert and we set off back to the house.

Back in the lounge the others were lolling about reading back issues of *National Geographic*. David burst into the room and, finding the others engrossed in the magazines, sat down next to me.

'Ah, hello!' he said. 'You're back. Good! Now, I was wondering, do you like birds?'

For a split second I was slightly taken aback. In London, if a fourteen-year-old boy asked me if I liked birds, it would probably have a whole different meaning. But I was in the home of the wholesome family Kusserow, where bird actually means, well, bird.

'Er . . . yes, I suppose so,' I replied. 'I feed the birds back home in my garden.'

152

'Would you like to come and see my pet egret?' asked David keenly. 'I found him with a broken wing and rescued him.'

'I'd love to,' I said, following him out into the garden.

'And I've got a snake, and we've got a dachshund called Kobi, and under that stone there's a chameleon,' he continued proudly, leading me around the garden.

Once I'd had the full tour of David's menagerie he went to return his egret to its cage and I walked back to the house through the garden, but as I was about to step inside I noticed that Angel was sitting alone in the Land Cruiser, fiddling with her hair.

'Are you all right?' I said, knocking on the window.

She opened the door and took a quick glance around.

'Yeah, it's just like, I'm like so freaked out!' she said, once she'd made sure the coast was clear.

'What's the matter?'

'All this religious stuff, it like, just does my head in.'

She was wearing one of her marginally less dirty T-shirts, which said 'No Wucking Forries.'

'Oh, it's fine. They're nice people, they're not going to sacrifice you or anything.'

'I know, but it's like, there are Bibles everywhere and stuff.'

'Well, they're missionaries, what d'you expect?'

'I don't know, it's just totally freaking me out!' She widened her eyes in exaggerated fear.

'What happened to all your lectures on tolerance?' I said with a grin.

'They're not lectures, Lois, that's what I believe in, but personally, I'm anti-religion. Although I respect the rights of others,' she added quickly.

'Well then, let them get on with it, we'll be out of here tomorrow.'

'Yeah, but what should I do if they try and convert us tonight?'

'Angel,' I said, trying not to laugh, 'why don't you just chill out?'

Preparation of dinner was a group effort, and once the pot of hearty bean stew was on the table, it was time to pray. There was a distinct sense of discomfort among us non-believers, and Angel was visibly squirming in her seat, but we avoided eye contact and kept our heads down, staring at the table. Tim's prayer was heartfelt and had a homemade sensibility about it: he thanked the Lord for our food and asked that our onward journey be successful. I was worried about our hosts picking up on our atheistic vibes, so when the 'Amen' came at the end, I joined in with an overly-enthusiastic bellow, rather than the reluctant mumble of my church-going childhood.

While we were washing up the dishes Barbie and Tim took care of the drying and entertained us with more of their missionary tales, mostly concerning the heathen ways of the locals.

'We try to educate them about healthcare, contraception, but it is very difficult,' Barbie was explaining.

'Yes, they still make the tribal marking on the faces of newborn babies. That's one thing we're trying to bring to an end, but tradition runs very deep here,' added Tim.

'And the population growth is out of control, it's only foreign aid that keeps Niger going, there's not enough food for everyone, and it's only getting worse.'

'Yeah, I can imagine,' I said. 'I read an article not long before I left the UK, saying that Niger is the worst place to give birth in the world.'

'And it has the highest birth rate in the world too.'

'Yes, an average of eight children per woman.'

'Jesus!' I exclaimed automatically. There was a moment of awkward silence, but Tim, ever the diplomat, smoothed over my blasphemy and carried on talking, while I cringed inwardly and busied myself with the scrubbing of a saucepan.

'Yes, it's interesting because men get automatic custody of the children, but most marriages end in divorce, something like eighty per cent I think,' Tim was saying.

'So what happens to all the children, if their fathers can't afford to feed them?'

'Everyone ends up getting remarried and the kids get spread around the family, so there are very few actual orphans or abandoned children in Niger.'

'It just means that everyone's related to everyone else in some way,' added Barbie with a laugh.

'So is there no contraception then, or is it not allowed?'

'No!' Barbie said, almost exasperated. 'The Pill is available, but it's not very popular because it's considered a good thing to have loads of children.'

'Even if you can't afford to look after them,' added Tim.

'Oh dear, you must think we're terrible, the Americans in their nice house criticising the locals. We don't mean to sound judgemental, we're here to help.'

I reassured her otherwise and we left the last of the dishes drying while we retired to the lounge. The evening was rounded up with the most middle-class of pursuits: a political quiz from an old *National Geographic*, in which David demonstrated the benefits of home-schooling, putting the rest of us to shame with his encyclopedic knowledge of world leaders, workers' revolutions and military coups.

We were up the next morning at what I considered to be an ungodly hour to help the Kusserows load their pick-up, ready for the journey to Diffa. Breakfast kicked off with another prayer, which I managed to avoid by making Tim's coffee in the kitchen. But when I sat down at the table and spotted the toast, marmalade and English Breakfast tea, I too came pretty close to thanking the good Lord. Our hosts had been house-sitting here for several months, so there was a lot of clobber to shift, but with all of us forming a human chain, by 9.30 there was nothing left to pack except David's animals. The caged snake was squeezed into the back of the pick-up, the ailing egret got boxed up and wedged under a chair, and Kobi the dachshund rode shotgun with Tim. Our mini convoy was ready to hit the road.

'I hope you guys are ready for this road!' Tim called out of the cab.

'Why, what's it like?' I said as I mounted the bike.

'You'll see!' he replied with a grin, and we motored down the path and out of the gate, back into the real world.

We were trucking along at a good pace to start with and I wondered what all the fuss was about, but after thirty miles it became all too apparent. The route to Diffa degenerated into the worst tarmac road I had ever encountered, although to give it such a title is misleading; the tarmac was all but gone. The potholes were enormous, so enormous that entire sections of the road had disappeared completely, leaving long sections of deep rutted sand. These sections were often a foot deep, so riding into them was like bumping down a big step, which I tried to do as gently as possible to save the bike's suspension. But as soon as I'd landed, I was forced to accelerate immediately to get through the sand without sliding around and falling off, before finally giving an extra blast of revs to get up and out the other side. Occasionally I would try circumventing these sections by riding up the steep grassy verges, but I could see that trucks had been trying the same trick and had rutted and chewed up the ground. Both methods were as onerous as each other but there was nothing to do but plough on. It was exhausting riding, both physically, due to the heat, and mentally, owing to the concentration required, but at least it was doable. Tim and Jacques in their cars were forced to a walking speed, crawling in and out of the giant holes at two or three miles an hour, so at least I was able to catch my breath and gulp down some water while I waited for them to catch up.

There was a brief respite when we came upon a truck that had become stuck in the sand. Another truckload of people had stopped to try and help but they weren't making much headway. Most of the passengers were milling about, seemingly unconcerned about this interruption, as if this was all part of normal life in Niger, and no doubt it was. What wasn't part of normal life, however, was an Englishwoman arriving on a motorcycle, so when I pulled up at the scene I was soon surrounded by a group of inquisitive young men fawning over the bike and barraging me with questions in the nicest possible way. As I was going through the standard responses of where I was from, where I was going, Tim, Jacques and the others turned up. I barely had time to greet them before Tim was out of the cab and attaching a tow-rope to the marooned truck.

I watched in admiration as he chatted with the Nigerien guys and exchanged a few jokes, always smiling and laughing despite the fearsome heat and the laborious nature of our travel. He climbed back into his pick-up, fired up the engine and successfully hauled the stranded vehicle out of the hole to much cheering from everyone. The truck rumbled off filled to the brim with waving smiling passengers and our convoy was once again under way. I suspected it was just one of many Good Samaritan acts that Tim performed, almost unconsciously, as part of his daily life, and I had to admit to my atheist self that the Kusserows' unconditional generosity and non-judgmental approach, along with their all-round affableness, was in danger of giving religion a good name.

After many more tortuous hours of banging in and out of potholes and slithering through sand we arrived at the house of Kusserow, just a few miles from Diffa, where we made our farewells. I thanked them from the bottom of my heart; unwittingly or otherwise, they had brought a much-needed dose of warmth and bonhomie into what had been threatening to become an arduous slog. We said our goodbyes and made the last few miles into Diffa before darkness.

'You can stay with us if you want!' said Tim, but Jacques wanted to get going as soon as possible in the morning and turned down his offer of hospitality.

It would be our last night in Niger and tomorrow we would make our uncertain step into Nigeria and our mad dash across the country to the Cameroon border. As I lay in my tent, restless in the heat of the night, I remembered my visit to the Nigerian embassy in London. It seemed a long time ago now but the memory of the unbridled chaos was still fresh in my mind. Now here I was, poised on the frontier of the country itself, about to plunge into what I suspected was going to be more than just a 'bleedin' palaver'.

EIGHT

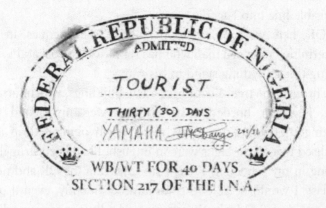

A brutal dawn start was motivated by the urgency of the mission we had set ourselves: to get in and out of Nigeria in one day. Jacques was adamant that tonight we would sleep in Cameroon, no matter what. Adrenalin spurred us on, and we were rolling up at the border post as the sun gave its first hint of the heat that lay ahead. The drowsy customs officer at the Niger exit point looked surprised to see us and was a little befuddled by our request to officially leave his country. But we weren't complaining; we wanted a sleepy little border crossing and we had got one.

After muddling his way through the necessary red tape he sent us on our way with a bemused but amiable farewell, and we set off along a winding gravel track to a newly built bridge over the Komadougou River. On the other side a rope was slung across the route, next to a tin hut occupied by a camouflage-clad soldier, cleaning his teeth with a twig. He was almost as lethargic at his counterpart on the other side of the river, but he managed to scribble our names and passport numbers into a book, and with the twig still dangling from his mouth, he untied the rope to allow our passage across the invisible line into Nigeria.

'OK, here we go. Cameroon or bust,' said Jacques, in the determined tone of a man who has set himself a goal and is not going to let anything stand in his way.

Through the trees I could see a few buildings, which formed the Nigerian border post, and as we approached the immigration office my heart made an involuntary leap as I realised that all the signs were in English. I had been struggling along in my schoolgirl French since leaving the UK and now, at last, I would be able to communicate fluently, even if only for one day. Suddenly Nigeria seemed a little more appealing. But most reassuring of all, this little border post was almost tranquil, the very antithesis of Nigeria House's chaotic, anger-fuelled visa office. There were none of the usual rogues that congregate in the shifting netherworld of a frontier; no hawkers or sleeve-tugging kids, no pushy money-changers or dreaded hordes of 'helpers'. Instead just a few officers lolling about in the shade next to a couple of makeshift stalls selling Tupperware boxes and the ubiquitous Chinese laundry bags.

'So far, so good,' muttered Jacques as we made our way single file into the hut marked 'Immigration', nervously clutching our passports.

The hut was tiny and occupied by a very large immigration officer who could easily have found alternative employment as an Idi Amin impersonator. His uniform was at least two sizes too small, suggesting a previously svelte figure, but now the buttons of his jacket strained across his ample stomach and the starched collar of his shirt dug into his neck like a garrotte. He was sitting behind an old-fashioned wooden desk, surrounded by piles of yellowing paper and tie-bound manila files, and on the wall behind him hung a picture of Tower Bridge illuminated at night, a token nod to the erstwhile colonial rulers.

'Good morning!' he boomed, standing up to greet us and almost filling the room. 'Welcome to Nigeria.'

Although he was making a good show of being convivial, he wasn't smiling, and there was a sternness about his manner and a look in his eyes that said: Do Not Mess With Me Or You Will Be Very Very Sorry, I Can Make Your Life Hell. I had seen the look before, in the faces behind the glass screens at Nigeria House.

'Where are you going?' he demanded.

'Cameroon.'

'And where have you come from?'

'Niger.'

'No, no! Where are you from, what is your country?'

'We're from Belgium,' said Jacques.

'And I'm from England.'

'Aah, England,' he said, turning to me with an appraising eye. 'You used to own us.'

I had no idea what would be an appropriate response to this statement, so I just smiled in an encouraging manner and made what I hoped were some non-committal, non-colonial noises.

'Do you have visas for our country?'

'Yes,' we piped up in unison.

'Please,' he said, holding out a massive hand. 'Give me your passports.'

He spent ages examining them, holding them up to the bare

161

bulb that hung from the ceiling, studying every stamp and visa, looking at our photos, then back at each of us in turn. Remaining silent, he stared out of the open door, squinting into the sunlight at where the Land Cruiser and my bike were parked outside the hut.

'So, you, from Belgium, are in the car,' he said slowly, as if trying to clarify a matter of great confusion. 'And you' – he gave me a quizzical look – 'are riding the motorcycle?'

'Er, yes. That's right,' I replied.

'Maybe you are a man, yes?'

I wanted to laugh but it didn't seem like a good idea, so I assured him of my feminine attributes with poker-faced earnestness. He didn't look very convinced.

'And you come all the way here from England on your motorcycle?'

'Yes.'

'And where do you go?'

'I'm going to South Africa, to Cape Town.'

He stared at me aghast.

'But why?' His voice bounced off the corrugated iron walls of the hut as it increased in volume. 'Why do you do this, why do you ride a motorcycle all the way through Africa?'

'Um . . . for fun, for an adventure I suppose,' I replied.

'Women do not do that in Africa!' he bellowed, although I wasn't sure if he was angry or merely baffled. 'They stay at home and look after the house and the children. I wouldn't let my wife go off on a motorcycle in the name of, of . . .' – he spluttered out the word – 'adventure!'

He then proceeded to narrate a detailed account of a day in the life of his wife, starting with her making the breakfast at 7 a.m., then ironing his uniform, taking the kids to school, going to the market, cleaning the house, picking up the kids from school. By the time we'd got to the bit where the wife was cooking his dinner, another immigration officer had entered the hut, stamped our passports, filled out the necessary forms and informed us that we were free to go. It was a shame, as I was looking forward to hearing how the wifely duties shaped up after the kids had gone to bed, but we never got that far as we were ushered out of the hut, back into the blinding light and white heat of a Nigerian morning.

The others were climbing into the car, getting ready to leave, but as I fumbled in my pockets for my ignition key a horrible reality made itself known to me. The inside pocket of my jacket, where my address book should be, was empty. In a moment of panic I ran through the events of the morning and realised with mounting dread that I had left it where we had camped last night after I had written some letters home the previous evening. This wouldn't have been a problem; it was only a couple of miles away, I could be there and back within ten minutes, so I wouldn't hold up the others too much. No, that wasn't the issue. The problem was that those two miles were in another country, on the other side of an international border that I had just crossed, in a country that I had officially exited. I considered the amount of African bureaucracy involved and wondered if it was worth the hassle. After all, I reasoned, as my mind raced through the various options, I didn't actually need my address book while I was in Africa; but what about all those phone numbers and addresses I would lose? I groaned inwardly at the thought of collating them all again when I got home. No! It was too much to bear. What would Theresa Wallach have done, I wondered? She would rather grapple with the sands of the Sahara than the sands of contemporary society. And I would rather grapple with a giant Nigerian immigration officer than go through all the hassle of starting my address book again from scratch. My decision was made, I was going back.

'You ready to go Lois?' Jacques called out of the car.

I pulled up next to them and explained my predicament. Their faces filled with dismay.

'Oh no! I don't think he's going to let you go back out of Nigeria and back in again' said Josianne.

'Yeah, he's scary!' said Angel in a baby voice.

'And what about on the other side, in Niger, you'll have to explain it to them in French' said Jacques.

'I could write out an explanation for you to show them' suggested Josianne.

'I reckon I'll be OK in Niger, as they're all so dozy anyway' I said, but I can't see our new Nigerian friend being very helpful, he's a bit of a stickler.'

'Hmm, and he's not very keen on women on motorbikes either by the sound of things!' added Josianne

I glanced over to the hut. The immigration officer was standing by the door, staring at us.

'I'll give it a go.'

I walked towards him, trying to look purposeful yet friendly, but not too desperate.

'Is there a problem?' he asked, his tone and expression as stern as ever.

I took a deep breath and explained my plight.

'I see' he said, nodding slowly, 'your address book is in Niger. And you,' he paused for effect, 'are in Nigeria'

'Er, yes'

There was a moment of silence as his eyes bored into mine.

There was no way he was going to let me do it.

'GO!' he boomed so loudly it made me jump 'Go now! You are a STRONG WOMAN!' There was an imperceptible twinkle in his eyes and I thought I even spied a hint of a smile but I didn't hang around to check. I was on the bike and tearing it up back into Niger as fast as I could go.

Sure enough the border guards on the other side didn't notice as I whizzed past them. The first one was still busy with his dental hygiene and the customs officer was nowhere to be seen. I was relieved to find my address book where I had left it, in the grounds of an aid agency where we had camped for the night. Well, it was almost where I had left it. The caretaker, a wizened old man who lived in a small one-room shack on the site, had found it and was looking after it for me, which of course incurred a charge. Sitting on the bike with the engine still running, I emptied the contents of my purse into his open hand; it seemed like a good way to get rid of the last of my West African Francs. He gave a surprised toothless smile as I crossed his palm with a fistful of silver and stood there staring after me as I disappeared off in a cloud of dust, as quickly as I had arrived.

'That was fast!' exclaimed Josianne upon my return. 'Did you get it?'

'Yep, let's go. Do you think we can still get across Nigeria today?' I asked Jacques. He was studying the map and looked twitchy.

'Yes, I think so. It's still early but we've got to go through customs.'

'Oh yeah, of course, where's the customs building?'

'It's in the next town, Damasak.'

My map revealed that this was only about fifteen miles away

along a dirt track, but when I looked in the direction of the route I realised that the map in no way reflected what was on the ground. Rather than one clear trail leading off into the distance, instead was a bewildering maze of sandy tracks, winding through the small thorn trees and low scrub.

'Do you know which track to take?'

'No, but don't worry, there's a couple of guys here from the customs office that need a ride back, so they're going to come in the car with us and show us the way.'

'OK, fine! Let's go.'

'And after customs: Cameroon!' Jacques declared. It was almost a battle cry.

We were guided out of the border post by the two customs men and I followed along behind. I was glad of their help, as the network of tracks became more and more confusing as we progressed deeper into the scrubland. We were still in the Sahel here in northern Nigeria, and the ground was soft sand carved up into deep ruts which made for tricky riding and required maximum concentration. But occasionally I caught flashes of bright colours through the trees, where women in patterned robes and headdresses were collecting firewood or washing their clothes in the tributaries that fed into the main river. Huge herds of black cows roamed freely among this activity, appearing out of nowhere round a bend or drinking at a silty watering hole.

But after a while I began to suspect that our new passengers were not quite as sure of the route as they had made out. We were doubling back and driving round in circles a little too much for my liking, but I just hung back and followed the Land Cruiser's cloud of dust until we reached a clearing in the trees, where Jacques brought the car to a sudden halt.

'I don't like the look of this,' he said, climbing out of the driver's door.

We were faced with a big mud-hole, about twenty yards in diameter. It was blackish brown in colour, thick and sticky, with a foul odour.

'Oh my God! It smells like an enormous cowpat,' Angel said, climbing out of the car to have a look. 'We're not going in there, are we?' she asked the customs men, her eyes wide with exaggerated horror.

'No. We are not,' Jacques said, before the customs men got a chance to speak.

It was strange to see mud after spending so long in arid conditions, but I had no urge to be reunited with it in more than a passing fashion and we started scouting round for an alternative route.

'It's still too wet,' Jacques said as we tested the surrounding areas, prodding the muddy ground with sticks.

'Yeah, but what about up there?' I suggested, pointing fifty yards to our left where the mud petered out into a large area of grassland. 'I'll go first on the bike if you want.'

I rode away from the mud-hole, with the others in the car following behind, and set off across the grassy terrain without much thought. But after just a few yards I felt the bike's power being sapped from under me, and I realised with despair that beneath this stretch of innocent yellow grass lay a vast festering swamp. It was already sucking me down and I knew that if I didn't act immediately I was going under. I stood up on the pegs, opened up the throttle and blasted across the bog as fast as possible, drenching myself in a bow wave of stagnant brown water.

On the far side was a small embankment which I ascended

at speed, landing on a dry sandy trail. I was soaked and stinking, but I had made it. I turned around to see how the others were progressing, to find a scene of saturnine inevitability. They were up to their knees in the swamp, pushing the steadily sinking Land Cruiser with all their might. It was only 10.15 in the morning, but the Cameroon finale was already looking unlikely.

'Are you OK? Do you need me to come over and help?' I yelled to them.

'No, it's OK, you stay there,' Josianne called back. 'There's no point in you getting covered in mud as well.'

This was very gallant of her, so I set about trying to clean up my mud-spattered belongings, but after a while I couldn't bear the guilt of being on dry land, watching them shoving and rocking the car to no avail.

'I'm coming in!' I shouted to Josianne as I removed my boots and socks and rolled up my trousers. At around the same time two local men passed by on a little moped, and, spotting the chance to make a few *naira*, pulled over and prepared to wade in too. They were dressed in the Muslim apparel of a long tunic, loose trousers and small round hat, and although their outfits were of impeccably clean white cotton, they wasted no time in stripping off and striding forth into the bog.

I followed them a little more gingerly, trying not to look down at the ever-deepening quagmire. The mud was warm against my feet and the stagnant smell overpowering. I could feel insects flitting around the surface, brushing against my legs, but I tried to banish all thoughts of waterborne tropical diseases and continued squelching my way towards the stranded Land Cruiser. Jacques was at the wheel, revving the engine in an attempt to reverse out of the swamp and looking thoroughly flustered by the whole affair. The two customs officers didn't seem in the least perturbed and were throwing themselves into the rescue mission, as were Josianne and Angel, but the customs guys almost seemed to be enjoying themselves.

'You did not drive fast enough! You go too slow,' one of them was telling Jacques, much to his annoyance.

'You must not be scaredy-cat!' said the other one and they both broke into fits of laughter.

Jacques was steaming with rage but keeping a lid on it, and ignored the two men's taunts. All four of them were now up to their knees in the mud and pushing with all their might against the bonnet. The two passing locals and I joined in but it was obvious that the car wasn't going anywhere.

'Have you got anything you can lay under the back wheels, to get some traction?' I suggested.

'We've already tried that,' Jacques replied with a hint of irritation.

'What about those old tyres over there?' said Josianne. 'Could we use them somehow?'

Jacques didn't answer but gave her a look instead.

'I knew we shouldn't have come this way. I said so, didn't I?' said Angel.

Josianne glanced at me with an incredulous expression and dragged Angel out of earshot.

'Let's leave them to it, shall we?' she said as we sludged through the mud, away from the car to a thorn tree where we took shade from the burning sun.

'Yeah, best bet,' I said. 'I've been in this kind of situation before with blokes, and the worst thing a woman can do is to offer suggestions.'

'Male pride, eh?' said Josianne, lighting a cigarette and grinning. 'I'm so glad we're not like that, it must make life difficult, all that pride at stake!'

We exchanged anecdotes of male vanity in our new roles as spectators, while the men continued with their revving and heaving and pushing.

Eventually one of the customs guys began scooping up armfuls of sand from the nearby track and pouring it behind the rear wheels of the Land Cruiser. It was a slow, tedious operation, but once there was enough sand to cover the mud we ladies were roped in again for tow-rope duty. With Jacques in the driving seat and the other seven of us pulling on the rope like a tug-of-war, we finally freed the Land Cruiser from an ignominious demise.

'Hurrah!' we all cried as Jacques backed out on to dry land.

The two guys with the moped were paid handsomely and trudged back through the bog to the far bank, where their clean clothes awaited them. The customs officers, feeling left out, made it known that they too would need to be rewarded for their labours.

'But you're meant to be guiding us!' he protested. 'Why didn't you tell me to stop!'

The customs officers just giggled uncomfortably and with a noisy sigh, Jacques doled out a handful of *naira* to each of them.

He was patently irritated and embarrassed by his ineptitude and the constant teasing from the customs officers was only making matters worse.

'Right,' he said, cleaning spatters of mud from his glasses. 'Which way are we meant to go?'

'Ah yes, it is over there,' said one of the officers, pointing at a track on a raised embankment a hundred yards away which skirted the swamp and eventually led to the far side, where my bike was parked.

There was a moment of awful silence as Jacques's logical cartographer's mind struggled to come to terms with this showcase of African absurdity.

'Then why the fuck did you not tell me that before?' he said slowly and quietly, only just suppressing his rage. It was the first time he had sworn in two months of African travel, and even Angel managed to restrain herself from telling him to chill out this time.

I walked back to my bike, wiped my muddy feet as best I could and followed in the trail of the Land Cruiser, feeling particularly glad that I wasn't in the frosty confines of the car. The remaining few miles of the journey to the customs office were mercifully straightforward, continuing through the scrubland on a mixture of sandy rutted tracks interspersed with a few muddy sections and a couple of small rivers to cross. But just as we were becoming complacent, a couple of armed police jumped out of a bush into our path, forcing us to stop. They had their intimidation down to a fine art, but the customs officers proved themselves useful at last, doing all the talking until we were allowed to continue.

'It is OK, no problem,' they explained afterwards. 'The policemen say people are coming over the border from Chad, and they kill the Nigerian people for their cows. But I tell them you are good people!'

Jacques made some sort of harrumphing noise and set off again in silence.

In Damasak the two customs officers directed us to the office without further ado. Our arrival caused much furore, and as soon as we stopped outside the building we were surrounded by an inquisitive but friendly mob of boys and men. There seemed to be far more people than was necessary around the place, although only a couple of them appeared to be doing any work. The others were employed in that most African of activities: sitting around. But the presence of visitors from overseas spurred everyone into action and soon we were being ushered into the office, while the older men instructed the younger members of the group to relinquish their chairs and fetch us water.

'Would you like to wash your feet?' said the chief officer to Jacques, Josianne and Angel, glancing down at their mud-encrusted toes.

Although this was worded as a question, it was quite clearly meant as an order and without waiting for their reply the chief led them to an outdoor tap, where they removed their sandals and washed away the last traces of the swamp. My muddy feet were hidden away in my boots and I was in no hurry to wash them. I was hot, tired and permanently grubby. Life on the road had lowered my standards of cleanliness and I was happy to wallow in my own grime for a bit longer; after all, I was happily installed in the chief officer's room with a fan blowing cool air on to my face while I watched BBC World on satellite TV. I had to take my moments of contentment where I could find them.

Nigeria was already an obviously richer and more advanced country than neighbouring Niger, where even the official buildings were constructed from mud and sticks. Here in Nigeria there was even a bit of business flannel seeping into the culture, with posters on the walls of the customs office waffling on about 'good practice' and a 'commitment to our customers'.

I supposed they were meant to inspire confidence and put Nigeriaphobic minds, such as ours, at rest. But like the festering swamp beneath the layer of innocent grass, I suspected that this cleverly worded cant merely camouflaged a deeper layer of rot below the surface.

'Everything all right?' asked Jacques, as the three of them returned to their seats. The cleansing of his feet appeared to have had a similar effect on his mood, and he was back to his usual self, uncontaminated by either mud or fury.

'Yeah, fine, the chief has gone off somewhere with our documents. But I think everything's OK, he seems all right.'

'Good! I don't know what we were worried about!' said Josianne.

'You see, I told you it would be OK!' said Angel. For a minute there was a flicker in Jacques's eyes, but it was quickly extinguished.

'You see, northern Nigeria is the most stable part of the country,' Angel continued in her foreign-correspondent tone. 'The north is Muslim and it's under Sharia law, which might explain why there is less crime and . . .' she tailed off when she noticed that no one was listening, preferring instead to watch Gordon Brown on BBC World making a deadly dull speech about interest rates.

'I guess we're not going to make it to the Cameroon border now, are we?' I asked Jacques gingerly. I knew he was dead set on this target, but it was past midday now and the chief officer was still busy with our papers. Reaching the border by nightfall was beginning to seem less and less likely.

'I think we could still do it, if we drove in the dark. We could get there tonight.'

The rest of us groaned in opposition.

'What's the point? We'll get there tomorrow. I think we can survive one night in Nigeria,' Josianne said.

'Yeah, chill, Jacques, we'll get there when we get there. You can't be in a hurry in Africa!' Angel's smugometer was off the scale.

I agreed with the other two, and, worn down by his female companions, Jacques conceded defeat and no further suggestions were forthcoming from his lips.

By the time the chief was finished with his many rubber stamps we had cooled down, cleaned up and caught up on world news. It was time to get moving again. The same group of curious guys who had greeted us followed us outside to give us a rousing send-off. As I mounted the bike and fired up the engine, one of the men stepped forward and took my hands between his. Oh no, I thought immediately, he's going to ask me for money.

'I am full of inspiration when I see you on the motorcycle,' he said, his face beaming. 'It is good to have adventures, not just for you, but also to tell your grandchildren.'

I smiled back gratefully, thoroughly touched and not a little guilt-stricken at having my suspicions shot down in such style.

'Well, if I ever have any I will tell them about you!' I said, and I rode away with a light heart and the image of his smiling face burned into my memory.

We decided to head for Maiduguri, the only big town between Damasak and the border with Cameroon. The road was quiet, with little traffic, passing through grassland which remained largely undeveloped except for the small villages of circular thatched huts that cropped up every few miles. The villagers were endlessly busy, the men collecting firewood on donkeys, bicycles or their heads, while the women, many of them with babies slung on their backs, pumped water from the well, lugging it back to their huts in vast tin buckets. We were stopped several times at police and immigration checkpoints, but tedious as they were, the bribes and intimidation for which we had steeled ourselves never materialised. Our only sniff of the legendary Nigerian corruption came from one officer who showed a particular interest in Jacques's pen, and after dropping numerous clumsy hints he was eventually granted ownership. We all agreed we had got off lightly, although he was quite annoyed as he claimed to have a certain attachment to that particular pen.

One of the checkpoint charlies hitched a ride into Maiduguri with us and led us to a hotel. It was dark by the time we had checked in and unpacked, but I was taken by an urge to see Nigeria by night; we would be leaving tomorrow and now that my fears had been somewhat tempered it seemed a shame that we would only be spending two days in the country. Maiduguri was a big, dirty, hectic town by day, but by night its main drag sizzled with another kind of energy. I could almost chew the air, still thick with the day's diesel fumes, which now mingled with the smoke of the many fires that burned on the pavement, barbecuing goat and corn. Hustlers, chancers, mobile phone pedlars and watermelon sellers moved noisily among each other, jostling for pole position while music blasted out of the shops and cafés. I was the only white face in this black night, but apart from the occasional greeting I was left alone to wander among this acutely African scene.

I did my bit to boost the local economy by phoning home with the assistance of one of the many young men who were sitting at their tables with their array of mobile phones fanned out in front of them. It took several attempts to get through, and when it came time to pay up, the cost of the call was twice the price I'd been quoted, but somehow I'd known that would happen. After all, as I had declared excitedly on the phone to Austin, 'I'm in Nigeria!'

Another day, another dawn start, another border crossing; and for the others, today was the end, their adventure would be over. They were in excitable spirits about their imminent homecoming, and although on the one hand I envied the cosiness of their Christmas with friends and the home cooking that awaited them in Cameroon, I was also excited about setting off on my own across the rest of Africa. Now, almost halfway through my journey, the qualms and uncertainties that had dogged me back in Tunisia had long since been quashed by a good old-fashioned urge for adventure. I was well into the swing of it now and I wanted more.

As I gave my bike the usual daily once-over in the hotel car park, I was soon surrounded by the entire male contingent of the staff. Unlike the more reserved Arabs I had encountered in North Africa, they thronged around me firing questions and trying to help by holding the bike steady as I checked the oil level or spinning the rear wheel while I lubricated the chain. Most of the conversation involved them trying to wangle my address and phone number out of me with lame explanations about becoming penpals. But wise to every Nigerian scam, thanks to my stepmother, I waffled my way out of it with bogus excuses that my husband would be very angry if I was to enter into such a relationship with a strange man! This concept they understood and the subject was closed.

'Yesterday I seen you come in here on your motorbike,' said one of the hotel porters, 'and I do not know if you are man or woman, and now I see you working on your motorbike, and I think, she is a woman, but she is like a man!'

'What do you mean?' I exclaimed, feeling slightly offended. After all, what red-blooded heterosexual woman wants to be described as a man? I wear make-up, I have opinions on soft furnishings, I own too many handbags – of course I'm a woman, I wanted to protest. But I kept quiet and continued topping up the oil with a slightly peeved expression.

'Because you work on your motorbike, you do the maintenance, it is only men who do this.'

I laughed out loud as the realisation dawned on me: he was giving me a compliment. In the harsh world of the African pecking order, to be a man is the greatest accolade, even if you're female.

'I'm most definitely a woman,' I assured him.

'Ah yes, but you are a manwoman,' he said, shaking my hand.

In a bizarre segue the conversation then turned to the subject of Tony Blair's 'interference' in the Israel/Palestine situation. But Jacques and the girls were ready to go, so I bade my farewells and rode out into the turmoil of Maiduguri's morning rush hour. The streets were jam-packed with every kind of dilapidated vehicle; a polyphonic blare of horns played out across the city, exhaust fumes filled the air and the potholed tarmac bubbled beneath my tyres. It was a hot and gritty grind across town but soon we were out on the open road, sharing it with livestock and convoys of thundering trucks. Decrepit pick-ups overtook us with inches to spare, crammed full of young men holding transistor radios to their ears, singing and shouting as they flew past.

I noticed there was a fashion among the truckers to paint

177

slogans pertaining to their life philosophy on their bumpers. No doubt their intent was genuine at the time of application, but the statements seemed to be at odds with the reality of life on the road in Nigeria. 'Take It Easy' overtook me with such speed that I was nearly sent flying into a huddle of goats nibbling at the roadside. 'No Hurry in Life' was the next culprit, who came hurtling round a corner towards me on my side of the road. A more serious-minded truck driver had chosen to declare that 'Islam is My Religion' but he was driving as if Allah had promised him a seriously good time in the afterlife.

There were absolutely no signposts anywhere, so a fair amount of our time was taken up with stopping, asking and doubling back. But a few hours later we arrived at the border post, where the smashed-up tarmac dwindled into a bumpy dirt track leading to a cluster of small official buildings that were steadily being subsumed into an unruly market. After getting vaguely lost in a labyrinth of Chinese laundry bags and mobile phone accessories, we discovered that, in an unusual stroke of logic, the immigration and customs offices were sited next to each other, just before a metal barrier marked the border between Nigeria and Cameroon.

'Oh! But you have only been in Nigeria for two days!' exclaimed the immigration officer, as he inspected our passports. 'You cannot see anything in two days! Why did you not stay longer? You must come back to see all the attractions, all the sights you have missed. There is so much to see in Nigeria.'

We made a few mumbled excuses to explain our mad dash across his country while he busied himself with his collection of rubber stamps.

178

'OK, OK, all finished!' he announced, banging his final stamp over my visa and collecting the four passports together into a little pile.

We reached out to collect them but he seized them back with a mock serious expression and wagged his right index finger at us.

'First, you must promise that you will return to Nigeria,' he said. 'Will you come back one day?'

'Yes!' we all lied, except for Jacques, who remained silent, but the immigration officer didn't notice his reticence, and with a big smile he handed our passports back to us one by one.

NINE

On the other side of the metal barrier lay Cameroon, and with it, the raw essence of Africa that had, until this moment, eluded us. From the chilly reserve of the Algerians, through weary Niger and then rural northern Nigeria, the change had been gradual as we had moved south into black Africa. Now here we were in the pounding heart of the continent, where the tasks and trials of everyday life are played out against a milieu of constant chaos. The streets were packed solid with people shouting, pushing and shoving, making it almost impossible to make any headway. We were mobbed instantly, or to be more accurate, I was. In the car with the windows up and the doors locked, the others were sealed off from the noise, the smell, the dust, the heat and the sheer overpowering sensation of being surrounded by hundreds of human beings literally rubbing up against each other; peddling one thing, hustling another. There was no escape.

I was hit with contradicting emotions. Instantly a surge of excitement and the feeling that yes, I'm here, I'm in Africa! This is like nowhere I've ever been before. But this was quickly tempered by the reality of the situation, of having to undertake the tedious minutiae of border-post bureaucracy against this highly charged backdrop, and the paranoia of leaving the bike unattended as I sweated it out in some hot, poky little room waiting for that vital stamp in my passport. As ever the bike attracted a crowd of boys who touched and pulled at every feature that took their fancy, tooting the horn and tugging at my sheepskin saddle. At first I was a bit taken aback, but although boisterous they seemed harmless enough, more curious than threatening, and it occurred to me that the notion of private property, and certainly personal space, was a concept I had brought with me from a faraway land. It certainly didn't exist here in Cameroon.

Unhelpfully the customs, immigration and police offices were spread far apart, providing maximum harassment opportunities as we made our way between them. But after several hours of unrelenting heat and pestering we were given our final stamp at the police station and we made our getaway, almost tripping over a man who was sitting half-naked on the floor, handcuffed to a bench, his glazed eyes staring out at nothing. Our attempt to speed out of town proved extraordinarily difficult without causing a small-scale massacre, but eventually the throng fizzled out and we found ourselves on a bumpy dirt road leading to Maroua, where Angel's friend Max lived, sixty miles away. We arrived by late afternoon and followed his directions to his home, which he shared with his girlfriend; it was a big house by African standards, down a small side street in a walled compound and

181

shaded by palm trees. Among the excitement and jubilation of their long-awaited arrival there was also a distinct sense of relief for Jacques and Josianne, but Angel was already complaining about the fact that her grand adventure was over and she wished she could do it all again.

'What? Even the bit when we got lost in the Sahara?' said Josianne, but Angel ignored her and continued bombarding Max and Bernice with her tales of the desert, omitting her night of Saharan hysterics.

But while the others reflected, I was busy thinking ahead. For me this was my halfway mark, from where I would be setting off alone towards Gabon, Congo, Angola, Namibia and finally South Africa. A whole new adventure started here.

'So how are you feeling about the rest of your trip?' Jacques asked me later that evening, as he celebrated their arrival with an ice-cold bottle of beer. He was really letting his hair down and hadn't even filled in his notebook yet this evening.

'Oh, you know, a bit of everything,' I told him. 'Excited, nervous, depending on what mood I'm in. When I'm knackered and hot and filthy dirty it seems like the worst idea in the world, but then the next day I'm raring to go! I dunno . . . I'm taking it in small steps; first off, I've got to get some visas sorted out.'

'I'm sure it'll work out fine,' he said, somewhat unconvincingly. 'You must have got the hardest part out of the way, crossing the Sahara?'

'I don't know, I think the Congo and Angola will throw up a few challenges.'

Bernice turned and looked at me alarmed, 'Oh, no, girl, you're not serious are you? You really don't want to go to the Congo!'

182

'Well, I've got the visa for Congo-Brazzaville already, it cost me a hundred quid in London, so I might as well get my money's worth.'

'You're not planning on going to the other Congo are you, the Democratic Republic of Congo?'

'Maybe, it depends how I can get into Angola. If I can get a boat from Congo-Brazzaville, I can avoid DRC.'

'You must!' she insisted. 'Congo-Brazzaville is bad enough but DRC is crazy, and Kinshasa is out of control, it's a dangerous city, not somewhere you want to be alone, certainly not for a white woman.'

Max was nodding in agreement.

'Some bad shit has been going down there, y'know,' he said. 'I've travelled all over Africa, but you couldn't pay me to go to Kinshasa.'

Although I tried to ignore doom merchants and naysayers as a general rule, I was more inclined to take notice of Bernice. After all, she was a born and bred African and had lived in both Europe and Cameroon, and she was no fool. Everyone back home had said I should avoid the Congo, but I had put that down to the usual fear-mongering and there was a part of me, maybe a lingering remnant of my teenage self, which, when told not to do something, just wanted to do it more. But this wasn't simply a case of rebelling for rebellion's sake; it was curiosity too. The more I learned about the Congo, the more I wanted to see it with my own eyes. How awful was it really? I had read somewhere that during the civil war the militia used to drive around Congo-Brazzaville with the severed heads of their victims impaled on their car aerials, and this was back in 1997, just ten years ago, the same time that Tony Blair had swept to power back home, declaring that 'things can only get better'. But some 5,000 miles south, in the heart of Africa, things were only getting worse. The stories and news bulletins of corruption, torture and even cannibalism were mind-boggling, but the Congo had stirred a morbid fascination in me, and as I heard myself assuring Bernice and Max that I would try to find another route, I already knew I was definitely going.

After a couple of days I was back in my 'raring to go' frame of mind. It was mid-December and I was on a mission to get to Cameroon's capital, Yaounde, to arrange the visas for my onward journey before the embassies closed for Christmas. I stuffed my panniers full of my standard supplies of white bread, Laughing Cow cheese and tomatoes before bidding the others farewell.

'Oh, I hope you'll be all right,' said Angel, coming over all worried about me. 'Just take it easy, don't get too stressed about anything, remember . . .'

'Yes, yes, I know, Angel, "chill out", is that what you were going to tell me?'

Jacques laughed for the second time in two months.

'TIA,' he said with a sly smile, but Angel was too busy doling out her advice to notice her cousin's uncharacteristic cheekiness.

'*Bonne chance!*' said Josianne, kissing me on both cheeks.

'Yes, good luck!' shouted out Max from the doorstep.

'And don't go to the Congo!' added Bernice.

They waved me off out of the gate and back into the heat, dust and havoc of life on the road in Africa.

It was strange to be suddenly out there alone. In one way I relished the heightened sense of adventure, but in another I missed the ready-made company of my travelling companions. I knew I would get used to it soon enough, but the adjustment period was a short sharp shock to the system and I tried to fill my head with positive thoughts, doing my best to banish any rumblings of fear or loneliness that threatened to bubble up and over into my conscious mind.

As ever, the geography made a more gentle transition. There was still a dry, sandy feel to the land as I set off from Maroua, but soon the semi-desert of the Sahel was behind me and as I continued ever southwards, towards the Equator, the scenery changed daily and it wasn't long before I was deep in the jungle of Central Africa. Now I was riding through dense, luscious greenery, along rust-red dirt roads lined with banana and mango trees, while exotic birds in Technicolor plumage darted past me and lizards scuttled in front of my wheels.

But it wasn't just the vegetation and the wildlife that had suddenly burst into action: there was another discernible energy in Cameroon, an industrious vigour and enthusiasm for life that had been noticeably absent in the Saharan countries. Maybe it was the sheer hardship of existing in the desert that created such solemnity in its inhabitants. And although life certainly wasn't easy here, there was no shortage of water, making for an abundance of fresh fruit and vegetables. As I rode through the little villages of thatched huts the women and children flagged me down, waving huge bunches of bananas or beckoning me towards the papayas, mangoes, guavas and watermelons piled up on rickety tables at the roadside. The rambling markets in each town were equally well stocked, and there were plenty of trucks on the road, exporting Cameroon's harvest to other Central African countries and creating a source of income for the many enterprising men, which as far as I could make out was spent largely on football shirts and mobile phones.

The expression 'in yer face' could have been invented for the people of Cameroon; there was nothing reserved about this nation, and as I watched the boys in the towns ferrying passengers around on the ubiquitous yellow moto-taxis, dodging potholes and traffic while shouting greetings and hi-fiving each other as they passed, I wondered if it was even possible to grow up shy here. A timid child would surely be trampled underfoot, metaphorically and possibly literally. It was dog eat dog, albeit in a strangely cheerful, upbeat manner.

Travelling solo again after so long in company, I felt painfully conspicuous at first. During the first couple of days this manifested itself as shyness; reminiscent of how I had felt on the ferry crossing to Tunis, I wanted to run away and hide from the staring and the cat-calls, the jokes and the inquisitions. But the Cameroonians were never going to let me get away with that kind of behaviour, and the only thing I could do was lighten up and go native. At first I was doubtful whether I could grow to love the scousers of Africa, a nation of football-crazy wheelers 'n' dealers, but after a few days on the road, like a snake shedding its redundant skin, I began to lose my British reserve; it was no use to me out here, and I found myself warming to the energetic hustle of Cameroon.

The country fairly buzzed with something I found hard to define at first, until I recognised it as simply humanity in its rawest form, a phenomenon that was almost alien to me after thirty-three years in sanitised, organised, convenient Britain. And I was surprised, if not a little saddened, at how awkward it made me feel to begin with. Like the Londoner who takes a walk in the country and responds with alarm when greeted by jolly, green-wellied strangers, I just wasn't prepared for these new rules.

Everybody struck up conversations with me, in the street, in cafés, in shops; they looked me in the eye and sometimes held my hand. Most of the time they weren't even trying to sell me something, it was just what they did. They were the same with each other, too: friends and strangers exchanged greetings, news or just gave a friendly slap on the back or a touch to the arm. It was impossible to do anything in Cameroon that didn't involve real human contact, and I wondered how and when this simple ingredient of our existence had ebbed away from our lives back home. Did it all come down to the fact that, unlike in England, there was no sense of immediate distrust, that people weren't scared of each other here?

I thought about the routine of everyday life in London and realised it was technically possible to go about one's business without speaking to another person all day. You could shop for groceries online, pay for your petrol with a card at the pump, post a letter with stamps bought from a machine, even trawl the anonymous mire of the internet in search of your life partner. And as I watched a group of giggling girls pretending to ignore the whistles of some likely lads hanging around the petrol station, I wondered how the age-old method of drinking, dancing and screwing had given way to sitting in front of a screen, downloading the data of a potential mate. Here in jostling, down 'n' dirty, real-life Cameroon, these images of twenty-first-century Britain seemed quite bizarre, almost science-fictional. I may have been hot, grubby and essentially alone, but as I flew along those dirt tracks in a cloud of red dust I knew I was alive every second.

However, it was fortunate that I was a happily married

woman and not on the pull on this occasion, as travelling in the tropics had its fair share of unsavoury drawbacks – namely masses of mosquito bites, buckets of sweat, and very frizzy hair. I was certainly no catch, but had I been an overweight, middle-aged white man it seemed that Lady Luck would have been smiling on me. I spotted several examples of this not-so-rare species, usually in a bar sinking ice-cold bottles of Cameroon's Trente-Trois beer, and always surrounded by a group of their natural predators. These blubbery, pale-skinned mammals were hunted ruthlessly by impossibly curvaceous young black women, sporting outfits that would cause Jodie Marsh to blush, and slathered in the kind of make-up favoured by novice transsexuals.

A few days after leaving Maroua I arrived in the small town of Bertoua and happened upon what appeared to be a fully functioning hotel. This was something of a novelty, having spent the last few nights in various cockroach-ridden dives or the Spartan bunkhouses of the many religious missions along the way. It was hard to resist the lure of a shower and the chance to hand-wash my sweat-soaked, dust-caked clothes, so I motored up the drive, passing a lawn with a sign forbidding anyone to set foot on its lush grass. Back home in green and pleasant Blighty there's nothing quite like a 'Keep Off the Grass' sign to get my back up, so I was most surprised, and alarmed, that this particular directive actually had the opposite effect on me. It found it quite soothing and reassuring that among the wham-bam bedlam of Cameroon there was a little piece of order here on this small but perfectly formed patch of turf. I laughed out loud at my bourgeois inner self as I pulled up outside the front door, wondering if at last I might be able to get a decent cup of non-instant coffee.

188

The hotel, like the worker's restaurant we had visited in Niger with O.B., was another example of groovy 60s aesthetics gone to seed. There were some fantastic orange plastic lights that would have fetched a few quid in Camden Market, and the once striking dining-room curtains were now a torn and frayed shadow of their former psychedelic selves. A sign behind the reception desk confirmed that the hotel had indeed been built in 1966, back in the early days of independence, when so many African countries were at last allowed to govern themselves after hundreds of years of colonial rule. It must have been such a time of optimism, I thought sadly as I rang the bell on the desk and waited for someone to appear. What happened? Why did they let it all go so wrong? And this was Cameroon, one of the better-off African nations, one of the few that could feed itself. What hope was there for poor old Niger, with its spindly animals and scrawny crops, and its mushrooming population? It was no wonder Africans lapped up religion like a drug.

The hotel staff were thin on the ground but they still outweighed the guests by a ratio of about five to one. In fact there appeared to be only two guests at large: me and a textbook example of the fat middle-aged white man. I could see this particular specimen from the window of my room, lolling about by the grubby pool on a white plastic sun-lounger that bowed under his bulk. True to form, a bevy of lithe young Cameroonian girls encircled him, all of them wearing skin-tight, buttock-skimming Lycra dresses. I couldn't see all their faces, but the rear view was a topographical sight to behold and confirmed my suspicions that there wasn't a single VPL to be seen, largely due to the fact that there weren't any P's to make an L in the first place. As dusk fell, the man lumbered to his feet and waddled off to his room with three of the five girls in tow. My night's activities were not to be as eventful: I washed my knickers, fleetingly considered donating them to the ladies by the pool, but instead hung them over the futuristic light fittings before climbing into the musty sheets. The bedside cabinet contained a condom and a Bible but I had use for neither, so I switched off the gentle glow of my illuminated undies and fell into a deep sleep.

In the morning I was up before my fellow guest, who I assumed was catching up on some much needed kip. I was hoping to make it to Yaounde by the end of the day, so with a fond glance at the immaculate lawn, I rode out of the gate and back into the fun and games of Cameroon's road-surface lottery. These final 200 miles were a classic African cocktail of potholed tarmac, half-decent red dirt, and the worst of all, washboard corrugations that steadily shook me and the bike to pieces and left my body juddering gently for several hours long after I'd stopped riding. As I neared the capital the muggy tropical heat became ever more oppressive, the thundering trucks and dilapidated cars multiplied every mile and I began to see signs of the modern world pushing their way into the landscape. Up in the far north of Cameroon the villages had been formed of small circular huts made from palm leaves and sticks. A couple of hundred miles further on, the materials remained the same but the huts had become more house-shaped. Now the first breeze-block homes with tin roofs started appearing and by the time I reached Yaounde the glossy green jungle had been trodden into submission by its concrete counterpart.

I entered the outskirts of the city feeling pretty confident that I could find my way into town without too much trouble; after all, I had a map of the city centre that I'd cut out from a guidebook. But as I plunged optimistically into the mayhem I realised that this was in fact the equivalent of arriving in Croydon with a map of the West End. Utterly hopeless. The complete lack of any signs or street names only added to the confusion, but even if I had known where I was going, it was almost impossible to move through the turmoil that swirled around me. There were thousands of people everywhere; in the road, on the pavement, crammed into the back of pick-up trucks, on the roofs of overloaded buses. All of them swarming about among the hordes of street-sellers who were flogging sugar cane, plantains, batteries, phone cards, beans, nuts, screwdrivers, bananas, sacks of rice . . . anything, everything.

Maniacal taxi drivers who cared for no one wreaked havoc among this scene of Third World enterprise, sending bags of peanuts, slices of watermelon and sometimes even people flying in their wake. Eventually I was forced to admit defeat and hailed the nearest cabbie, shouting, 'Centre ville! Je suivre vous!' without a care for the cost, or the correct French grammar. 'Oui, oui! Follow me!' he replied with a huge grin, and without looking or indicating, he pulled out into the traffic, narrowly missing a car bearing a bumper sticker that read, 'Fear not! Jesus is in Control.' I proceeded to follow him on a death-defying tour of Yaounde before he deposited me, slightly traumatised but eternally grateful, in the centre of the city.

In the car park of a slightly shabby hotel I spied a Toyota Land Cruiser with British plates, which was a good enough reason as any to check in there for the night. As I unpacked my gear the owners of the car appeared, introducing themselves as Eric and Sherry-Kay, who despite their UK licence plates were in fact an American couple who had been living in London before setting off on their grand tour of Africa.

'Yaounde's a total dump!' announced Sherry-Kay, with a friendly grin. 'But we've been fixing our car here and getting visas. We're leaving the day after tomorrow, thank God!'

'But we have found a decent restaurant that serves pizzas,' Eric added. 'We're going there tonight, d'you want to come along?'

'I'd love to; I've been surviving on Laughing Cow cheese sandwiches for God knows how long.'

'Yeah, tell me about it!' said Sherry-Kay, laughing.

At the restaurant we sat outside amid the traffic fumes and honking horns and perused the menu. As a vegetarian in a carnivorous world I'm used to picking bits of meat out of my food, or, if politeness dictates, just gritting my teeth and swallowing it quickly. It would never have occurred to me to try to persuade an African restaurant to cater to my whims, so I watched with a mixture of toe-curling British embarrassment and genuine admiration as Sherry-Kay did what North Americans do best.

'OK, I'll have the fried chicken with salad, but go easy on the chicken, not too black and just breast meat, no wings or legs. Hold the onions in the salad, but I want the carrots, but only if they're raw, not cooked. And the lettuce, and the tomatoes, but no sweetcorn, OK? And hold the dressing, no dressing. Oh yeah, and one Coke, with ice. Thank you!' she handed back her menu to a bewildered waiter who was still busy scribbling on his pad.

Eric and I made our less ambitious orders, and while we waited for our food we sipped ice-cold beers and discussed our respective journeys. It was a providential meeting for me, as

Sherry-Kay was full of tips about picking up the visas I needed for the next few countries on my itinerary and was also a fount of up-to-date knowledge about the routes and border crossings that were closed, out of bounds, or just downright dangerous.

'OK, so where are you going next, and what visas do you need to get?' she quizzed me.

'Well, I need Gabon and Angola and maybe DRC. But if I can get a boat to Angola, it means I can avoid DRC.'

'Forget it! The boat goes from Cabinda, it's an Angolan enclave in Congo-Brazzaville, but you won't be able to do that because you can't get the right Angolan visa any more.'

'You need a multiple entry visa,' Eric explained, 'first to get into Cabinda to get the boat, and then to get into Angola itself.'

'Yeah, and for some stupid reason that nobody understands, they've stopped issuing them,' added Sherry-Kay.

'I thought you could get them in Gabon, at the Angolan embassy in Libreville,' I said.

'Not any more. That's what we wanted to do, but they've stopped issuing all tourist visas.'

'You used to be able to get them at Point Noire in Congo-Brazzaville, but they've stopped doing them there too,' said Eric. 'We met a French couple who had waited there for three weeks before they were told they couldn't have one.'

'So are you saying that it's currently impossible to get into Angola?' I asked, worried that my carefully laid plans were about to be stymied by a tangle of African red tape.

'No, it's not impossible, we met some people who had done it, but it looks like the only place you might be able to get a visa is Matadi.'

'Where's Matadi?' I asked, trying to keep up.

Sherry-Kay pulled a map out of her bag.

'There,' she said, pointing to a town in the Democratic Republic of Congo on the border with Angola.

'Oh right, so I've definitely got to go to DRC then?'

'Yeah, it looks like it. That's what we're going to have to do. You can get the DRC visa here in Yaounde, but be warned, the women in the embassy are total bitches; I had a screaming row with them yesterday.'

Eric stared intently at his pizza as she recounted the story of her face-off with the troupe of catty Congolese bureaucrats.

'Oh yeah, and the Gabon embassy has a goddam dress code! We were turned away because I was wearing flip-flops! I mean, Jesus Christ, who are these people?'

'They're Africans,' replied Eric with a resigned, but amused look.

'We met some other Brits on motorbikes,' said Sherry-Kay, changing the subject. 'A couple of guys from Portsmouth, one of them was on a big red and white bike – d'you know them?'

'No, I don't think so. Which way are they going?'

'South, same as you, but they left Yaounde a couple of weeks ago and they were on a mission. They said that if they weren't back in England for Christmas their girlfriends were going to dump them!'

'Ha! Oh, in that case I probably won't catch them up. Sounds like they'd be better off taking their time and getting dumped!'

We walked back through the unlit backstreets of Yaounde with little incident except for a proposition by a group of prostitutes of debatable gender. Male or female, they'd certainly made an effort, but with their drawn-on red mouths, sequinned boob tubes and unfeasibly high heels, they looked more like a fancy-dress version of a hooker. I was intrigued by the fact that they were obviously making a feature of their fat stomachs, which bulged over their miniskirts, and as we walked past they shook their wobbly bellies and called out a list of their services in English, accompanied by shrieks of laughter.

It was a shame that Eric and Sherry-Kay were leaving so soon – they were good company and it would have been fun to hang out with them while I killed time waiting for my visas – but I could see why they were so keen to get out of Yaounde. It was an oddly soulless city, with no sense of history or even reason for being: it wasn't a port on a great river, or the site of an ancient fort high on a hill; there were none of the fine old buildings or grand parks that one associates with capital cities. It was almost as if Yaounde had come about by accident as more and more people had gravitated here, forcing it to expand accordingly with no sense of planning or order. Most of the buildings dated from the 60s onwards, ugly concrete monoliths, strewn randomly across the city. The only exception to this was the diplomatic district of Bastos, where stately embassy buildings and ambassadors' homes lay behind tall whitewashed walls, protected by armed guards on every corner.

After being on the bike all day every day, and aware that my Laughing Cow diet was in danger of turning my figure into that of a Yaounde hooker, I decided to walk the few miles to the embassies. But even at eight in the morning the heat was unbearable, and bearing in mind Gabon's dress code I decided to go for the Democratic Republic of Congo first, in the hope that they wouldn't object to a sweating, red-faced, frizzy-haired Englishwoman wanting to visit their country. From what I knew about DRC, they had much bigger problems to worry about. But what I hoped would be a gentle amble through

Yaounde soon turned into an urban assault course, as I dodged the homicidal taxis, leapt over open drains and scrambled up and down piles of rubble in my flip-flops, thinking how a pavement and a couple of zebra crossings wouldn't go amiss. To add to the fun, my entire journey was accompanied by the calls of the local men, who found my presence highly entertaining, shouting at me as I passed by, '*La Blanche! La Blanche! Bonjour, La Blanche!*'

I had a good hour's walk ahead of me, so I spent the time noting the various items that the citizens of Yaounde carried on their heads. By the time I had spotted a bowl of cow's feet, a tray of eggs (very bold), a stack of books and a bedside table, I had arrived in Bastos. Just around the corner from the heavily fortified Israeli consul was the embassy of the Democratic Republic of Congo, and with quaking knees I pushed open the gate and wondered, for a brief moment, what on earth I was doing, applying to visit one of the most lawless and dangerous countries in the world, alone.

Sherry-Kay was right; the women behind the counter raised the bar on bureaucratic surliness, and I made it my secret mission to force one of them to smile before I was through. A photocopied form was shoved my way with sullen instructions to fill it in and hand over a large amount of money. The décor of the embassy was pure dictator chic, or at least it had been once; now it was more a case of shabby dictator chic and there was something slightly tragic about the clumsy attempts at grandeur. The grubby cream leather sofa had a distinctly sticky, PVC feel, the rococo style lamps were missing a few shades and on closer inspection the gilt mouldings and picture frames turned out to be gold plastic. I took a seat in the empty waiting area and began filling in the form, resting it on the one magazine in the place, a copy of *Poultry World*, bearing the ominous headline, 'Dark Clouds Hanging over the European Poultry Industry'. I burst out laughing at finding this banal publication in the wannabe opulent surroundings of the DRC embassy, but my merriment was quickly stifled by a sharp look from the stroppy madam and I continued my form-filling in silence.

I collected my visa three days later, and after a bit of gooning around and excessive friendliness I managed to wring a smile out of the younger woman behind the counter. One nil to me! I declared as I headed straight for the Gabon embassy, just a few blocks away. It was a similarly austere affair, with lots of marble and dark wood panelling. But judging by the 'Elf' logo that accompanied the framed posters of Wildlife of Gabon, I guessed that there was plenty of oil money lubricating the wheels of this small country. Sure enough, the leather sofas really were leather and the antique desks were solid mahogany, not the veneered repro affairs they favoured up the road. In fact the only thing that the two embassies had in common was a snooty staff that would barely deign to speak to me. After the usual paperwork and handing over of cash, I was instructed to return forty-eight hours later, but I feared that a smile would not be forthcoming here.

When I turned up two days later, at the appointed time, the sour-faced, middle-aged clerk I had dealt with was reclining on a velvet chaise longue next to her desk, chatting away with a colleague. The door to the office was open, so I stepped inside.

'*Bonjour, madame*,' I greeted her. 'I've come to collect my visa.'

She glanced over and briefly looked me up and down before turning away and continuing her conversation. Resisting the urge to rush over and bundle her, I took a deep breath and made what I hoped was a sweet smile. OK, I thought, I'll play your game. I stood in the doorway staring at her in silence as she continued to ignore me, while I wondered if embassy employees became like this because of the job, or if they were born like this and that was why they got the job. Eventually, with an exaggerated sigh, making it quite clear that I was causing her enormous inconvenience, she eased herself upright with great effort, squeezed her swollen feet into a pair of painfully tight high heels and tottered the four steps to her desk where a pile of passports sat, waiting to be collected by some other poor hapless travellers.

'*Voilà*,' she said with a sarcastic sneer, handing my passport to me. I recoiled slightly when her talon-like fingernails scraped against my hand as I took it from her. She returned to her supine position as I flicked through the pages, checking the details on the blurred inky stamp.

'*Merci beaucoup!*' I called out, and not waiting for a reply I ran down the steps of the embassy, back into the sweltering, syrupy heat of the afternoon, looking forward to the freedom of hitting the road again.

TEN

I was all ready to leave Yaounde and make my way over to the beach town of Limbe on the Atlantic coast when I received an email bringing some unexpected but exciting news from home. A few years earlier, when I'd come up with the grand idea of writing for a living, I had boosted my non-existent income by working as a motorbike courier for a TV equipment company in North London. It was run by a fiery Iranian man by the name of Ahmad, who in between sending me off around London delivering lenses and tripods had kindly tolerated me tapping away on the stockroom computer, writing what he used to refer to, not a little sarcastically, as 'your memoirs'. It was in this very stockroom that I had received news of my first book contract, and my courier career had gone steadily into decline thereafter.

But now here was an email from Ahmad himself, telling me

of an old school friend named Ekoko Mukete who lived in Cameroon's second city, Douala. Although a born and bred Cameroonian, Ekoko had been sent to school in Britain and, according to Ahmad, was now a high flyer in his home country. As I read on I discovered this was something of an understatement. His CV included a top position in Cameroon's Chamber of Commerce, ownership of a TV channel and some vague references about royal blood. And according to Ahmad, this man was waiting for my call.

I scribbled down his number and found one of the street-corner phone booths where a group of teenage boys were hiring out their mobiles. Ekoko answered the phone and sounded very jolly and pleased to hear from me, despite the fact that I was a total stranger.

'We live in Douala,' he said, 'but in a few days it is the Christmas holidays and we'll be in our beach house in Limbe. You must come and visit us there.'

'Limbe!' I said, surprised. 'That's where I'm heading to today.'

'Excellent, it couldn't have worked out better. Call me on Friday and you will come to our house that evening.'

This new turn of events put a spring in my step and I set about packing up my bike, ready to leave. I was glad to be getting out of Yaounde, but as this was probably the last big city I would see for a while, I decided to make the most of its few amenities and change some money before I set off. After the visas, the hotel bill and a few lengthy phone calls, I was running low on my stash of Central African francs. I made my way to where my bike was parked behind the hotel and, with a quick glance to make sure no one was around, removed the side panel from the left side of the bike, unscrewed the cover of the air-box and slid out a roll of Euro notes that I had hidden in there when I left the UK. I had taped them up in a plastic bag and they seemed to have survived, despite having spent the last few months wedged alongside a very dusty, hard-working air-filter.

I nipped across the road to the nearest bank, but the snotty woman at reception made it known in no uncertain terms that as I was not a customer of the bank, I would not be allowed to set another foot inside the building, let alone use their foreign exchange service. Maybe I had strayed into the Cameroonian equivalent of Coutts, I thought. Thankfully, the more approachable security guard at the door took pity on me and pointed me in the direction of a bank that catered to the needs of the hoi polloi. I slogged over there in the boiling heat, with my bankroll shoved in my bra, to discover that indeed, this was the bank for me. A formless queue of Cameroon's great unwashed filled the entire building and snaked out of the front door on to the street. There were no signs at the cashier's windows to give me any clues as to what I should do or where I should go, so I resigned myself to joining the back of the line and settling in for a long wait.

As the throng moved slowly forward I shuffled along with it and after twenty minutes I had actually made it inside the building. Unlike the Cameroonian Coutts there was no air-con, and after a while the overpowering heat from hundreds of people crushed together in this airless room was starting to make me feel a little dizzy. There was the usual pushing and shouting that I had come to expect now, but the security guards ignored it and stayed put at their posts, letting the people sort out their grievances among themselves. After an hour of this self-imposed torture I was feeling distinctly wobbly and light-headed in the sticky heat and was considering giving up, when at last, my turn came round and I lurched up to the counter, fishing inside my bra for the cash.

'I'd like to exchange these Euros for Central African francs,' I said in French, peeling the notes out of their plastic wrapping.

The woman behind the counter nodded as I passed the money under the glass screen. She picked up the notes, flicked through them and then wrinkled her nose.

'Where have these been?' she asked.

'Er, I've kept them on my motorcycle,' I said, trying to keep my explanation as simple as possible.

She held them up to her nose, this time making a face of pure disgust before calling over a few of her colleagues. They stood there in a huddle sniffing my Euros, while I waited in silence, already knowing what she was going to say.

'We cannot change this money. It smells bad,' she said and pushed the bundle of notes back in my direction. 'Next!' she yelled at the baying mob behind me.

I swore loudly in English, but the annoying thing about swearing in your own language in a foreign country is that nobody understands what you're saying, which somehow lessens the effect. Making a mental note to learn some French swear words, I stood there sniffing my cash and wondering what to do next. I had spent the last hour queuing in this suffocating hellhole for nothing, and true, the money did smell of engine oil, but the notes were still crisp and new, and goddam it, they were real hard cash! I pushed my way through the crowd out into the boiling streets, shoving the dosh back into my bra, and set off in search of another, less fussy bank.

But it was not to be. The cashier in the next bank I tried also objected to the oily odour, and the third one was the same. I was beginning to wonder what on earth I was going to do when I remembered I had spied a cashpoint machine at a bank in the centre of town. I had noticed it because it was something of a novelty; it was the first one I had seen since arriving in Africa. Naturally there was a queue to use this modern miracle, but when my turn came round I whipped out my credit card and went through the usual process, only to have my card spat out with a definite negative. Lordy! Even the cashpoints are surly in Yaounde. I had another go using a different card, but the result was the same. After rejecting me a third time, the bank's logo appeared on the screen with the uncannily accurate slogan 'Meeting Your Expectations.'

I made my way back to the hotel, grumbling to myself the African traveller's standard complaint: why is nothing ever straightforward? Sod the vibrant humanity of Cameroon, just gimme some soulless convenience for once. I'd hoped to be on my way to Limbe by now with a wad of CFA in my pocket. Instead it looked as if I would have to spend the afternoon in my hotel room doing a spot of money laundering, quite literally. Back at the hotel I turned to my last hope, the guy on reception with whom I had become friendly over the last week. He was a classic example of the Cameroonian wide-boy and was always offering to wash my bike or do other odd jobs in return for what amounted to a few quid. With a wink and a nudge he relieved me of my smelly Euros, promising to return with the equivalent local currency, minus a generous commission for his troubles. I was hot, sweaty and knackered, so this sounded OK by me, but after an hour had gone by I was beginning to wonder if I'd been a little hasty, sending my cash off with a near stranger. Thankfully my suspicions were unfounded, and two and a half hours after he'd set off, there was a knock on my door and he was standing outside, clutching a handful of used notes.

'*Très difficile*,' he said. I got the hint and peeled off a couple of extra thousand for him.

My bike was already packed and waiting outside, ready to hit the road, and I weaved my way out of Yaounde without too much trouble, thanks to an unusually accurate set of directions from my Boy Friday at the hotel. Christmas was just a week away now, and its associated tat had begun to infiltrate the markets and street sellers of Cameroon. Big black men roamed the city wearing plastic Santa Claus masks complete with silky white beards, and carrying artificial Christmas trees on their heads. They stood on the street corners, waving lengths of mangy tinsel and hollering out their bargain prices, competing with the tinkle of 'Jingle Bells' and 'Silent Night' that blasted out from every shop, all of this under the blaze of a tropical sun.

Having bestowed a little attention on the bike while in Yaounde, it felt in good shape after a dose of fresh oil, a clean air-filter and a good wash. I was relieved to be back on the road again, and especially to break away from the city and back into the dark green, steamy wilderness of the jungle. But my relief didn't last long, as my route took me through Douala, which although it bears the title of Cameroon's second city, is actually bigger and even more frantic than Yaounde. I spent a good couple of hours getting lost in its sprawling outskirts, trying to find the road to Limbe, and suffered further setbacks when I became entangled with a wedding party that had brought the road to a near standstill.

A troupe of ten dancing girls led the way, wearing matching

pink dresses, singing and clapping as they performed their choreographed moves. Behind them was a patched-up 1970s Mercedes carrying the bride and groom, followed by a convoy of other cars crammed full of family and friends dressed up in their finery. Bringing up the rear was the strangest sight of all, a group of men, naked from the waist up, who were carrying spears, and chanting and stamping their feet to the beat of their leader's drum. I assumed it was some sort of ancient tradition, but their outfits looked distinctly confused, as if they'd forgotten to get dressed properly. They wore feather headdresses and big, chunky necklaces made of beads and bones, but below the waist they were sporting the archetypal outfit of the middle-aged English schoolmaster on holiday: shorts and sandals with socks pulled up to the knees.

The whole entourage was travelling between three and four miles an hour and I managed to get past the stamping, chanting men before whizzing alongside the line of cars, but the dancing girls were now ten abreast, taking up the entire width of the road. There was no way I could get round them, and the pavement next to me was packed solid with the usual African bustle, so I found myself trapped, riding alongside the bridal car at walking pace. I gave the happy couple a supportive grin through the window but they just looked at me alarmed. After several miles of us exchanging awkward glances with each other, the car came to a halt behind the dancing girls, who had stopped suddenly in a flurry of pink satin. A logging truck had fallen over, shedding its cargo and blocking the road. Seeing my opportunity to get away, I waved goodbye to the bride and groom, accelerated round the now stationary dancers, hopped over one of the errant logs and sped off in what I hoped was at last the direction of Limbe.

I was glad to have my hopes confirmed by Cameroon's Trente-Trois beer, whose makers have had the decency to erect hoardings at an appropriate thirty-three kilometres outside every major town. As these are the only road signs you ever see in Cameroon, they always come as a welcome sight. Arriving in Limbe was like entering a different world. As the former capital of the British part of Cameroon, the lingo in the region had remained defiantly English, although not quite as I knew it, and Limbe itself was laid out in a style more akin to a Buckinghamshire village than one of Africa's sprawling metropolises. There were picket-fenced parks of trimmed grass which were crying out for a duck pond or a few croquet hoops. The roads and shops bore names like Church Street and Victoria Bakery (The Pride of Limbe), but most English of all were the magnificent Botanical Gardens, where a humble war memorial remembered the African soldiers who had fought for the British: 'Their glory will not be blotted out,' read the inscription. There was one aspect to Limbe, however, that was distinctly unlike dear old Blighty: the weather. It was hotter than anywhere else I had been in Africa, and the humidity was so dense it hit you like a warm, wet sponge.

Down a bumpy side street I found a small hotel going by the name of the Holiday Inn, which bore no likeness to the chain of international hotels of the same name, and I suspected that the real Holiday Inn bigwigs wouldn't have been too worried about this shabby little impostor trading on their name. After my morning of money-changing madness, followed by the standard trauma of riding 200 African miles, I collapsed on the bed in my now customary state of filthy, sweaty exhaustion and reached for the TV remote control. Naturally, it didn't work. Summoning up my last shred of energy, I staggered the few steps to the television only to find that I was offered just one choice of viewing matter: the terrifying prospect of God TV, an American cable station made by, and for, religious maniacs. With a morbid fascination I reclined on the bed and watched a screaming preacher hollering and howling in a voice like Cleetus from *The Simpsons*, while his 1,000-plus congregation swayed, wailed and cried, fell to the floor, writhing around and speaking in tongues, while he stood over them shrieking, 'Y'all are sayuhved! God lurrves ya! God has sayuhved ya!' It was all rather disturbing and I tried in vain to find another channel, twiddling with the knobs and pressing buttons at random. Then I noticed the laminated sign taped on the table next to me. '*The TV is already programme. Consequently do not fidget with the TV.*' There was another sign next to it, recommending an alternative source of enter-tainment should the urge to fidget become too much for the Godless hotel guest: '*Please try to take a look at the hotel garden, telling people you have been there by suggestions and complaining.*'

I had a few days to kill in Limbe before Ekoko arrived in town, but my first stop was not the hotel garden, but a trip to the somewhat grander Botanical Gardens, a haven of calm and serenity where vast tropical trees cast much-needed shade for anyone seeking a break from the sweltering bustle of the town. There were several locals snoozing on the grass or stretched out on benches, including one woman who had fallen asleep with her Bible open, mid-read, and I wondered if maybe she would find God TV to be a more stimulating way of getting her religion fix. As I strolled through the banana trees, admiring the little bunches of green fruit in their early stages of life, I heard a man's voice calling out, 'Hello, hello.' Looking through the trees I caught a glimpse of a beautiful whitewashed house in the colonial style; it was set back from the banana plantation in its own grounds, and standing outside, among a scattering of chickens, was a middle-aged black man, smiling at me and beckoning me over.

'Oh, hello,' I greeted him back with a wave.

'Welcome, please come over!' he insisted. 'I saw you looking at the banana trees, are you interested in them?'

'Er, yes, I suppose so. I mean, I like bananas,' I added, somewhat unnecessarily, unsure where this was leading.

'Where are you from?'

'England, from London.'

'Aah! I lived in Wales for three years, my wife studied forestry at the University of Bangor. I loved it there,' he said, looking dreamy for a moment. 'We were married in Wales.'

'Yes, Wales is a beautiful country,' I agreed. 'So do you live here now, in this house?'

'Yes, my wife works here, at the gardens. They gave us this house to live in.'

'Wow, you're very lucky,' I said, admiring the solid but elegant Victorian building.

'Yes, I suppose so,' he agreed, but he didn't sound like he felt lucky. 'My name is Charles – welcome to Limbe and to the Botanical Gardens,' he added in a formal manner. I made my introduction and he insisted I sit down on the porch while he fetched me some water from inside the house. I wasn't quite sure what I was meant to be doing here, but he seemed keen to talk, even a little lonely, and I didn't want to appear rude by rushing off.

Charles made some more small talk and then his motive became clear as he began to fill me in on his life story.

Currently an out-of-work accountant, he was trying to start up a charity for lepers in Cameroon and struggling to get the necessary funding; he was coming up against the usual brick wall of African red tape and didn't know what to do next. He went about his tale in a subtle way, but after lots of tiptoeing around he finally got to the point: 'Maybe you can do something to help me? Maybe you know someone, an organisation? Perhaps you know how I can get financial assistance?'

I didn't know what to say, and I sighed inwardly at the insidiousness of his tactics. I'd rather he'd have shouted out: 'Hey you, white person in the banana trees, what can you do for me?'

I'm a nobody, I wanted to explain to him, I'm just a normal person from England. I don't have any connections, or influence, or access to funds. My assets amount to one boat and three tatty motorcycles. But in his eyes, I was white so I was rich and maybe, with a bit of luck, I was important too. I felt awful about shattering his hopes, and as he continued talking I found myself coming up with ideas to help fund his leper colony.

'Well, I know a woman in Maroua, in northern Cameroon, who's involved in charity work,' I said, thinking of Bernice. 'Maybe she would be able to help. I can email her and give her your details.'

'Yes, that would be very good,' Charles said, brightening up a bit. 'And what about your husband? Maybe he could help?'

I hadn't even mentioned Austin, but one thing I had noticed over the last few months was that Africans are quick to spot a wedding ring.

'Um, well . . .' I faltered, a bit taken aback. I was torn between wanting to help someone who had made a direct appeal to me, and resenting this stranger who had wangled his way into my conscience.

'What does your husband do for work?' Charles asked, warming to his new subject.

'Er, he's a teacher.'

'Ah! A teacher!' He looked pleased about this. A respectable, useful profession. 'Maybe he could help?' he pleaded again.

'Um, well, I don't know. I mean, I suppose he could send some textbooks over here or something. I can certainly ask him.'

'Very good, that would be most excellent!' said Charles with a big smile.

I didn't really see how a few old maths books were going to help the lepers very much, and there was already a glut of cast-off English school-books in Cameroon; no doubt an easy way for the white liberals of Britain to assuage their middle-class guilt. I had seen the books piled up in the street stalls; dog-eared, dreary tomes from the 70s, their covers showing obedient, studious children wearing flares. They made me shudder with memories of my own school-days, and judging by the surplus that was sloshing around the markets here the Cameroonians were none to keen on them either. But Charles was very excited about the idea.

'Yes, yes, thank you! But you must not use the postal service, the books will be stolen. I think maybe you should talk to the Cameroon embassy in London and they can send them out.'

'Er, right, OK,' I heard myself saying, and then, as if I was a puppet being controlled by some invisible strings suspended from the banana trees, I found myself exchanging email addresses with Charles and promising that I would 'see what I could do'.

I finished my round of the gardens, wondering how on earth I ended up getting myself into these things, and walked back to the hotel, taking a circuitous route to see the town. It was my first time walking through Limbe, and I quickly realised that Charles was in no way unique among its residents. He was just one of many, albeit an eloquent, educated one, who viewed me as a potential bankroll, a UK visa, a ticket out of here, or hopefully, all three. Every few hundred yards I was pounced upon by a young man with big plans for his future. Sometimes they would start by offering to 'show me around' or claiming they wanted to 'be my friend', but some took a more direct approach, stating quite plainly that they 'needed connections in Britain', and would hassle me for my phone number and address. Sometimes they walked along beside me, making jokes and cajoling me while spinning out long-drawn-out tales about their family or friends in Manchester, or Birmingham, or wherever, who needed them to go out and join them. The problem was that they couldn't get a visa, they just needed a contact address, some money, a little help . . . And so it went on. It wasn't threatening, more wearing; they were just having a go and I couldn't blame them for that. Thankfully they lacked tenacity, and I found that a friendly but firm 'no' would get rid of all but the most persistent offenders.

My meandering route took me along the coastal road that led to the nearby fishing village. Although this makes it sound picturesque, St Ives it wasn't. However, I didn't realise this until I strolled on to the beach straight into the arms of 100 drunken, marauding fishermen. There were masses of long, wooden canoe-style boats, carved out of tree trunks, pulled up on the beach, and a general air of raucous activity as the men traded their catch with much bartering, boozing and general hubbub. The arrival of a white woman on this scene was something of a novelty and caused quite a commotion; this was no place for *La Blanche* alone. I tried to make a fast retreat, wrenching myself free from one particular old fisherman who was grabbing my arm, trying to pull me into one of the bars along the shore. Fortunately he had only three fingers remaining on his right hand, so his grip wasn't as tight as it could have been.

'No thank you! No! Thank you, NO!' I protested as firmly as possible, before resorting to more salty language that I guessed would be understood by the fishing community of Limbe. It seemed to do the job and I yanked my arm away from the inebriated angler's grasp, causing him to stumble in the soft sand and fall over backwards into a pile of nets. I pegged it off back to the road as fast as possible, with a just a quick glance over my shoulder to see him struggling to disentangle himself, surrounded by a group of his friends who were roaring with booze-fuelled laughter.

By the time I made it back to the hotel I was thoroughly drained. Even the smallest task was an effort in the stifling heat, and tackling the non-stop circus of Limbe's streets had finished me off for the day. I was ready to collapse into bed, but as I turned the key in my door I heard a nervous little voice behind me, coming from the reception desk.

'Mrs Lois, excuse me . . . sorry . . .'

I turned round to see the receptionist looking at me with a pleading face.

'I'm sorry, excuse me, I . . . I . . . would like to talk to you, please . . .' she trailed off.

'Oh yeah, sure, is everything OK?' I asked, wondering if I was in trouble for fidgeting with the TV.

'Yes, yes. I would like to ask you something. Can I please come and talk to you, in your room, when I finish here?'

I groaned silently. All I wanted to do was crash out, but as with Charles and the lepers and the maths books, I stood there thinking 'NO!' and heard myself saying, 'Yes.'

A couple of hours later there was a timid knock on the door and I let her in. She introduced herself as Jane and sat down on the bed next to me. For the first few minutes I couldn't get a word out of her, but with a bit of coaxing she began to speak in a tiny, tremulous voice, as if she was about to cry.

'I . . . I wanted to talk to you about er, schol . . . er . . . scholarships,' she whispered.

'Oh! Well, oh dear, I'm afraid I don't really know anything about scholarships,' I told her as gently as possible.

'Oh,' she said, and sat there for a few moments. 'Um, can I ask you about tourism?'

She said this so quietly that I had to ask her to repeat it three times.

'Oh right, tourism. Er, yeah, sure, what is it you want to know?'

Again she stared at the floor in silence for a couple of minutes, before turning her face towards me for the first time and then bursting out in a voice full of desperation and frustration: 'How do you do it?'

'What, tourism? You mean how do you get to work in tourism, or . . .'

I wasn't quite sure what she was getting at.

'No, no! You! I mean *you*! How do *you* do it? You are here, riding a motorbike in Africa all on your own, how do you do it? I want to know.'

I didn't know what to say, so I just stuck to the facts.

213

'Well, I saved up some money and borrowed some more. I did lots of research, plotting my route and organising everything, and I hoped that luck would be on my side.'

It sounded easy when I put it like that, but our lives and experiences were so disparate that I could see she barely understood what I was talking about.

'Tell me what you want to know, and I'll try to help,' I said to her.

She sighed and spent another minute staring at the floor.

'Oh, I don't know, it's just that, well, I don't want to work in this hotel for my whole life,' she said. 'I have a BSC in environmental studies and geography, but I can't get any work in that area, and I have been working here for five years now.'

'Right, so you've been to university, you've got the qualifications and you live in Limbe, so have you applied to work at the Botanical Gardens here?'

She nodded miserably.

'I wrote to them but they did not reply.'

'OK, well, why don't you try calling them or, even better, go round there and introduce yourself? You could offer to work there for free in your spare time.'

'I can't do that, I only get one day off a week, and if my boss found out I was working at the Gardens, he would make me leave here.'

'OK, but still, go round there and start talking to people, make sure they know about you, try to get involved.'

She nodded but still looked unconvinced.

'There are lots of European charities and organisations involved in African environmental stuff,' I continued. 'Y'know, saving the rainforests, endangered species and all that. Get on the internet, look them up and write to all of them.'

'I've written lots of letters,' she protested, 'but they never reply.'

'Then call them up, write again, keep at it.'

She looked at me, shaking her head, and I could tell she was thinking, *you don't understand, it doesn't work like that here.*

'Is it difficult to find work because you're a woman?'

'No, no, that is not the problem. It is tribalism; that is the biggest problem. The jobs go to the people who are the right tribe.'

'Look,' I said, 'I know things are very different for you than for me, but perseverance is the same the world over. You mustn't give up just because you don't get a reply to your letters. Never stop trying. Make a decision that you're going to write one letter a week and if you don't hear back then follow it up.'

But my pep talk seemed to be falling on deaf ears and she still looked utterly downcast. 'I'm twenty-nine,' she said, 'and I don't want to find a man just to get money, that's what all my friends have done. I have studied at university, I have moved away from my village where my family are to work here, but now I will never get out because nobody will give me the work that I am trained for. I will never leave this hotel!'

'Yes, you will!' I told her. 'Because you want to, so you'll make it happen. It's not easy, but you mustn't give up!'

She nodded but didn't speak, continuing to stare at the floor in silence, and I felt sad and helpless about the huge gulf between our worlds, and the hand of fate that had cast me into twentieth-century Britain, and her into darkest Africa. By sheer luck I had grown up in a land where anything was possible, but Jane would never know that magical feeling. Although I feared my attempts at motivational waffle would come to nothing, I couldn't bring myself to just give up on her. Her misery was universal; I knew only too well what it was like to work in a hellish job with an idiot for a boss. And I also knew the sweet feeling of telling them to shove it.

'Look,' I said, 'I met a man at the Botanical Gardens today, his wife works there as a forester. I'll go and talk to him and tell him about you, maybe see if his wife can give you some advice. She might even be able to get you some work there.'

Jane looked pleased by this suggestion and after another hour she set off for home, looking a little more cheery than when she had arrived. To be honest, I felt a complete fraud, giving out career advice; after all, what the hell did I know? And I was ashamed to admit it but I felt slightly irritated too. I was becoming tired of being pounced on by every Cameroonian who saw me as the answer to their problems, and I resented the false friendliness that barely disguised their ulterior motive. It wasn't that I didn't have sympathy for their plight, but I felt uncomfortable about the fact that I could never make contact with anyone without this subtext floating up to the surface. Their eyes lit up as soon as I appeared and the underlying message, sometimes left unspoken, but usually not, was, 'What can this white person do for me?' All I wished for, somewhat naively perhaps, was to interact with my fellow human beings as equals, but there was no getting round the truth of the matter; in the eyes of the Cameroonians I was one of those lucky ones who had been born more equal than the others.

Despite my discomfort surrounding the whole situation, my conscience wouldn't let me walk away from Jane's predicament. If I could help I would, so next day I set off in search of Charles to see if we could cut a deal: a bundle of old maths books in return for saving a budding botanist from extinction.

ELEVEN

If the amount of sweat generated was anything to go by, the next couple of days were quite productive as I scuttled around town between the Holiday Inn and the Botanical Gardens, trying to broker meetings between Jane and Charles, these two strangers who had suddenly loomed large in my life. It wasn't until Friday afternoon that I remembered that today was E-day, Ekoko's arrival in Limbe, and sure enough, a call to his mobile prompted the words I never thought I would hear on my trip through Africa: I'll send my driver to collect you.

A hasty attack with the eyebrow tweezers and a liberal helping of red toenail varnish went some way towards preparing me for an evening with a local dignitary. I had only two sets of clothes: one for riding in, the other for everything else. Neither outfit was very dashing and both had seen plenty of action over the last few months, but I did my best to scrub up, and at the appointed time an immaculately dressed young man arrived in a blacked-out 4 × 4. He greeted me with a small bow and held the rear door open for me to climb inside, while Jane watched agape from behind the reception desk at this turn of events.

Despite having been in Limbe for just a few days, I was already on friendly terms with the family down the road from the hotel that sold tomatoes outside their house, and the old lady at the banana stall next to the Botanical Gardens, and the guy with a plate of watermelon slices on his head who hung out near the petrol station. It wasn't a big town, and as far as I had seen I was the only white person here; and despite their attachment to English, they still called me *La Blanche*, the standard nickname for a white woman in Cameroon. But after all my walking around town, working up a sweat, it felt odd to be whisked past these familiar faces in the air-conditioned comfort of a big fancy car on my way to visit a high-flying member of Cameroonian society. And when I remembered my grovelling for visas and begging to be allowed into banks in Yaounde, the whole thing seemed quite absurd. Not that I was complaining; I was happy to take my good times where I found them, but I recalled my silent protest to Charles in the banana trees: *I'm a nobody, I don't have any connections, or influence!* Now, a few days later, I was being carted off to the beach house of a member of the Chamber of Commerce! It was a bizarre turn of events, but I marvelled silently at the strange twists and turns of my African adventure.

The driver sped up the coast road for about ten miles before turning off into a village of tumbledown shacks and breezeblock dwellings. He twisted and bumped his way along a series of rutted stony tracks before pulling up at an ornate metal gate set into a high wall. This was the entrance to Ekoko's beach house, and, once inside, with the gate shut tight behind us, we cruised along a bougainvillaea-lined drive until the Atlantic Ocean came into view. The setting sun was melting away into the sea and the sound of waves crashed against the rocks below us. I was in high-security paradise.

Standing by the swimming pool was a jolly-looking man, dressed casually but expensively in a short-sleeved checked shirt and cream trousers. He beamed an enormous smile as I stepped out of the car.

'Ah! So you are Lois! Welcome to our house!' Ekoko greeted me with a big bear hug before introducing me to his beautiful wife Nadya, who didn't look old enough or weary enough to have produced four children. Nadya took this compliment gracefully while Ekoko exploded in a big booming laugh.

'Oh yes, we have four wonderful children, three girls and a boy. Our eldest daughter is ten now.'

A drink was thrust into my hand and we sat at a table overlooking the sea and catching the last pink streaks of the sunset.

'This place is amazing,' I told Ekoko, glancing around at the spacious villa and its well-tended gardens.

'Thank you. Come with me, you must have a tour!' he declared, standing up and leading me across the garden. 'As you can see, we have a car-port, behind is the garage, and this building here is the guesthouse . . .'

'Wow, a whole extra house just for guests!'

'Oh yes, we have many guests so it is better for them if they have their own house. We had a most eminent politician visiting us last year but he did not like our pillows. The next time I invited him, he wrote to say that he would be bringing his own pillow!' Ekoko roared with laughter at this memory

219

and I found myself joining in. He seemed to be amused by everything and his good humour was contagious.

The guesthouse was decorated in a modern minimalist style: lots of plain dark wood, off-white walls and leather furniture.

'We wanted a contemporary, European feel,' explained Ekoko as he opened the door to the swanky bathroom, where glass and chrome fittings gave an air of clinical chic. 'But I bought all of this from China,' he said, sweeping his hand around the room. 'You can get everything there now and it is so much cheaper.'

'But not these?' I guessed, pointing to the paintings that hung on the walls throughout the house. They were avant-garde in style but the subject matter was definitely African, depicting the continent's wildlife and musical instruments.

'Ah yes, this is my favourite artist. He is from Cameroon – his name is Otheo, I have hundreds of his paintings in all my homes,' Ekoko said, and I wondered how many homes that was in total. It was obvious that Ekoko had some seriously highfalutin lineage. I knew he had been educated at Gordonstoun, one of Britain's super-élite public schools, which claims Prince Charles and the Duke of Edinburgh among its old boys. It also spawned 'Nasty Nick' of *Big Brother* 'fame', Jasper Duncombe, a toff turned porn film-maker, and Michael Forwell, an international drug smuggler. So I reckon Ekoko came out of it pretty well.

'I had the garden made on two levels,' Ekoko continued as we stepped back into the muggy heat of the evening and moved towards the sea. 'The patio is built on to the rocks below, and we are having an extension built here.' He led me to where a couple of men were digging and hammering in the fading light. 'I am having a hot tub built, so you can sit in it and look out to sea.' He beamed with pleasure at the thought and then burst out laughing for no apparent reason.

'Come with me into the house, Nadya is putting the children to bed but she will come and join us shortly. Then would you like to eat something?'

'Oh, well, yes, if that's OK with you. I brought a bottle of wine, but, er, I'm not sure what it'll be like.'

It had been hard to find anywhere in Limbe that sold wine, but eventually a little grocery store had come up trumps, although the bottle looked as if it had been sitting around for a while: it was covered in dust and the label had been faded by the sun. I had a sneaking suspicion that the shop wasn't the kind of place Ekoko would go for his booze; he probably had a cellar somewhere, jam-packed with cases of vintage Bordeaux.

As we toured the inside of the villa I realised that Ekoko and Nadya had staff, not just the driver and the workmen I had met, but a fleet of assistants, including a cook, who was given orders to rustle something up for dinner. Outside by the pool the lights were switched on and a supper of fish, spinach and plantain was served, but not touched until grace had been said. My bottle of wine was placed on the table and when the time came to raise a toast Ekoko showed his true breeding. Not a wince or a splutter did he make as the vinegar-like plonk met his exclusive, Gordonstoun-educated tastebuds.

The three of us shared our stories over the meal, and when I told them about my unintentional foray into the wedding party outside Douala Ekoko hooted with laughter and shook his head despairingly.

'It is a big problem in Cameroon,' he said. 'The weddings cost so much and they go on for days, it is getting out of

221

control. But the funerals are even worse! There is one province in Cameroon where they have banned funerals that are longer than one day. People are spending their life savings, and borrowing more, just to have these lavish weddings and funerals; it is a real problem throughout the country. There is one man I know of, he spent the equivalent of fifty thousand pounds on just the champagne for his mother's funeral, and another fifty thousand pounds on the wine! It went on for weeks! The whole thing is crazy!'

Luckily for Ekoko, Nadya had no truck with such lavishness and despite her privileged lifestyle she radiated a homely, gentle kindness. After dinner she told me how she had been trained as a chemist but no longer worked, as she preferred to concentrate on her family and her charity work.

'What charity do you work for?' I asked.

'I don't work *for* a charity, it is just my own charity, nothing big,' she said, becoming a little bashful.

'Oh, right. What's it called?'

'Well, it doesn't have a name, it's just something I do myself.'

'Oh, I see. So what is it you do exactly?'

'I work with street kids in Douala. It started because I used to drive past the same junction every day and there were always these children there, the same boys, trying to sell things or asking for money. One day I tried to talk to them, but they ran away, they thought I was going to get them into trouble with the authorities, but I kept going back to see them. I am a religious person,' she said, looking me in the eye, 'and God spoke to me, about those boys. He told me to help them.'

'Wow! So what did you do?'

'I kept going to see them and in the end they started to trust me. I met their families, but some of them were not very friendly towards me. But I kept on helping the boys. I try to get them to attend school and church, which is quite difficult,' she added with a laugh. 'I organise activities for them and they have got to know our children too. Sometimes it is very hard work, and I feel as if I am not making any difference, but I keep trying. Ekoko thinks I work too hard for them but I cannot give up on them, it is God's wishes.'

I had to admit that I was thoroughly awed at this story of sheer selflessness. No charity dinners and a cheque to Oxfam for Nadya; she was getting her hands dirty, chipping away at the coalface.

'Well, I'd better get going, it's gone eleven,' I announced, and the driver was duly summoned.

'We are having a party for Christmas,' said Ekoko as I clambered into the car. 'You must come and meet our friends, it starts at two in the afternoon. It is nothing formal,' he added kindly, as if he already knew that I would show up wearing the same outfit.

'Thanks, I'd love to. See you then!' I called out as the car set off down the drive.

Back at the Holiday Inn, all was quiet but something strange had happened. Someone somewhere had been fidgeting; where once there had been God TV, now there was CNN, and a blonde, blue-eyed anchorwoman with expressionless features was reading the news. 'The police have arrested a suspect in the inquiry of the murders of five prostitutes in the town of Ipswich in eastern England . . .'

She continued talking as the faces of the dead women appeared on the screen before cutting to a shot of police and dogs searching a Suffolk field. The sky was grey and the trees bare; I could almost feel the cold seeping out of the TV. The police and reporters were wrapped up in scarves and heavy winter coats, their breath visible in the freezing air as they spoke urgently into their microphones. This story from my homeland was one of the lead items on CNN and appeared to have been running for a few days, but it was the first I had heard of it, and I realised how out of touch I had become with world news and, more notably, how I didn't mind. The CNN reporter was now interviewing the people of Ipswich, who didn't have much to say, except, 'Oh dear, and oh my, and isn't it awful,' while they huddled together, fenced off from the action by a perimeter of police tape.

'A book of condolences has been set up for the victims in Ipswich town hall,' the reporter was saying as the camera showed a wide shot of the hall before zooming in on a close-up of the book's pages, where it lingered for a few seconds on the condolences. Someone had taken the trouble to come all the way to the town hall and had used up an entire page with their message for the murdered women.

'THE WAGES OF SIN ARE DEATH. REPENT NOW,' it read in big, neat capital letters, and as I switched off the TV and climbed into bed I wondered what Nadya or the Kusserows would make of this fellow Christian of theirs.

I was looking forward to celebrating Christmas with Ekoko and his friends and family, but after the fun was over it would be time to get going. I had been in Cameroon for several weeks now; I still had plenty of miles ahead of me, and they were tinged with uncertainty. My inquiries by phone and email regarding the Angolan visa had confirmed the bad news that I had learned from Sherry-Kay: Angola's embassies were no longer issuing tourist visas and my only option was to head for the border town of Matadi in the Democratic Republic of Congo and hopefully get one there. So it was official, my route would now take me through DRC, a change of plan that was threatening to keep me awake at night. Every piece of evidence suggested that DRC was the scariest country in the world; that the capital, Kinshasa, was a raging, lawless hellhole full of crazy people and gun-wielding soldiers. I had read books about the place, horror stories from when the country had been called Zaïre, and steadily decaying under the corrupt dictatorship of President Mobutu, or to give him his full (and self-appointed) name, Mobutu Sese Seko Kuku Ngbendu Wa Za Banga, which, in case your Lingala is a little rusty, translates as 'The All Powerful Warrior Who, because of His Endurance and Inflexible Will to Win, Will Go from Conquest to Conquest, Leaving Fire in his Wake'. Mobutu had spent the best part of his rule plundering his nation's wealth, spending it on palaces, villas on the Côte d'Azur and chartered Concorde flights, while Zaïre descended into a seething pit of anarchy and violence. And to think people complain about Tony Blair's legacy.

But Mobutu's taste for looting and personal gain was nothing new. A template for greed and brutality had been set in the late nineteenth century when King Leopold II of Belgian had claimed the country as his own private kingdom, naming it the Belgian Congo and exploiting its resources and people alike. Most notorious was the Belgian traders' practice of chopping off the hands of rubber plantation workers who failed to reach their quotas. Things had looked hopeful when Mobutu had come into power in the 60s, renaming the country Zaïre and promising a new era of African 'authenticity' and black pride, but the optimism didn't last long, and by 1997, when Mobutu was overthrown, Zaïre had descended into a state of anarchy,

225

a nation riddled with corruption and brutality. The new leader, Kabila, immediately outlawed political opposition and, without irony, renamed Zaïre the Democratic Republic of Congo, showing an almost laughable lack of awareness that sums up the terrifying absurdity of this apocalyptic and tragic country.

As for Angola, well, I could hardly bring myself to think what that would be like: a country in ruins after twenty-seven years of civil war, landmines strewn all over the place and Portuguese as the lingua franca. But there was no point in worrying about it yet: my brain couldn't get past the impending dread of DRC at the moment. I remembered my survival tactic that I had employed when I set off from home, heading for Portsmouth: one small step at a time. I was halfway through my journey across the African continent now, but Cape Town still felt like a distant fantasy, as remote and out of reach as ever.

It was under this cloud of anxiety that I set out the next morning to send some 'Happy Christmas' emails on a painfully slow computer in a nearby café. Someone, whether it was the God of Motorcycling or my old friend Lady Luck, had been busy during the night and a message from a stranger greeted me. The stranger's name was Chris, he was from Tunbridge Wells (which for some reason, I found strangely reassuring), he was riding his motorcycle through Africa, and guess what? He was just a little way behind me, about to enter Cameroon from Nigeria. Did I want to meet up and ride together through the Congos and Angola? In other words, the scary bit. It would better for both of us to travel in a pair, he reasoned.

A wave of hope surged through me and I replied something along the lines of darn right I do! Afterwards I went about my day's activities with a new spring in my step. Compared to my previous journeys around the globe, other travellers were a bit thin on the ground in Africa. I had met a few people driving across the continent in their Land Rovers, but my fellow motorcyclists, it seemed, were a rare breed out here. But now Chris of Tunbridge Wells had appeared on the scene I felt altogether more positive about the next leg of my journey.

I checked out of the Holiday Inn the next day, intending on riding to Ekoko's party and then continuing my journey south. I wished Jane good luck with her ambitions but she didn't look very hopeful, and her expression was as mournful as ever.

'Charles is going to speak to his wife about you, so if you don't hear anything, go round there and talk to him.'

She nodded, but her face told the true story of her despair.

'Don't give up!' I said as I walked down the hotel steps into the car park. She stood there staring after me and waving as I climbed on to the bike. I hadn't ridden it for a week and it felt enormously heavy and unwieldy. The rest of the hotel staff had downed tools to watch me set off, and as I heaved the bike upright to kick up the side stand, I lost my balance and my motorcycle and I toppled over on to the ground. There was a gasp from my audience followed by raucous laughter, which I forced myself to join in, despite feeling like a prize idiot. But Jane was still standing in the doorway, looking sad and hopeless; not even my display of bungling incompetence could bring a smile to her face.

I arrived at Ekoko's Christmas party just a few minutes before the recently appointed Ambassador for South Africa turned up with his wife. He cut an impressive figure, tall and imposing, dressed in a lightweight black tunic-style suit with a map of Africa embroidered on the chest, each country picked out in a different colour. His wife was equally glamorous and they both had the diplomatic thing down to a T. They made admirable small talk with everyone, were effortlessly polite and gave non-committal answers to any question that was even vaguely personal. There was no way you were going to find them slightly tipsy in the kitchen, raiding the fridge and gossiping about some ambassadorial scandal. Although I had never considered such a career move, I realised I would never be able to cut it in the diplomatic world; I just wasn't, well, diplomatic enough, although I did rather like the way everyone called the Ambassador 'Your Excellency'.

More guests were arriving: the head of the Chamber of Commerce, a bigwig from an oil company, some high-flying Cameroonian businessmen, a couple of doctors and the top bods from STV, Ekoko's television channel. They were all nattily dressed, with beautiful wives and little broods of impeccably behaved children. Ekoko, being the excellent host, steered me around the party, booming out, 'This is Lois from England, she is riding her bike all the way to South Africa!' Thankfully, my fellow guests found the scruffy English bird and her even scruffier motorcycle to be an entertaining story, and furnished me with travel tips, places to visit (and avoid), and hotels that were way beyond my budget. 'You must stay at the Nelly,' urged the Ambassador's wife. 'You know, the Lord Nelson – it's the best hotel in Cape Town and they do a wonderful afternoon tea.'

By the time the party was coming to an end Ekoko had arranged for me to be interviewed about my journey on STV, and after a few calls were made I was given instructions to show up at the station the next morning. I made my way through the manic streets of Douala to STV's headquarters, a high-rise building in the centre of the city. I left my bike in the underground parking and ventured past the security guards to the lift, which whizzed me up several floors to the reception area. The offices of STV weren't that different from a TV station back home: a little more scruffy maybe, but populated by super-fashionable bright young things rushing about with mobile phones permanently glued to their ears, and although it was Boxing Day morning, Cameroon was back to work.

Eventually the door swung open and I was greeted by a tall, astonishingly handsome man dressed in an expensive camel-coloured suit. This was Eric, the presenter who was going to interview me. He led me back to the lift up to the top floor, and through a maze of corridors to the studio, which was decked out with plastic plants and 80s décor.

'This is where we will be filming,' he explained, 'but first you must go into make-up. Come with me.'

I followed him into a tiny room across the corridor, where a matronly woman was crammed into a corner, surrounded by hundreds of pots and tubes and tubs and brushes and even a selection of wigs.

'Please sit down,' she said, ushering me into the only chair in the room, and set about preparing me for my first, and what would no doubt be my last, appearance on Cameroonian television.

The make-up woman worked away in silence, and although there wasn't a mirror in front of me to see what she was doing, I was beginning to get a little worried as she continued to pile on the slap. My face felt as if was covered with pancake batter, and that was before she'd applied several dollops of red blusher to my cheeks. My eyelashes were soon clogged into a sticky black lump and then, to my horror, she came at me with a palette of sparkly blue eye-shadow. Just when I thought things couldn't get any worse, a rummage through her box of lipsticks resulted in a shade of iridescent purple being applied to my reluctant lips. It reminded me of the horribly 80s 'Twilight Teaser' my friends and I used to wear when we were thirteen, in our (unsuccessful) attempts to catch the eyes of the bad boys who hung around at the local shopping centre.

Eventually the make-up 'artist' laid down her tools and, with a satisfied smile, held a mirror up to my face. The look was pure teenage hooker. An eighteen-year-old might have got away with it, but on my thirty-three-year-old face it had more than a hint of the *Rocky Horror Show*'s Frankenfurter about it. I looked revolting.

'OK?' she asked as she laid down the mirror.

'Yes, very nice, thank you very much,' I replied and legged it out of the room, rubbing away at my face with the sleeve of my shirt.

I felt ridiculously self-conscious, but Eric was a consummate professional and managed not to laugh when I appeared in the studio in my transvestite make-up. He positioned me on a high stool next to a plastic fern and, with the camera rolling, proceeded to ask me the usual questions about my trip: where are you from, where are you going, isn't it dangerous? Are your family worried about you? I was so used to being asked these questions now that the answers tripped off my tongue without much thought. Then Eric came in with a non-sequitur.

'If in the future you have children, would you encourage them to ride a motorcycle around the world?'

'Oh yes, of course!' I replied. 'It's a great experience, I would recommend it to anyone.'

Eric's previously calm composure faltered slightly and his

immaculate features rearranged themselves into an expression of mild disapproval. The cameraman and the sound man looked also a little concerned at my response, as if they felt that someone should contact British social services as a pre-emptive measure. But Eric quickly regained his polished presenting face and rounded off in a suitably slick manner. The interview wasn't going out live and I doubted very much if it would ever be beamed into the homes of Cameroon, but I didn't really mind; in fact I was quite relieved, considering the purple lipstick.

It was time to move on. I rode out of STV's car park and after dodging the traffic out of Douala I was out on the open road again, heading south down the Atlantic coast towards the beach town of Kribi, seventy miles away, where I had arranged to meet Chris from Tunbridge Wells. It's not hard for two English motorcyclists to find each other in a small town in Cameroon, and sure enough, as I sat outside a little restaurant on the main road from Douala, I heard the telltale rumble of a mighty single-cylindered motorcycle approaching, a rare sound in a country where a 125cc bike is considered big, and certainly powerful enough to transport the whole family.

Chris pulled off the road in front of the restaurant and parked his bike next to mine. It was a giant of a machine, a 600cc Yamaha with an oversized tank and big metal boxes as panniers. Chris, however, was not a giant of a man and confessed to finding his bike a bit challenging in the more tricky sections, particularly in the sand.

'And I'm not really looking forward to all the mud,' he said, as we ordered a couple of beers and took our seats on the patio at the back of the restaurant, overlooking a tropical beach.

'Yeah, I know what you mean,' I agreed.

'And the rainy season is about to start,' he said, looking worried.

'Well, if we travel together, at least there'll be two of us to haul the bikes through the mud!'

'I've still got to get my visas for next few countries,' he said, 'so I'm going back to Yaounde tonight. It'll probably take me about a week to get them all.'

'Yeah, that's what it took me, but I've got to leave Cameroon soon, my visa is running out in a couple of days, so we'll have to meet up in Gabon, I suppose.'

I had already committed an act of forgery by altering the expiry date of my visa with a biro, so as to give me a few extra days in Cameroon, but I didn't want to push my luck with any more homemade falsifications.

'OK, well, I'll let you know how things are going with the visas and I'll keep in touch by email. You should be able to pick them up OK – there seem to be internet cafés in most big towns, so I guess Gabon will be the same.'

'OK, that sounds like a good plan. I'll go into Gabon and wait for you somewhere. Once you've got your visas you'll probably be able to catch up with me quite quickly, seeing as your bike's bigger and faster than mine.'

Our plan was agreed, and we spent the rest of the time sharing stories of our respective journeys, which had brought us, two strangers who lived less than 100 miles from each other, here to the African jungle. It turned out that this was the second time Chris had set out on a motorcycle journey across Africa. His last attempt, a few years before, had ended abruptly with some mechanical disaster in Mauritania, and he had shipped the bike back to England and travelled around West Africa on public transport instead. But this time he was determined to make it all the way to South Africa on two wheels, and if time and funds allowed, he would ride back up the east coast of Africa and finally home to Tunbridge Wells, where he would return to his job as a central heating engineer.

Chris didn't strike me as a typical motorcycle adventurer, although I knew by now that there was really no such thing, despite BMW's best efforts to create a worldwide army of identically dressed middle-aged men striking out on their massive machines. I had met all sorts of motorcyclists on my travels, and the motives that propel these ordinary folk out into the world on a motorbike are as diverse as the people themselves. Married couples having the final hurrah once the kids have left home; divorced, disillusioned men trying to create the youth they never had; likely lads chasing adventure and a girl in every port; and the romantics, the aimless wanderers for whom life on the road means never having to commit to anything, trying to convince themselves that there's poetry and meaning to be found among the fleapit hostels and the Laughing Cow cheese.

But Chris didn't fit into any of these categories. He seemed a nice, mild-mannered guy, polite and intelligent, but from the little time I had spent with him he struck me as having something of a cautious disposition, a trait not often to be found in a man about to motorcycle across the Congo. But maybe he was just a little shy, and to be honest, his anxiousness made me warm to him; like me, he was nervous, but he was doing it anyway, and I remembered Dominique's toast on the Tunis ferry to this spirit of wary adventure. Chris and I might make an unlikely couple of travelling companions, but if I was going to ride through the Congo and Angola with a strange man, he

233

would certainly be preferable to some macho tough guy with something to prove.

Chris set off for Yaounde and I waved him goodbye from the restaurant car park.

'Good luck with the visas!' I called after him. 'See you in Gabon!'

I rode slowly towards the border with Gabon over the next few days. The rainy season was beginning, although so far it had mercifully confined its downpours to the nights. But I was waking up to a new smell: wet leaves and swampy forests and a dankness in the air. The red dirt roads were no longer the dusty highways I had ridden in the north of Cameroon; now the dust was turning to a slippery, cloying mud and my progress was already being hampered by the churned-up ruts caused by the logging trucks that rumbled past me, carrying huge tropical tree-trunks destined for ports all over the world. My average speed was falling as I plodded onwards towards the border, juddering along miles of corrugations and skirting around deep mud-holes. And I feared this was just the beginning: I could only imagine what the terrain would be like in Gabon and the Congos, the very heart of Africa's equatorial jungle. The map showed very little tarmac and an awful lot of green rainforest for the next 1,000 miles, but I was cheered by the thought that I would be travelling with Chris for most of this. I had clocked up over 5,000 miles since leaving home, so I had passed the halfway mark, and I ploughed on towards Gabon, feeling hopeful about the next leg of my journey.

TWELVE

I approached the frontier with the usual trepidation that accompanied each of my African border crossings. The Cameroonian exit post appeared to be deserted and I rode around, knocking on doors of empty buildings, searching for the men in uniform, but to no avail. The river Kom lay before me, a muddy brown strip of no man's water separating the two countries. In a rare show of progress on this crumbling continent it was crossed by a newly built modern bridge, which had replaced the ferry, leaving its wooden jetty abandoned and rotting away into the river.

My initial anxiety was unfounded; there wasn't a pushy 'helper', a grabbing kid or even an official of any kind in sight. Eventually I found a couple of immigration officers and the customs man down by the river, sitting in a palm-thatched hut eating their lunch of rice and fish. There was an open bottle of whisky on the table in front of them, which may have accounted for their good humour and work-shy ways. They were in no hurry to do anything and could barely be bothered to raise their rubber stamps to send me on my way, but I was glad of their laissez-faire approach, as it meant my modified visa expiry date slipped by unnoticed, and after a bit of banter and a slug of whisky, I was on my way out of Cameroon. At the bridge a lone sentry appeared from a tin hut, a young man who made a show of examining my passport but actually wanted to practise his English rather than conduct any official business. Once we'd got the preliminaries out of the way he launched into the usual drive to wheedle my address and phone number out of me.

'I learn English, but I must come to England to learn more,' he insisted.

I sighed inwardly at the predictable nature of his conversation.

'Well, your English is very good,' I assured him, trying to sound interested.

'Yes, but I need improve. Where do you live?'

'London.'

'Ah! I always want to come to London! I come and visit you in London?'

'Er, well . . . I don't know when I'll be going home. I might never go home!' I said, quickly inventing myself as some eternal drifter, roaming the globe.

'Please you tell me address, and telephone, and I write you.'

'I don't have an address, or a phone, I have left England to travel all over the world!' I declared, warming to my new itinerant alter ego.

'OK, I email. You have email?'

'No, no email.'

He looked at me in disbelief and shook his head.

'OK, I write you my address and email, and one day, when you home in London, you call me. You say, "Alfred! Yes, I remember him in Cameroon, he is good man." And I come visit you.'

'OK,' I agreed, realising that I was never going to get across the bridge if I didn't agree to enter into some sort of penpal relationship with Alfred. And he did have a gun, I reminded myself, so it was in my interests to play along.

He dug out a piece of scrap paper from his trousers and carefully wrote his name and contact details in block capitals, before passing it to me and gripping my hands in his.

'Alfred. You remember me, Alfred. Yes, OK?'

'Yes, I will. Goodbye Alfred, it was nice to meet you.' I put the folded piece of paper in my jacket pocket and set off across the bridge into Gabon.

On the other side of the river, things were just as quiet but remarkably efficient, and I was stamped in, signed off, and delivered into Gabon within half an hour, reeling in shock at this distinctly un-African border crossing experience. My astonishment continued as I headed south on the most silky-smooth tarmac road I had ridden since the south of France. Apart from a few logging trucks it was empty, winding its way in great sweeping curves through the rainforest, where impossibly tall trees towered over the impenetrable mass of bright green ferns and palms on the jungle floor below. Turquoise butterflies fluttered around my face and tendrils of vines wormed their way on to the highway from the forest, as if trying to claim back the tarmac, reminding me of the sand drifts in the Sahara that crept across the road, eventually engulfing the blacktop altogether.

237

My culture shock deepened further when I approached my first road junction to find proper signs, road markings and even distances shown to the major towns. I felt almost cheated by Gabon. What was going on? Where was the real Africa, the Africa of unrideable roads, miles upon miles of mud, gun-toting military men and trigger-happy bandits? But at the same time I revelled in the ease of it all, unsure as to whether I really craved the action and adventure of slogging my way through the jungle up to my knees in mud, or if I should just sit back and enjoy some easy road while it lasted.

My map was way out of date when it came to road surfaces, and I had learnt long ago not to take get too excited about a solid red line, or to let my heart sink at the sight of hundreds of miles of dotted yellow. Where once there had been tarmac, there could easily now be knee-deep mud, and conversely, but less likely, a potholed, corrugated dirt road might well have been transformed into a superhighway. It certainly seemed as if Gabon was working towards the latter, with the superbly named President Bongo being a rare case of an African leader spending his nation's riches on something useful, rather than pink champagne and presidential palaces. The drilling of offshore oil had made this tiny African nation a relatively wealthy place; under Bongo's rule it was one of the most stable countries in the continent and here I was, reaping the benefits.

But I was definitely still in Africa. The verges of the road were inhabited by the local women, collecting firewood and transporting it on their heads back to their villages; and every river I crossed was being used as the community bath, although it wasn't just the people that were getting clean. Women were washing up piles of crockery and pans, while the men drove their cars and motorbikes into the water, turning the river into an improvised carwash. As I rode across these rivers everyone would stop whatever they were washing, even if they were stark naked, to wave and shout greetings at me. These scenes of diligent cleanliness reminded me how I, my bike and all my clothes needed a thoroughly good scrub, and I realised I had reached that point that occurs on all long road trips: the liberating moment when you stop caring how dirty you are. I was glad it had arrived; it meant one less thing to think about and brought with it a certain freedom.

After a few hours I arrived in the small town of Mitzic; it wasn't much more than one wide street lined with shops and market stalls, with various rubbish-strewn dirt tracks leading off the road into the bush. I rode down the main drag and, seeing a tumbledown shack purporting to be an internet café, pulled over and went inside to see if Chris had been in touch. Sure enough there were two messages from him and he was making good progress. It was almost a week since I had seen him off in Cameroon, and he had managed to get his visas and was already on the move again, heading my way. Feeling cheered by this news, I decided to call it a day and spend the night in Mitzic. It was late afternoon and still stiflingly hot, but not dark yet, so there was plenty of time to find somewhere to sleep.

Alongside the internet place was a little shack selling mobile phones and offering international calls. Although not much bigger than a British phone box, it managed to contain hundreds of phone accessories, leaving just enough room for the proprietor, a flashy young guy with a gold tooth who had successfully cashed in on the mobile phone mania that was sweeping through Africa. The walls of the shack were plastered with phone cards, chargers, hands-free kits, leopardskin cases, pink ones for the ladies, even little red and white Santa Claus hats for your phone (now half price).

'Excuse me,' I said, stepping into the hut, 'can I phone the UK from here?' I had spoken in French, but he replied in English.

'Oh yes, lady, you phone anywhere in the world from here,' he announced with pride, 'and you speak English to me, I speak English, German, French, whatever you like.' He gave me cheeky wink. 'So, you from the UK, white girl, you from Manchester, Manchester United? Haha! You a long way from home. Why you here in Gabon?'

Oh Lord, why do they always want to talk about soccer, I wondered, but I continued smiling and entered into the loathsome football banter.

'Who you calling in England?' he said with another wink. 'Is it your lover boy? Haha!'

'I'm phoning my husband,' I replied in what I hoped was a prim tone of voice.

'OK, OK, I just joke with you, yeah, you want to make call?' he said eventually. 'You take a telephone here' – he pointed at an array of handsets on a little table – 'you buy this card, you put in card number, like this, yeah? You call number in England and you say "Hello lover boy!" Hahaha!' He screeched with laughter at his punchline which was delivered in a mock girlie voice.

I couldn't help but laugh at his ridiculous patter; he was certainly entertaining and I was relieved that so far he hadn't made any attempt to arrange to visit me in London. I tapped in the phone card details, treating myself to a whopping 5,000 francs, which I reckoned would give me at least five minutes to exchange soppy declarations with Austin. I positioned myself at the entrance of the booth, facing inwards with my back to the street, while the proprietor leant against the back wall facing me, giving me encouraging smiles and occasional winks, making no secret of the fact that he was going to listen in on my conversation.

After a few seconds' delay I heard a faint, faraway ringing tone and then Austin's voice crackled on to the line, 5,000 miles north of where I stood in the middle of Africa. It never failed to amaze me that this was possible; it seemed almost supernatural.

'Hi darling, it's me!'

'Oh great! Are you OK? Where are you?'

'I'm fine, I'm in Gabo . . . eeeeeurgh!' I screamed as I felt a pair of slobbery lips on my neck and an arm around my shoulders, wrenching me out of the booth on to the street. But it was the putrid smell that hit me the hardest.

'Get off!' I yelled, almost retching with repulsion. My eyes met those of my assailant and I recoiled with involuntary disgust. I was being jumped by a stinking, drunken, albino man. I had never before been face to face with anyone or anything so utterly repellent. His ghost-white skin was covered in open sores, and his eyes glowed pink out of his ghoulish face. In contrast, his few remaining teeth were black and rotten, and his odour of stale urine mixed with his breath of methylated spirits and general decay was pure *eau de tramp*.

'*Ma chérie, ma chérie,*' he slurred into my ear, still slobbering down my neck and clutching me in his foul-smelling arms. It was less Charles Aznavour and more Silas, the mad monk from *The Da Vinci Code*.

'Hey you! Get out of here!' shouted the proprietor in French.

'GET OFF!' I screamed, louder, choking with nausea. I

shoved him away with all my might, sending him staggering back into the street. Then I remembered I was still holding the phone, with Austin on the other line.

'Oh my God! Austin, are you there? I just got . . .' I was about to explain what was happening when the pink-eyed monster lunged back into the booth for another ill-judged attempt at seduction, this time shoving me up against a wall of Santa Claus mobile phone hats that came tumbling down on to the dirt floor. I yelled every swear word I could think of and aimed a knee at his groin, hopefully doing the world a favour by rendering him infertile, not that he would ever get the chance to find out, I imagined. But he barely flinched and yanked again on my left arm, pulling me out into the street. I winced as I got a waft of his flammable breath; it was ninety per cent proof, and ten per cent jungle dentistry.

'Get off! *Laissez-moi!*' I screamed again, but just as I was lurching out of the booth, an opposing force pulled on my right arm, hauling me back inside. It was the proprietor, come to my rescue, but the albino was still gripping my left arm, slobbering and slurring his amorous declarations into my ear. His stink filled the small space and I was trying not to breathe through my nose, instead gasping audibly through my mouth. One of the stickers from the now demolished display of Santa hats had attached itself to his right arm, bearing the unlikely missive, '*Papa Noël! Demi Prix!*'

I was still clutching the phone in my right hand, but with each man tugging me in a different direction, I couldn't get it close to my ear, so I tried shouting in its general direction.

'It's OK, Austin, I've just been . . . OW!' I yelped as the tug-of-war shifted to a new level of intensity, pitching me back and forth, in and out of the booth. In a split second of wisdom I decided to keep quiet and phone him back later. After all, what was I going to say? *I'm being assaulted by an alcoholic albino tramp, but don't worry because a mobile phone salesman with a gold tooth is rescuing me.* Even in my traumatised state, I realised that this is not what a man wants to hear when his wife phones home from Africa.

Quite a crowd had gathered outside now, and a couple of young lads, who appeared to be friends of the proprietor, were pulling the tramp off me and shoving him back into the street, where he landed, sprawled among a pile of rotting bananas. He made an attempt at being angry, waving his fists and shouting, but he was too drunk even to make it to his feet again, and in the end he resigned himself to collapsing among the bananas with the half-price Santa Claus offer still stuck to his arm.

Meanwhile the mobile phone proprietor and his bunch of merry men were laughing and hi-fiving each other as if this had been the best entertainment Mitzic had seen in years.

'Heeheehee!' he squawked, his gold tooth glinting in the evening sun. 'He crazy man! Crazy man!'

'Yes, quite clearly,' I agreed. I was still flustered and trying to collect up the Santa Claus hats.

'Were you scared? Were you? You scared of the crazy man?' he asked me, giggling hysterically.

I didn't know what to say. He seemed to want me to answer in the positive, but I didn't want to give him the satisfaction.

'No, not really,' I insisted, somewhat unconvincingly, and he laughed harder and louder than ever.

'I think you scared. You scared of the crazy man! Hahaha!'

I tried to make another call to Austin but my previously bountiful phone card had run out of credit due to the broadcasting of my ordeal to the UK at a pound a minute. I wanted to get the hell out of this place, so I decided to get going and find another phone shack, with hopefully less drama. There was just one thing delaying my escape: during the course of the day I had drunk my usual two gallons of water and I was now bursting for the loo.

'Have you got a toilet anywhere here?' I asked my gold-toothed rescuer. It was a silly question, seeing as his premises were about seven square feet, but I was desperate. He looked a bit uncomfortable at my request and shifted his gaze around his modest surroundings before admitting in a roundabout way that there were no such facilities.

'Next door,' he said, jerking his head towards the internet café. 'At the back.'

Sure enough, among the rubble and general detritus behind the building there was a shack made of corrugated iron. It housed a deep hole in the ground and a couple of splintered planks on which to balance while hovering over the hole. The smell was what you would expect from a pit of raw sewage, but the vile stench of the albino tramp was still troubling my nostrils and I was almost glad to have a different odour, any odour, to replace it. As I hovered and held my breath it occurred to me that there was no toilet paper; not that this was a surprise, there was never any paper in African toilets, and I usually came prepared, but not on this occasion. I rummaged through my pockets, finding some mini cable ties, a length of string, my Leatherman, a couple of expired credit cards (for muggers), some Algerian coins and finally, a folded piece of paper in my jacket pocket.

'Sorry Alfred,' I apologised silently, 'but that's the end of our penpal relationship. 'And I sacrificed his particulars for what I considered to be a worthy cause.

It was almost dusk now and I hadn't even started looking for somewhere to stay. My gold-toothed friend had somehow reached the conclusion that as he had rescued me from the drunken albino I would be spending the night with him. I put him clear on this matter, and thanking him for his chivalry, made a speedy getaway on the bike. Thank you, thank you, thank you bike! I thought, as it whisked me away from the scene without a fuss; you're the real hero around here! I considered what it would be like, making my trans-African journey on public transport, and I shuddered at the thought. Nope, you've got to have your own wheels, I concluded. Once again, the motorcycle had come through for me.

I rode to another phone booth at the opposite end of the main street and phoned home. I poured out the story of my saga to Austin, who confessed to having been worried when the drama unfolded live over the phone but now managed to see the funny side of his wife being pulled apart by an albino Negro and a regular black one.

'Hmm, sounds like you were in something of a grey area,' he surmised.

I could appreciate the comedy element but I was still feeling quite distressed, not because I had felt my safety to be under threat – nothing too awful could have taken place on such a busy street – but because there was something so utterly chilling about my assailant, something alien and grotesque, even monstrous about him. And his fetid smell continued to haunt me, as if it had soaked into my skin by osmosis. I suppose I should feel sorry for him, I thought; life's hard enough out here, even if you're a fit young man, but talk about being the odd one out, an albino Negro in darkest Africa! It was bad enough being *La Blanche*, but I didn't have to live here;

I could go home whenever I wanted. I tried to summon up some sympathy for my assailant, but the way I felt at that moment, I'm sorry to admit that I failed.

Having only just reached that pivotal stage of my journey where I was happy to wallow in my own dirt, I now felt a huge urge to wash, but this was looking increasingly unlikely. I couldn't even find a place to stay. According to the man at the phone shack there was no guesthouse, hotel or even mission in this godless town, and this was confirmed by the other people I asked in shops and cafés. Just when I was starting to give up hope, a woman selling vegetables in the market responded by pointing in a general direction back down the main drag and then drawing a rough map in the dust on the ground. She didn't speak much French, just the local dialect of Fang, but she said the words '*Maison blanc*', which sounded hopeful, and between her and her fellow market traders I managed to work out what they were telling me. I thanked her a little more effusively than was necessary and she gave me a big smile, which was just what I needed at that moment (as well as a hot shower and a double gin and tonic). I set off, following her directions.

I ended up at a white-painted house on the outskirts of the town. It was a little run-down and there were a few broken-down cars in the front garden, but at least it was a house, a real house. I had gathered from my conversation with the market traders that the owner rented out rooms, so I knocked on the door, praying that I had got the right end of the stick. It was dark now and the last thing I wanted to do was set off on another hunt. So I almost wept with relief when a young man with a friendly smile opened the door, confirmed that I could indeed stay the night, helped me carry in my bags and proceeded to rustle up an omelette for me on a one-ring camping stove. There was no running water or electricity but I didn't care any more; there was a bed in the room but I didn't really need that; by this point I was so shattered that I would have lain down and slept on the floor. Three generations of the young man's family watched me wolf down my omelette in the kitchen before I made my excuses and staggered off to bed. But sleep wouldn't come and I spent the night scratching my mosquito bites and tossing and turning in the heat, haunted by the leering spectral face, pink eyes and vile odour of Mitzic's only other pasty-skinned inhabitant.

I must have slept eventually, as I awoke early the next morning still feeling tired, but less spooked, and keen to get going. I was soon on the road and glad to be making progress away from Mitzic; the very act of movement was itself soothing and reassuring, and it seemed to me that trouble only started when the moving stopped. My mobility was everything; it was my greatest strength, my guardian angel and my best friend. Going off on a strange tangent of thought, as is the luxury of the long-distance motorcyclist, I found myself feeling quite annoyed on behalf of the women of Saudi Arabia, who aren't allowed to drive. It's one of the greatest gifts of modern life, being able to get around of your own free will. And learning to drive is a rite of passage, up there with losing your virginity; the two of them should be dealt with as soon as possible, so you can get on with driving and fornicating, surely two of the fundamental pleasures of adult life.

I was riding through more deep jungle on another of Gabon's perfect roads, following the course of the vast Ogooue River, which swept through the forest in huge, sweeping brown curves. The trials of the previous day were slowly

247

evaporating with the morning dew, while my mood brightened with the rising sun. Last night had been a 'What the hell am I doing here?' moment, but I was getting used to the African mood swings now; it seemed I had unwittingly signed up for 10,000 miles of PMT. But for every moment of despair I knew its opposite number would appear soon enough, and I spent the rest of the morning running through a list of all the things that *hadn't* gone wrong, just like those motivational 'life coaches' tell you to do. I was more than halfway through my journey – I'd crossed the Sahara, for crissake! The bike was running well, I hadn't had a crash, got a puncture, been mugged or got ill. I would be meeting up with Chris soon, and after yesterday's events I reckoned that having a male escort would be pretty useful. My halfway mark was further confirmed by a sign at the side of the road informing me I was crossing the Equator. I was now officially in the southern hemisphere, and all in all, I decided, things were looking pretty good.

At a petrol station in Lambaréné, a large town built on an island in the middle of the Ogooue River, I pulled up alongside a seriously kitted-out Land Rover, complete with a roof tent, sand ladders, rows of jerrycans, a snorkel, a pickaxe, a spade and various other bits and bobs for the serious overland driver. It had Swiss plates and looked like it had seen some action, plastered in stickers proclaiming its many conquests and promoting the ethos of the 4WD brigade: 'One life. Live it', 'You can go fast, but I can go ANYWHERE!' and 'It's a Land Rover thing, you wouldn't understand.'

Tinkering with a bundle of firewood on the roof was its owner, a white guy probably in his late twenties, attired in khaki shorts and a photographer's jacket, which was equipped in a similar fashion to his vehicle, every pocket bulging with some gadget or another. He even had a hunting knife dangling at his left hip. He was tanned and lean, with just the right amount of stubble to win him a role in a Land Rover ad – enough to suggest he'd been out in the bush for a while, but not so much that it had turned into a full-blown beard. As I came to a halt at the pump opposite I noticed the other inhabitant of the car, a young blonde-haired woman who would be considered beautiful had it not been for her stony-faced expression. She was staring blankly ahead, wearing a mask of bitter disappointment. Beside her on the seat was a French edition of *Elle*, a pack of wet wipes and a pair of Jackie O style Chanel sunglasses.

'Hey there!' called the man on the roof, as he jumped down in what he hoped was commando fashion. 'Pete,' he said, offering his suitably rugged hand.

'Hi, I'm Lois. You don't sound very Swiss.'

'Nah, mate, I'm an Ozzie, but I bought this lil' beauty in Zurich.' He patted the side of the Land Rover. 'The car, that is.' He laughed at his joke then called to his companion. 'Hey, Katrin, come and say hi to this Brit chick on a dirt bike.'

The pale, made-up face with impeccable bone structure appeared out of the passenger window. The Chanel glasses had been donned for the occasion.

'Hi,' said Katrin in a vapid voice before disappearing back into the cab.

'She doesn't get on with the sun, with the heat, y'know,' offered Peter a little awkwardly. 'She's from the Alps! One helluva skier, though, that's how we met. I said to her, come with me to Africa, babe, I'll show you a real adventure!'

'How long have you been on the road?'

'Jeez, must be a couple of months now. Man, there's some serious driving to be done on this continent, we've been up to here in mud,' he said, offering his hand to the top of the window. 'Bow waves coming right over the top, I had to winch us out of a mud-hole in the Congo! Jesus, I love Africa, it's fuckin' wild! We're having a blast!'

Katrin was unavailable for comment on this last point.

'So where are you going, what's your route?'

'We're goin' fuckin' everywhere!' he declared excitedly. 'We're gonna visit every country in Africa.'

'What, every single one? Even the little islands, like, what's it called, San Tome or whatever?'

'Fuck, yeah! Every single one! The little ones, the big ones, the shit-holes, the war zones. Especially the war zones!'

He jumped up on the bonnet to adjust a strap on the roof-rack, pausing briefly to perform a couple of pelvic thrusts in Katrin's direction through the windscreen.

'*Do ya really like it, is it is it wicked!*' he belted out in an Ozzie-accented version of DJ Pied Piper. Unfortunately I wasn't able to see her response from where I was standing.

'Hey Lois! Where you staying tonight?' he hollered down from the roof.

'I don't know yet. I was thinking of going on to Mouila, but time's getting on a bit now.'

'Nah, forget Mouila, it's a dump, there's fuck all there. We've just come up that way. We're staying here, in Lambarene. Why don't you hang out with us for the night?'

'Oh, great, OK.'

'Yeah? Cool! And I can have a blast on your bike. Excellent!' he concluded in a Bill and Ted voice.

'Oh, er, yeah, sure, if you want. Where are you staying?'

'Katrin wants to stay in a hotel down the road. Says she needs a shower, not that I've noticed! But I probably stink myself. Haa!' He laughed loudly, sniffing his armpits. 'Oh yeah, smells good Petey-boy, smells gooood!' he said before jumping back down to the ground and into the driver's seat in one fluid movement. 'OK, saddle up! Let's go!'

Katrin wasn't consulted as to whether it was OK for me to tag along with them for the night, but I got the feeling that she wasn't consulted on a lot of things. But on arriving at the hotel I realised that when she put her foot down, Petey-boy jumped.

As soon as we'd checked in at reception Katrin trotted off to their room, leaving me and Pete to unpack our respective vehicles, but within a few seconds Pete was summoned back to the reception desk. I couldn't make out all of the conversation but it seemed that Katrin had deemed the room to be uninhabitable. It sounded as if Pete was making pacifying noises and then I heard the receptionist muttering something, before Katrin's voice sliced through the air, as sharp as Pete's hunting knife.

'Peter!' she spat. 'It smells. Of drains.'

The manager was called to the desk and a sullen receptionist was bullied into providing another, less pungent room. I made my way to my room, passing them in the lobby, trying to pretend I hadn't heard anything. Katrin wore an expression of cool satisfied triumph as Pete and the receptionist lugged her bags up the stairs for the second time, and I wagered there would be Gabonese phlegm in her breakfast tomorrow morning.

We met for dinner later that evening, and a shower and fresh clothes seemed to have thawed Katrin's chilly exterior. She even managed a thin smile. The hotel restaurant was empty,

251

verging on abandoned, with chairs piled up on the tables, but the waiter made a big show of preparing a table for us and fussing over our cutlery and condiments. The menu was the usual list of fantasy dishes and it turned out there were just two choices: steak with chips, or, for the vegetarian, chips. They had beer and Coke, the waiter explained, but if we wanted Coke we had to hand over the money now as they had to go to a nearby grocery shop to buy it. We opted for beer.

Over dinner we shared stories of our African adventures, our scrapes, our conquests, our disasters and our past lives, although when I say 'we', it was Pete who did most of the talking, with a liberal helping of hyperbole that prompted the occasional roll of the eyes from Katrin. He was an entertaining storyteller, so I forgave him his exaggerations, but when I talked about my experience of riding across the Sahara, he piped down for a moment and a sad, dreamy look came into his eyes.

'I wanted us to do this trip on a motorbike, y'know,' he said, 'but Katrin wasn't into it.'

'No, thank you,' she confirmed.

'I've ridden all over Europe and Oz, and New Zealand. That was before we met. I've always wanted to do Africa on a bike . . . Hey!' said Pete, remembering something. 'Lois, do you know two guys from England on bikes, they're riding to SA too? We met them coming the other way in Congo.'

'No, I don't know them, but I heard about them in Yaounde.' I guessed it must be the same pair that Sherry-Kay had mentioned. 'Are they from Portsmouth?'

'Yeah, yeah! That's them, one of them's riding an XT600, an old red and white one, the other's on a Beemer. They were really pissed off, moaning about everything, mostly about their sore asses!'

252

'I don't blame them,' said Katrin, then, addressing me for the first time, 'I mean, I just don't get it. Why would you want to ride a motorbike, especially in Africa. I just don't see the appeal.'

'Shit, man, it's the best! The freedom, the . . .' Pete launched into an impassioned piece of motorcycle propaganda which I suspected he had churned out on many occasions, trying to persuade the unwilling Katrin to take to two wheels, or at least to climb on the back.

'Yes, Peter, I know all that,' she said, wafting her hand as if he was an irritating insect she could brush away, 'but I'm not asking you, I'm asking Lois.' She turned towards me expectantly.

'Well, Pete's right about the freedom, that is the best. You can go anywhere, wherever you want, especially on a dirt bike . . .'

'But we can go anywhere in the Land Rover.'

'Well, there are certainly places you can go on a dirt bike where you couldn't get to in a car. If you see a goat track going up a mountain or a little trail going off into the woods, you can just nip down there and see where it goes. And a bike's portable, especially a small trail bike like mine; if it breaks down a couple of men can lift it into a truck or on to a train or something and I can pick it up, and haul it out of tricky situations.'

'Well, we've got a winch on the Land Rover,' she pointed out.

'Yeah, I know, but well . . . it's not for everyone I know, but I just love the act of riding along. You're out in the elements, smelling everything, feeling the warmth and the air against your face . . .'

'And the cold and rain,' she added.

I was already growing weary of her combative, competitive tone, but I continued out of politeness.

'Yes, true, but you know all these butterflies here in Gabon, the turquoise ones?'

'Yes.'

'You see them fluttering around in front of your windscreen and they're beautiful, but when I see them, I feel their wings touching my face too, d'you see?'

'Eurgh.' She shuddered and grimaced. 'Yes, and that means you feel the mosquitoes and the wasps too. No thanks.'

There was obviously no point in continuing this conversation, so I just shrugged and was about to change the subject when Pete, unused to being silent for so long, broke his gagging order.

'On a bike, you're *in* the picture, babe, not looking at it. You're *in* it. Know what I mean?'

I knew exactly what he meant, but I don't think Katrin did, and I doubted she ever would.

Pete and Katrin were hitting the road at dawn the next morning, heading north, so we said our farewells and Pete filled me in with tips and lurid tales of the road ahead towards the Congo border and of Congo itself.

'It's a crazy fucking place, Lois,' he assured me, shaking my hand, but I wondered if he would say that about anywhere. 'Good luck! Ride safe,' he said as they entered their odourless room.

'Goodnight, it was nice to meet you,' said Katrin with a watery smile, still as vapid as when she had greeted me in the petrol station.

I wished them farewell and good luck and settled into my bed to write my diary, noting a distinct smell of drains in the air.

*

Looking at the map the next morning over breakfast, I decided I would stick around here in Lambaréné to wait for Chris. It was the last big town before the Congo border and I would be able to keep myself occupied until he arrived in a few days. I went into town in search of an internet café, with the intention of emailing him with my plan. But I didn't get as far as writing the first line, as there was a new message from him waiting for me entitled 'Good luck with the rest of your trip'. I opened it, already sensing the nature of its content. I was right. Chris had had second thoughts about riding through the Congo and Angola. He was currently in Gabon's capital, Libreville, trying to arrange air shipment for his bike direct to South Africa. He was sorry, but he didn't feel confident about the bike, there were a few mechanical problems and this seemed like the best option. He feared the roads in Congo and Angola would be too demanding.

I sat there, feeling my stomach tightening in knots and a heavy weight descend upon me. Although I barely knew Chris and had only met him that one time in Cameroon, I hadn't realised until now how much I had been banking on his companionship on the tough roads that lay ahead. I wasn't annoyed with him; of course he had to do what was right for him, his bike and his trip. But I was annoyed with myself; I had allowed myself to be lulled into a false sense of security and now I had to reprogramme my brain. I would be riding through Congo and Angola alone, and I'd better get used to it.

THIRTEEN

Once I'd recovered from the initial blow, I decided to treat the news of Chris's change of heart as a positive development in my African odyssey. It would give me the adventure I craved, I told myself. The thrill of motorcycling through the Congo and Angola would have been diluted by having a male chaperone; now I would get the raw, unfettered experience. Ahead of me lay the very challenge that had inspired to me to make this journey in the first place. I scolded myself for having weakened, for having allowed myself to rely on the idea of Chris's companionship. I had set out to make it to Cape Town, and that meant taking the knock-backs as well as the good times. And, I told myself even more strictly, real adventures aren't meant to be easy. If I wanted easy I should have gone for a mini-break at Center Parcs. At this thought, I was relieved to find that the idea of holidaying at Center Parcs still filled me with more dread than the thought of motorcycling across the Congo. I'm not sure how much of my own pep talk I believed, but it was the only way to keep going. Optimism was as crucial to the success of this journey as my Michelin maps and my factor 30 sun lotion.

I spent the rest of the day doing some motorcycle maintenance, going through the usual routine of cleaning the air and oil filters, changing the oil and checking the bike over for any loose, rattly bits. I was amazed at how well it was holding up, but I feared that the toughest stuff was yet to come and I wanted to make sure everything was in good shape before I plunged into what I knew would be the most challenging riding of the entire trip.

Hitting the road again the following morning, I soon discovered that the funds for Gabon's fabulous road-building project had run out about halfway down the country, and in what I imagined was a taster for things to come, I plodded along the 160 miles to the Congo border at an average speed of thirty miles an hour, negotiating huge holes, corrugations, wash-outs, rocks, massive puddles and miles upon miles of mud. But most daunting of all were the numerous broken wooden bridges that spanned the rivers. Many of their planks had rotted away or been destroyed by heavy trucks, leaving big empty gaps where I could see the churning water, fifteen feet below. I knew there was nothing else to do but go as fast as I dared, skimming over these holes to avoid getting stuck or caught on a snapped plank, but my heart was in my mouth as I raced across each one, never looking down, and bumping and banging my way to the other side.

I arrived in the border town of N'Dende at dusk; Pete and Katrin had come this way and I tried to imagine Katrin here, staring out of the Land Rover window in her Chanel sunglasses, taking in its dirt streets and dilapidated buildings. N'Dende wouldn't be winning any Best Kept Village award: it was a classic frontier town, transient and unloved, with a whiff of desperation in the air, and I wondered what Katrin had made of it, and what she made of her whole trip through Africa, tagging along with the ebullient Pete, who relished every moment of discomfort and every scrap of dirt with boy scout enthusiasm.

N'Dende's one petrol station was open for business, despite its derelict appearance, and the guy pumping gas beamed like a ray of sunshine in this dreary setting. He smiled and joked while filling up my bike and even started trying to wash it, but I assured him there was no point.

'You go to Congo?' he asked.

'Yes, tomorrow. What is the road like?' I don't know why I bothered asking this question, as the responses usually varied from optimistic guesses to downright lies, but I suppose I just wanted to be reassured, even if it turned out to be nonsense.

'Bon, bon,' he assured me. 'Très bon.'

My spirits were cheered by this unsubstantiated piece of news, and when I asked about somewhere to sleep in N'Dende he offered me a hut at the back of the petrol station. There were a few of them dotted about in the back yard; they were nothing more than concrete cells but the doors were numbered so he obviously operated some sort of lodgings here. Either that or it was a Gabonese young offenders' institute. He opened the door of cell number 4 for me to have a look, and I recoiled as if I'd been smacked in the face with a warm sodden sponge. The hut had no window and had been cooking all day in the humid jungle heat; it was like walking into an industrial oven

259

and within a matter of seconds the sweat was pouring off me. Inside, a 1997 calendar hung on a bare wall and as I stepped in a few cockroaches scuttled away into a corner.

'I'll take it,' I announced, and threw my helmet on to the soggy mattress that lay on the concrete floor.

In the morning I awoke with mixed feelings: of excitement tempered with foreboding, and of being thoroughly knackered and soaked in sweat, having spent the entire night thrashing around trying to get comfortable on a lumpy mattress in the unrelenting tropical heat. As the day dawned I made my way through the empty streets of N'Dende and out the other side, through open green country along a reasonably decent dirt road, until across the track appeared an improvised barrier of tree branches bringing me to a halt. On the other side stood a group of camouflage-clad armed soldiers, leaning against a tree and eyeing me with wary curiosity.

'OK, this is it,' I said. 'Welcome to the Congo.'

I had to say it myself, as clearly, nobody else was going to, and there certainly wasn't a sign by the side of the road like when you cross the Severn Bridge into Wales.

The soldiers made no move to open the barrier so I skirted around it, up and down a muddy bank, and rode past them, feeling their stares boring into me. They said nothing and I passed by quickly without meeting their eyes. I had entered Africa with what I considered to be a valid wariness of the armed forces, but so far my fears had not been proved right. In Algeria the police and the army had been strict, fussy and misguided, but that was the worst I could say about them. Even in Nigeria, where I had expected the worst, I had never felt intimidated or in danger, but I knew that here in Congo, and particularly in DRC, the next country on my itinerary, the armed forces posed a genuine and terrible threat. Shafted by their superiors and the government élite, the underpaid, or often not paid at all, armed forces had rebelled and rioted on several occasions, particularly in Kinshasa, where in the 1990s they had practically destroyed the city. Angry young soldiers with no money but plenty of guns, and drunk on stolen booze, became the greatest menace to the country they were supposedly employed to protect. Widespread looting of shops, businesses, homes, farms, even entire villages was rife, and the raping of women and children was, and continues to be sickeningly commonplace.

'Ask a policeman', that comforting old adage instilled into British children of a certain age and class, could not be further from the reality of life in the Congo. Men in uniform are not the people you turn to here in a moment of crisis or danger; and even I, with my innate suspicion of authority figures, found it hard to make this mental shift. A new mindset was required and it was a difficult and disconcerting concept, because essentially, what it meant was that if anything should go horribly wrong for me here there was nobody I could trust, no higher power that could be relied upon to get me out of trouble and look after me. Out here in the Congo, the people, authorities and institutions that I could bank on at home were the baddies, not the goodies.

There were a few shacks ahead of me set back from the track among the trees, although none of them had any signs indicating what went on behind their mud-brick walls. I pulled up outside the first one to find I had by chance stumbled on the immigration office. A Gabonese family in front of me were involved in an argument with one of the officers about their passports but were shooed away when I arrived, and all attention was focused on the white woman on the motorcycle.

I stood there feeling unbearably self-conscious, but the immigration officials were welcoming, and although the process took far longer than it needed to, thanks to the multitude of forms that had to be filled in, I left the hut feeling a lot more relaxed than when I had awoken a few hours earlier, full of trepidation.

'Be careful,' said the chief officer, following me out of the hut to my bike. 'There is much rain, the ground is very wet, very dangerous, it is best if you go slowly. Last year, a German man came here on his moto, big motorcycle, very big.' He stretched his arms out to suggest the Teutonic vastness of the machine. 'It is the biggest motorcycle I have seen, not like yours. Much bigger. He stops here and when he leaves, he goes very fast and CRASH! He falls off because the mud, it is very dangerous.'

I laughed, thinking this was being told as an amusing anecdote, but the immigration officer wasn't laughing, so I quickly curtailed my amusement.

'Oh dear, was he hurt?'

'No. He was very angry.'

Now I desperately wanted to laugh, but it appeared that this Congolese immigration official was giving me a genuine health and safety lecture, so instead I nodded seriously and rode away at a measured pace.

The good, graded dirt road that had led me to the border was a strictly Gabonese phenomenon and had stopped abruptly at the barrier. On the Congolese side it was a muddy track and I continued slowly, fearful of emulating the German rider's pride-wounding fate. The entry formalities were predictably shambolic and dragged on along the route. Every couple of miles, another barrier made of tree branches would appear across the road, and another uniformed official would flag me down in order to inspect my documents and laboriously write my details into a huge old-fashioned ledger. Often I didn't even know the purpose of each checkpoint; I just handed over every official-looking piece of paper I could find and waited. At each one I asked about the state of the route ahead and received largely the same answer every time:

'*C'est bon, madame. Oui, c'est bon.*'

Well, that wasn't so bad, I decided, as I left the final checkpoint behind, encouraged by the fact that I'd not had to pay a single bribe or even been harassed by anyone. The police and soldiers couldn't be described as friendly exactly, but neither had they been intimidating, and there wasn't a severed head on a car aerial to be seen. So far, so good. Maybe the Congo's going to be all right after all, I thought; I've just been sucked in by the usual horror stories and exaggerations.

With the last of the border post shacks behind me, the track dwindled to a narrow muddy trail, lined on each side by shoulder-high grass, and more than ever before on my journey, I felt as though I was plunging deep into the jungle. There was no sign of human habitation here, or any suggestion that there ever had been. It wasn't like Gabon or Cameroon, where even the dirt roads were lined with villages and little stalls selling fruit and vegetables. This path of orangey-red mud would be considered one of Congo's main arteries, but apart from the fact that the track existed, there was no evidence of man's intervention in this wild corner of the world.

I was not surprised to discover that the reports of a '*bon*' route were way off the mark. The rainy season had arrived and the track had dissolved into a series of flooded trenches as long as Olympic swimming pools, endless stretches of thick mud, washed-out gullies and sections where the road had simply disappeared altogether, leaving clusters of sharp rocks jutting out of the ground. Within a matter of minutes I was soaked up to my knees and covered in mud from head to toe. And to think that I had been complaining about yesterday's ride in southern Gabon; I'd thought it was a taste of what lay ahead, and I uttered a dry laugh at my naivety. Compared to this Congo mud bath it had been a breeze.

I was heading towards the town of Dolisie, almost 200 miles away. Under normal circumstances it would have been a day's ride, but I knew that from now on my estimates of how far I could travel in a day would be just that: estimates. There was no way of knowing what was going to happen on a road like this, and there were plenty of routes in this part of the world that were seasonal, only navigable during the brief dry season. I could easily find myself stuck in some swamp or having to seek out an alternative route if the track became impassable. But I tried not to think about such dramas and instead I plugged away slowly, sliding around in the slippery mud and ploughing through yards of dirty brown water, concentrating on the more pressing matter of staying upright.

After a couple of hours I was beginning to feel I'd got the measure of it; if it carried on like this I'd be all right; it'd be slow, but steady. The hard-packed sections of dirt were wet and slippy, but at least I could get up a decent speed on them; however, the giant puddles needed a more cautious approach. Often they were too deep to ride straight through the middle and I would have to ride around the outside, sometimes battling my way through the tall grass that brushed against my face. This method was working out OK, and when I came upon one particularly deep, bike-swallowing pool of grey, clay-like mud I thought nothing of shimmying around its edge. Attacking what I thought was the least dicey side, I rode up and around the camber, keeping the revs high, but just when I thought I'd pulled it off, the back wheel slipped out from underneath me, and before I could say 'Um Bongo' I was lying next to my bike in the pool of hot, stagnant sludge.

I hauled myself up, swearing mildly, as the muddy grey water poured off me. It was my first spill since the Sahara, and I'd been pleased to be doing so well, but now the spell was broken. Thankfully, there was no damage done, to either me or the bike, and I knew I could pick it up, I'd done it before. But this time, whether it was due to plain tiredness, or the fact that the bike had fallen with the wheels higher than the handlebars, I couldn't get the darn thing to budge more than a few inches. I removed as much of the luggage as I could, but still I couldn't get the bike upright. The humid jungle heat didn't help matters, and by now I was boiling hot and dripping in sweat. I sat in the grass, catching my breath, before stripping off as many garments as I considered decent. Taking a deep breath, I garnered all my strength and plunged in for another go, but to no avail. The bike was now sinking deeper into the cloying mud and the possibility of me righting it was slipping further and further away.

My mind raced through the possible scenarios, my sense of desperation inventing ever more lurid outcomes. I would be stuck here for days, weeks even! I would run out of food and water, and then what? I hadn't seen another soul for hours, and I hadn't passed a single vehicle all day. I sat down, trying to keep calm, and considered my options, of which there were none. My only choice was to take a breather, gulp down some water, and keep trying to pick up the bike. But I couldn't shift it, no matter how hard I tried. I fished out a packet of chocolate biscuits and ate half of them in one go, in an attempt to inject some much-needed energy into my flagging reserves, but 500 calories just wasn't enough for me to raise my sinking bike from this slough of despond.

What the hell am I going to do? I cried aloud. What was I thinking of, riding across the Congo alone? My detractors were right, it was a ridiculous idea; something like this was bound to happen. And I couldn't understand why it was so difficult to budge the bike. I knew I could pick it up, I'd done it in Cameroon, when it had fallen over in the Holiday Inn car park. But now, for some reason, it was impossible, and with every attempt I became more and more exhausted.

An hour had passed now, and I was sinking into the depths of despair when faraway down the track I spied a lone figure in the distance. I couldn't believe it! My heart leapt with hope. He was ambling slowly towards me; it was a man, and hopefully, a big strong one. I waved my arms in the style of a castaway stranded on a desert island signalling to a plane passing overhead, although I realised as I was doing it that this was quite unnecessary, as we were the only two people for miles around. As he approached, our eyes met, and I realised instantly from the look on his face that while I viewed him as my knight in (slightly tatty) shining armour, he was eyeing me as a cashpoint machine.

He gave no greeting but just pointed to the bike.

'You want me to help?' he asked in French.

'*Oui, oui, s'il vous plaît, merci.*'

He looked at me with a stare so cold that my sweating, steaming brow dropped in temperature by several degrees. He said something else that I didn't quite catch, but I got the gist;

it included the word *argent*. My immediate response was to protest; but a split-second assessment of the situation forced me to accept the harsh truth. This man was my only hope. I was at his mercy and he could name his price.

'*Combien?*' I asked.

'*Cinq mille francs*,' he said.

Five thousand francs? That was five quid. It seemed pretty steep and I made a few hollow, British attempts at haggling, but as I did so, I remembered that I didn't actually have anything less than a 5,000-franc note anyway, and I guessed that, like a stroppy bus driver, he would demand the exact money only. And besides, I didn't have the nerve to ask for change.

'OK,' I agreed. '*Cinq mille*.' But he made it clear that he wouldn't so much as touch the bike until the 5,000-franc note was safely in his pocket. Grudgingly I handed over the cash, and he rolled up his trousers, removed his sandals and strode into the mud. I watched as he grabbed the bike's handlebars, heaved them towards him, and with a loud comedy squelch, the bike rose from the mire. He pushed it on to dryish land, wiped his hands on his trousers, and with that, he was off.

I estimated it had taken him about ten seconds to right the bike, and as I repacked my luggage and made a few fruitless efforts at wiping off the mud, I calculated that at this rate, he was on an hourly wage of £1,800 pounds an hour. Nice work if you can get it. I could hardly blame his entrepreneurial spirit; he'd spotted a way to make a fast franc and it was a simple case of supply and demand. In the business of picking up motorcycles for feeble English ladies in northern Congo, he had cornered the market. But the experience left me feeling vaguely depressed and resentful, and as I continued onwards, I tried to work out why.

Not in any of my travels had I encountered such calculating hardness in someone. In my experience it was the incidents such as these – the breakdowns, the accidents, the disasters – which brought you into contact with strangers and ended up restoring your faith in human nature. Someone stops to help and before you know it, you're invited back to their house for dinner, or they fix your bike and refuse to accept any money, or they adopt you for the day, show you around and introduce you to their family. These aren't romantic travellers' myths; all of these things have happened to me in various corners of the globe. But maybe the Congo was different? Had decades of brutality succeeded in eliminating the generous side of human nature here, the side that allows one to be kind for no reward? I was haunted by the expression on the man's face as he had approached me. I had never seen it in anyone before; it was cold and unscrupulous, but at the same time his eyes were utterly dead.

I was thoroughly filthy and wet through, but there was nothing to do but plough on towards Dolisie, and I attacked the muddy puddles with even more caution than before. I was trying to convince myself that the man who had picked up my bike was probably just a bit grumpy, and that there would be plenty of nice friendly locals along the way. After a couple of hours I came upon a small village; it was the first sign of human habitation since the border and I slowed down as I rode through, dodging a few scraggy goats in the middle of the track. The village was as basic as anything I'd seen in Africa, a mass of mud and sticks tucked among the trees. There was no colour to be seen in this landscape; mud covered everything, the people, the animals, the shacks – the entire scene was in shades of brown. The track through the village was badly churned up, with sticks and logs thrown down in the mud to provide some kind of surface, but this just made it more difficult to ride and I was reduced to a crawl, waving and smiling at the villagers as I picked my way through. But the welcome I had received in neighbouring Gabon was not forthcoming here and groups of men and women began shouting at me, brandishing sticks and running after me. I couldn't make out what they were saying, but it didn't sound as if they were inviting me in for a cup of tea. I gave it some revs and powered through the sludge, slipping and sliding, hitting hidden logs below the surface, almost sending me flying.

The hostility of the villagers and the demanding nature of the riding, plus the crushing heat and endless mud, were not making for high morale, and when I came upon a military checkpoint a few miles later I was almost glad of the break. It was staffed by a couple of boy soldiers who couldn't have been older than twelve or thirteen, but they had the confidence of grown men and flagged me down with authority, waving their sub-machine guns at me as I approached. They couldn't have been more different than the last African children I had encountered, the impeccably behaved, smartly dressed offspring of Cameroon's élite that had been seen but not heard at Ekoko's Christmas party.

'Your passport,' demanded the taller, cockier of the two as I came to a halt. 'Leave your motorcycle here. We go inside.'

I followed them into their hut; it was of the mud-brick and dirt-floor variety, and inside there was nothing but a desk and a chair, where the other boy was instructed to copy my particulars into a school exercise book. But over in the far corner of the hut, hanging on the wall, I spied a noticeboard covered in photographs, and while I waited for the boy to finish with my passport, I strolled over to have a look. I assumed they would be snaps of their fellow soldiers or maybe photos from the local village, but as I walked towards the board and the images became clearer, I felt a surge of horror rise up inside me. My stomach lurched as I stopped in front of the board; I had never seen anything like it.

Before I could speak, the boy soldier walked up behind me and, seeing me struck speechless with my mouth agape, began talking me through the pictures as if he was showing me his latest holiday snaps.

'This is someone who was shot in the genitals, this one had his head cut in half with a machete, this one drowned in the river, this one was found hanging in a tree . . .'

Sure enough, there were several pictures of each gruesome incident: a man, naked except for his underpants around his knees, with what had once been the family jewels now blasted into a bloody mess of raw flesh; literally shot to pieces. Next up was the blood-spattered, startled face of a young man whose skull had been split neatly in half by the clean slice of a machete. A man hanging by a noose in a tree, his tongue cut off and his face covered in dried mud; another lying dead and mutilated on the bank of a dirty brown river. I couldn't believe my eyes. The boy next to me was still recounting each gory detail in a flat monotone.

'But, but . . .' I faltered, trying to figure out what to say, what it was I wanted to ask – who were these men, what had they done, why were these photos here? But my French failed me, or maybe I was genuinely lost for words, even in my own language. The only thing that came out of my mouth was, '*Porquoi?*'

The boy turned and looked at me with dead eyes; it was the second time I had seen that expression today. He simply shrugged his shoulders and said by way of explanation, '*C'est la vie.*'

Well, it might be life round here, I thought grimly, but not where I come from. I had never felt so far away from home and so utterly out of my depth. What on earth was I doing here? What was I thinking of? This place was a living hell. I remembered a conversation I'd had with the grandmother of a friend of mine shortly before I had left England. She was a dear, white-haired lady of ninety-four who had lived in Africa during the days of the Empire, but when I had told her of my plans to visit the Congo she had looked quite horrified and clasped my hand in her soft, papery grasp.

'Oh my dear, no,' she had said in her wavering voice. 'They're savages, dear, absolute savages!'

My passport was handed back to me and I walked over to my bike, feeling spooked by just about everything. I had been in Congo for less than twelve hours and I was already in a state of high anxiety. As I was buckling my helmet and pulling on my muddy gloves, I heard the boy who had talked me through the pictures calling after me.

'*Madame, madame!*'

I turned round to see him running towards me with his hand outstretched.

'*Madame! Avez-vous un bonbon?*'

Now he was just a regular kid, asking me if I had any sweets. It chilled me to the bone.

The road continued to deteriorate as I headed south, and I passed several trucks, stuck in the mud or fallen over on their side, but the bike made it through everything and I was grateful for its dependability in these uncertain times. After a while the thick jungle ebbed away, making way for a strange landscape of small, neatly arranged hillocks, each one a perfectly formed, pointed cone, and all covered in grass so bright green that they seemed cartoon-like, even fake. I couldn't believe they weren't man-made, and in keeping with my newly acquired mood of Gothic drama, I convinced myself they were tumuli, burial mounds piled high with the bodies of the men in the photographs and countless others like them.

By the time I arrived in Dolisie, the day's cocktail of punishing riding, sickly heat and gruesome imagery had sent me into a strange state of numbness. It was easier to be numb than to get upset, to dwell on the horror all around me and what further horrors lay ahead the next day, and the next, and the one after that. It's easier not to think or care. But that's how the process of brutalisation starts, I realised; that's how you get those dead eyes. No one is exempt; if I stuck around here long enough, I too would end up with that empty expression carved into my face.

Dolisie itself did little to raise my spirits. It was a predictably grotty town, split into two by the railway that runs from the oil-rich city of Point Noire on the Atlantic Coast to the capital, Brazzaville. The railway tracks in the town were home to the less fortunate; street kids, invalids and the elderly gathered there, and the tracks were strewn with rubbish. Apparently Dolisie had once served as a weekend retreat for well-off Brazzavilleans, but it was hard to imagine this now. The civil war had seen them off, leaving a shabby, semi-derelict shell in their wake. I stopped by a bakery shop to buy some bread, but the shelves were empty and the man behind the counter informed me that there was no bread in town today, because there was no flour.

But among the grot and greyness of Dolisie's potholed dirt streets were huge, brightly coloured PVC banners, slung across the roads between trees and telegraph poles, as if the town was in the midst of a festival. However, these incongruous splashes of colour marked no celebration or carnival; they were adverts for MTN, the South African mobile phone company that was successfully conquering Central Africa. Each one bore aspirational images of beautiful young black people living the dream: a woman sipping an espresso while gazing at her snazzy phone, or a suited businessman striding through a modern city, his mobile glued to his ear. These pictures were about as far removed from life in Dolisie as I could imagine, but they were the only sign of progress amid the squalor.

As I entered the outskirts I was stopped at another checkpoint, and in my fragile state I allowed myself to be befriended by Serge, a middle-aged man who was there for no other reason than to hang out with his police buddies. He worked for the forestry department and flashed his ID card at me.

'Come with me, I will show you a good place to stay,' he assured me, jumping on his moped and beckoning me to follow.

I always found situations like this slightly tricky, trying to work out whether to trust these self-appointed 'helpers' or sussing out if they had an ulterior motive, but I pushed my paranoia to the back of my mind and trusted my instinct. So far it had never let me down and I was right again. There was nothing dodgy about Serge; he was that rare thing in Africa, just a friendly guy. I tipped him handsomely, not just for his trouble, but for being so guileless and for not demanding any money. He took me to a hotel that was owned by a friend of his and I collapsed into bed, still covered in dried mud but relieved that the day was over and trying not to think about what lay ahead.

I spent the following twenty-four hours washing the mud out of my hair and plotting the next part of my route. I had to get across the Congo River into DRC to get to Matadi, the only place I could procure the tricky Angolan visa. I had two options. Ride to Brazzaville and take the ferry to DRC's capital, Kinshasa, or take a short cut through the bush, crossing the river at some little out-of-the-way border post, thereby avoiding two of the world's most intimidating capital cities. I was at a loss what to do. Sometimes, as had been the case in Nigeria, it was best to seek out the back roads and the sleepy, isolated border crossings. But at other times, in other countries, sticking to the main road was the safest bet and the anonymity of a big city was preferable to showing up in a little one-horse town like a flashing white beacon. I usually had some innate sense of which option to go for, but here in the Congo, I was uncertain. It was the only country in which I had felt a genuine unease, and I feared that my nerves were affecting my judgement.

Luckily, I bumped into Serge the next day in the hotel reception. He was visiting his friend the hotel owner and they were sitting around drinking beer and watching TV. He didn't seem to do much forestry work, and I wondered if his ID badge was a fake, or whether he merely had a relaxed approach to his duties, having resigned himself to the fact that as most of the rainforest was being chopped down anyway, he might as well sit around and enjoy a cold bottle of beer.

I explained my predicament to the pair of them and showed them the map. But when I pointed to my possible route along the back roads they shook their heads with vigour.

'*Non, non! Très dangéreuse!*' They made shooting noises and imitated guns with their empty beer bottles to illustrate the point.

'Oh, so you think it's best to go via Brazzaville and Kinshasa?'

They looked at each, shrugging their shoulders, weighing up the situation.

'*Kinshasa, c'est très dangéreuse aussi . . .*' said the hotel manager.

'But not as bad as the other route?'

'No, not so dangerous,' said Serge, shaking his head and pointing to the squiggle of dirt roads leading down to the Congo River. 'This route, very dangerous. I do not go there. You must not go. But this route' – he pointed to the main road, leading to Brazzaville – '*c'est bon.*'

It was marked as a solid red line for most of its length; it was Congo's main road, the Route Nationale 1, and for a moment I allowed myself to indulge in a tarmac fantasy, but I didn't dare ask. I didn't want to have my dreams shattered.

Once I'd got my head round the idea that I would be riding through Brazzaville and Kinshasa, I began to get quite excited about the idea. It was a nervous excitement, but nonetheless, I was relieved that my thirst for adventure had returned, that the traumas of my first day in the Congo hadn't knocked it out of me for good.

As I had suspected, the RN1 to Brazzaville was in exactly the same state as the road from the border, only longer and wider, one of Africa's famous mud motorways, 220 miles to Congo's

275

capital. I didn't know if I would make it in one long day or two, but there were a few towns along the way where I could find somewhere to stay if need be. There was nothing to do but get on with it, so once again I plodded on slowly through the sludge, churning my way through vast stretches of filthy water and trying not to clock-watch my pitiful progress on the speedo. Again, I accepted the fact that I was going to be filthy and wet and knackered all day, and again, in an unwelcome repetition of yesterday's events, the bike slipped out from under me in a stretch of deep mud. But this time, no doubt spurred on by the thought of shelling out another fiver, I threw every single ounce of energy into hauling it upright, succeeding on the third attempt.

I was amazed at how quickly I'd accepted this grinding routine. The ride from the border had been a shock to the system, not just physically, but mentally and emotionally too. But I no longer felt the overwhelming despair and fear that had coloured that first day. It seemed I had unconsciously developed a pragmatic approach to the thought of carrying on like this for the next 2,000 miles. I had nobody to moan to except myself and that wouldn't do me any good, so I figured I might as well shut up and keep going. It was just another day in the Congo, and I could handle it. But then I reached the small town of Loutété and everything changed.

FOURTEEN

Loutété was just a little dot on the map, halfway between Dolisie and Brazzaville, but it was surprisingly busy, centred as it was on the railway. It was the typical collection of breezeblock buildings, tumbledown shacks, market stalls and general disorder. The streets were bustling with activity, but even among this scene of industrious hustle my arrival caused the now familiar furore, with people stopping in their tracks to point and shout and run after me, trying to sell me all manner of goods. I rode on through the town, making my standard gestures of what I hoped were non-committal friendliness, waving and smiling at the staring faces. The railway tracks cut through the middle of the town and as I approached the level crossing I was halted by the screech of a policeman's whistle. I had spotted their checkpoint hut but was taking my usual approach of not stopping unless ordered to do so. This method often worked in my favour with a lazy official waving me on, and I had even managed to pass by unnoticed on a few occasions, blending into the general hubbub. But not this time.

'Where are you going?' demanded the policeman, and as he stepped in front of the bike I noticed that half of his right arm was missing. The sleeve of his jacket was pinned up just above where his elbow had once been.

'Brazzaville.'

'You cannot continue.'

I was expecting the usual inspection of papers and possibly a request for '*un cadeau*', but not this. I wondered if it was a roundabout method of extortion, but I decided to hold tight until he asked outright.

An inquisitive crowd had already gathered around me and the noise of their animated chatter was at such a level that I could barely hear him speak.

'You cannot continue,' he repeated, motioning with his severed arm at the road ahead.

'Why not? Is there a problem with the road?' I asked.

He launched into a volley of high-speed French which I struggled to understand over the racket of the onlookers.

'I'm sorry, can you speak slower, I don't understand . . .'

'You cannot continue! It is dangerous! I must not allow you!' He spoke at a more measured pace, but his tone was tinged with irritation.

'But why?'

'Why? Why? Because of the Ninjas! The Ninjas!' he shouted, as if I was the most stupid person he'd ever had the misfortune to flag down. 'The Ninjas! They are rebels! The Ninjas! The road to Brazzaville, they control this area!' He waved his one-

and-a-half arms around, suggesting the scale of the Ninjas' operation.

I knew of the Ninjas; they were the former prime minister's own personal militia, but I didn't know to what extent they were still at large, and I didn't know what to believe. In my suspicious frame of mind, I wondered if it was all a big scam. Why should I trust this angry, bullying policeman?

'What do they do, the Ninjas?' I asked him. 'Hold up vehicles? Rob people?'

He stepped closer and stared into my eyes.

'Madame, they will kill you.'

Sure enough the policeman had an alternative plan all worked out for me.

'You must take the train to Brazzaville, you will put your motorcycle on the train.'

It was difficult knowing who to trust and what to believe, but the last thing I wanted to do was get on a train. I was here to ride my bike and that's what I was going to do, and if that meant running the gauntlet with the Ninjas, then so be it.

'No thank you,' I insisted politely. 'I'll continue on the road.'

'YOU CANNOT CONTINUE! YOU MUST TAKE THE TRAIN!' roared the policeman, utterly frustrated at my lack of compliance.

Fortunately at this moment a statuesque man dressed in an ankle-length white robe pushed his way through the throng. He was holding the hand of his tiny daughter, who looked at me shyly before burying her face in the folds of his robe.

'My name is Spencer, I speak English,' he said to me. 'Please, what is the problem?'

I liked him immediately; he had an air of calm authority about him that reminded me of Abba, the village chief at the

Niger border post, and I guessed he was high up in Loutété's pecking order by the way the policeman acquiesced to him. I introduced myself and explained my predicament.

'I'm on my way to Brazzaville, but he won't let me carry on.'

Spencer and the policeman entered into a lively discussion which involved much flailing of the policeman's stump.

'I am sorry, but he is right, you cannot continue on the road,' said Spencer. 'The Ninjas are very dangerous. After the civil war they refused to hand over their arms, and they control this area, here.' He pointed on my map. 'The road to Brazzaville is very dangerous now. Many people have been attacked and robbed. It is for his sake too,' he said, motioning to the policeman, who was looking thoroughly vexed. 'He cannot let you go – if something happens to you, it is his fault. You understand?'

It was unlikely that the expression 'covering your arse' had made it into the Congolese vernacular, but that's exactly what the policeman was doing.

The crowd had now swelled to the extent that they were taking up the entire width of the road and were looking on, laughing and shouting things I didn't understand, while the policeman tried to disperse them, yelling orders which went largely ignored. Frustrated at his ineffectiveness, he marched up to me and Spencer, exerting his authority.

'You, madame!' he said gripping my upper arm. 'You take the train. Come with me to buy ticket.'

The policeman was pointing to a building made of rusty corrugated iron, sited between the road and the train tracks.

I looked at Spencer but he just shrugged helplessly.

'You must go with him.'

I started pushing my bike over to the building but I barely had time to think before I was being shoved across the street, caught up in the swarm of bystanders. The crowd had burst into action and I was being mobbed by people who wanted to 'help'.

'I buy you ticket for train!'

'You pay me, I lift bike on train.'

'No! I put on bike on train – you pay me!'

'You need rope to tie bike to train – I have rope!'

'No, I have rope! You buy this rope!'

It was almost impossible to make any headway through the mob, and before long a couple of men had wrestled my bike from me and were lifting it over the railway sidings to the waiting train.

'Stop! Wait!' I shouted, but no one was listening. The policeman was striding ahead towards the building and I looked around for Spencer, but he was nowhere to be seen.

'Stop! Where are you going?' I shouted. 'Bring back my bike!' But nobody took any notice and through the crowd I could see a group of three men pushing it towards the train.

Several men in uniform appeared from out of the corrugated iron shack, shouting instructions at me.

'They've got my bike!' I shouted back at them, flustered by the way the situation was spiralling out of my control. I didn't know who to turn to for help; it certainly wasn't the policemen, and I couldn't see Spencer anywhere.

'There is no problem, madame, they will put your motorcycle on the train,' said the one-armed policeman, as if I was making a fuss about nothing. 'They are not stealing it,' he added witheringly.

But it's all I've got, I wanted to shout, it's not just a bike, it's my home too, everything I have is on that bike! Without it, I'm lost! I'm stuck! But I knew he wouldn't understand, or care.

281

'You! Madame! Come in here! You must buy ticket,' yelled a voice from inside the shack.

I stepped into the dingy, windowless room to find four uniformed men staring at me with grim expressions. One of them kicked the door shut behind me, leaving just the weak glow of a bare bulb illuminating their faces and glancing its dirty yellow light off their brass buttons.

'You go to Brazzaville, you must buy ticket,' said a man sitting behind a desk. He was obviously the one in charge here, as he sported the most stripes, badges and medals on his jacket. 'Forty thousand francs.'

'Look, I don't want to take the bloody train!' I protested one more time.

'The Ninjas! They will kill you!' bawled the one-armed policeman, utterly sick of me by now.

'And you must buy ticket for bike, thirty thousand francs,' continued the man behind the desk.

Seventy quid for me and the bike! I calculated, seething with frustration.

'And you must pay the men who lift your bike on to train,' added another.

'And you must pay the men who tie your bike to the train.'

I stood there in silence, trying to take everything in, not knowing what to say.

'But . . .'

'You pay the man now for the tickets,' said the one-armed policeman from the corner. It was an order. 'He is the chief of police,' he added.

'I don't have seventy thousand francs,' I told them, trying to keep my voice calm.

282

There was silence.

'How much do you have?'

My mind raced through my options, thinking about where I kept my cash and how I could avoid handing the whole lot over to these thugs. I reached into the inside pocket of my jacket, where I knew there were a couple of 10,000-franc notes. I kept them in case I ran into the likes of the Ninjas, but these guys weren't much different, they were just Ninjas in uniform. I fished out one of the notes and handed it to the man behind the desk. He looked at it, smoothed it out, placed it on the desk, and without saying anything, offered his hand again. His cronies watched in silence.

'You have more,' he said eventually. I wasn't sure if this was a question or a statement.

'No,' I lied.

'You give him more money,' said the one-armed policeman, with a meaningful look.

The four of them stared at me, succeeding in their attempt at intimidation. I fished out the other tenner.

'You must give him more,' he yelled, 'for the train ticket!'

'I don't have any more money,' I said very slowly in French, not making any attempt to keep the frustration out of my voice. '*Vous comprends*?'

'More! More money!' he shouted again.

Overcome with rage and frustration, I shouted back at him, even louder: 'I don't have any more!' My voice ricocheted around the metal walls.

They looked at each other, shrugged and muttered something unintelligible. The chief pocketed the two notes and nodded towards the door.

'Go,' he said.

I pushed open the door. I never thought to ask for the ticket and it never materialised.

As soon as I stepped outside someone was tugging at my sleeve, demanding more money to lift the bike on to the train; another was grabbing me, shouting about the rope he had bought. I was being propelled through the chaos, over-whelmed by all the yelling and pushing and shoving. The situation had slipped away from me – it was now completely out of my control and I felt overwhelmed with confusion. Then to my relief, I saw Spencer, standing among the chaos, his daughter still clinging on to his hand.

'Where's my bike?' I asked him desperately.

'It is over there, they are putting it on the train, but please, hurry, you must come quick, the train must leave soon. You have your ticket?'

'No, well, I mean yes, I mean I paid for it, but I don't have a ticket.'

'Never mind, you must come quick.'

'You must come now . . .' bawled someone in an army uniform, grabbing my arm, as I was swept along with the crowd of passengers that were pushing their way to the waiting train.

I was hauled over the sidings to find a couple of soldiers lifting my bike up on to a flatbed wagon at the rear of the train and lashing it to a metal post.

'You sit here,' said Spencer, pointing to a jerrycan that was wedged up against my bike, and I realised that I would not be travelling in a carriage, but out here on the wagon. That was OK, at least I'd be next to my bike and be able to keep an eye on my belongings, but as a rush of passengers climbed aboard I also realised that I would not be travelling alone out here. As well as me and my bike, the wagon was transporting a platoon of forty Congolese soldiers to Brazzaville, all of them wielding Kalashnikovs and sporting bandoliers of bullets slung around their upper bodies. I watched in mounting horror as they leapt on to the wagon, clutching bottles of whisky, shouting and laughing in drunken high spirits, and bellowing out army chants. I felt physically sick as the reality of my situation began to sink in.

'Hurry! Hurry! The train is leaving!' a policeman was screaming at me.

There was nothing else to do but clamber up on to the wagon and take my seat on the jerrycan. My embarkation prompted a rowdy cheer from the soldiers and I felt my stomach churn.

'It is OK, Lois,' said Spencer, seeing my face cloud over with despair. 'You must be strong.'

'But . . . but . . .' I bit my bottom lip, trying desperately to hold back tears of fear and anger and frustration. Spencer and his daughter stared up at me from the rubbish-strewn tracks.

'And Lois,' he said, beckoning me to crouch down so he could whisper, 'the military, the soldiers, they all smoke marijuana, OK?'

I nodded, thinking that this was the least of my problems, but he looked at me with a serious expression. 'It is OK. You understand what I am saying?'

I didn't really, but I guessed he was telling me to keep my mouth shut, not that I was in any mood for striking up a conversation with my fellow passengers.

Somewhere down the tracks a whistle blew and the big diesel engine shuddered into life.

'Be strong, Lois, you must be strong!' Spencer insisted, as the

285

train began to chug slowly out of Loutété station; tears rolled down my cheeks as I surveyed my new surroundings and, worse, my new travelling companions, who had been foisted upon me so suddenly. I nodded helplessly and managed a choked 'Thank you.' He stood there with his daughter, the two of them watching me and the marauding soldiers disappear off down the tracks into the jungle. I was taking the train, whether I liked it or not.

The jerrycan was leaking from the filler cap, and every bump and sway of the wagon sloshed a bit of diesel out until I could feel it soaking through my trousers. I could have sat on the floor but I couldn't bring myself to move a muscle. My arrival had caused quite a commotion and some of the soldiers had tried to engage me in conversation, but I pretended I couldn't speak French and ignored their attempts at a parley. A few of them entertained their colleagues with comments about me that I genuinely didn't understand, but which prompted raucous laughter and backslapping among them, and paranoid terror in me. I felt sick with dread, and my gut-feeling was to stay perfectly still in the pathetic hope that the soldiers would forget I was there. This response was strangely at odds with my usual approach to sticky situations – I normally relied on smiling, flattery and being ultra-polite to get me out of trouble. But this was different; something innate in me warned against making any kind of connection with these men. I knew what drunken soldiers got up to in the Congo and the very thought made me shudder with raw fear. *I'm not equipped for this*, I thought, *this wasn't meant to happen, I'm not cut out for this*. I felt a terrible, hopeless dread and, like a hunted animal, my instinct was to remain motionless until the danger had passed. But that was going to be an awfully long time.

Spencer had said the train to Brazzaville took eight or nine hours, at least twice as long as it would have been by road, even battling through the mud of the Route Nationale 1. I yearned to unleash my bike and for us to jump off and flee into the jungle; even if it meant dodging the Ninjas, at least I would be in charge of my own destiny. As I fantasised about my great escape, I realised why, along with the obvious sheer terror of what could happen to me over the next nine hours, I also felt so upset and angry. I had been robbed of my independence, one of the great joys and main reasons for travelling by motorcycle. My autonomy was gone; now I was at the mercy of a semi-derelict public transport system and a platoon of drunk, armed Congolese soldiers. It had all happened so quickly – within a matter of minutes the freedom of the road had been snatched away from me and I felt as if my bike and I had been taken prisoner.

The train was old and rickety and moved at a painfully slow pace, winding its way through dark, thick rainforest where tenacious vines coiled around the vast tree trunks and the swampy jungle floor never saw the light of day. Occasionally we would stop at a little halt that seemed to service nothing but a couple of shacks in the middle of nowhere but was overrun with people. They looked as if they'd crawled out of the bush, and maybe they had. They stood by the tracks, half-naked, barefoot and muddy, hollering and waving at the train. The soldiers would shout back at them but I couldn't understand if this was an exchange of greetings or if they were protesting about something. The only other time the train stopped was for the passengers to answer the call of nature, grinding and creaking to a standstill while the soldiers jumped off, took a leak by the side of the tracks and hauled themselves back up before it set off again on its excruciating crawl. I was desperate to make use of these toilet breaks, but I couldn't bring myself to join in with the soldiers, so I just sat there, crossing my legs and praying for the nightmare to end.

As predicted by Spencer, the soldiers were soon passing round giant spliffs, and mixed with the whisky their bullish spirits reached bursting point. They sang in raucous discord, shouted mock insults and threats at each other, pretending to push one and another off the train in play fights. Most of them still wore their AK47s slung on their backs, but a few of them had removed their weapons, casually discarding them on the floor. Occasionally one of the soldiers would direct a comment at me and they would all burst out laughing, but I did my best to ignore them or at best, managed a weak smile. It was like being trapped on the world's worst stag night. I had never felt so small and acutely female. I had grown up with two brothers, I've always had male friends and plenty of fruity language has passed my lips, but this was too much machismo for my tender heart; I was drowning in a sea of testosterone.

It wasn't the yelling and shoving that bothered me, or the boozing and smoking, it was the call and response army chants that chilled me to the core. I don't go for men in uniform, quite the opposite in fact, and as a champion of individuality I have a deep-rooted mistrust of most organised group activities. A friend of mine almost persuaded me to join a yoga class once, but just the sight of everyone doing the same thing at the same time sent me running for the door; it was all a bit Hitler Youth for my tastes. Ergo, the armed forces and I were never going to hit it off, and the mindless, boorish chanting of my travelling companions epitomised everything I loathed and feared in our species.

I didn't know what else to do but sit there on the jerrycan and avoid all eye contact with the soldiers. I stared at my bike, tied up next to me, and concentrated on its smallest details, its scratches and scrapes, each one telling a story, reminding me of happier times. Although I've never been one for bestowing names or human characteristics on my vehicles, at this moment just having my bike next to me gave me comfort. It was more than merely a means of transport; it had become my home over the last few months but most of all it represented fun and freedom, two things that were sorely absent from my current situation.

The time dragged by with unbearable slowness and after a while I could hardly bring myself to look at my watch. But every minute that passed by without incident gave me hope and I knew that I was another minute nearer to Brazzaville and the end of this nightmare. However, my hope that I would blend into the background was way off the mark and a couple of young soldiers, tired of shouting and pushing each other around, looked to me for their entertainment. They were probably as bored as I was, but bored young men plus booze plus drugs does not make for a pretty combination, as any English town centre on a Saturday night will attest. I froze with unadulterated fear as one of them sat down on another, vacant jerrycan and put his arm around my shoulders. I had spotted him earlier when he had climbed on to the wagon; he was one of the youngest of the soldiers, probably in his late teens, and a brash, aggressive show-off. He was the loudest, the cockiest, and I despised him already for his attention-seeking behaviour. His entire upper body was slung with rows of brass bullets over his black string vest and his machine gun swung around carelessly, hanging from his right shoulder.

'What is wrong with you?' he said in French. 'Don't you like us?'

I could smell the whisky on his breath. I didn't know what to do or say, I didn't know if he was being facetious or genuine.

'What is wrong with you?' he said again. 'Why don't you speak?'

'I'm fine,' I muttered. 'Just tired.' It was a lame answer, but the last thing I wanted to do was to engage in conversation with him.

His friend was examining my bike with great interest, looking at the luggage and opening and closing my panniers. I turned away from the younger soldier so I could keep an eye on the bike, but just this move was enough to provoke him.

'You think he will steal something?' he said, and gave a harsh, loud laugh. 'She thinks you are stealing from her!' he said to his mate, who shouted something back that I didn't understand and spat on the floor of the wagon.

The rest of the platoon were still carousing, shouting and chanting, but the young soldier's arm remained around my shoulders and I could feel the hard metal ridges of his bullets pressing through my clothes. My stomach was knotted tight and I was desperate to shake off his arm but instead I sat there, tensed for what might happen next. His tone and his eyes scared me; he was that dreadful combination of young, cruel and vainglorious, and I feared the lengths to which he would go to impress his fellow soldiers.

As I sat there perfectly still, breathing heavily and trying to stay calm, the train groaned and screeched as it slowed down and then jolted to a sudden stop. The soldiers lurched and steadied themselves and there was a loud clamour as they leapt off the train and busied themselves in the bushes. The young soldier stood up to follow them and grabbed my arm.

'Get off!' I shouted, and my sudden burst of anger caused him to jump in surprise. It was the loudest noise I had made in hours, and even though I had spoken in English, he had not failed to understand. He laughed in a patronising way, as if to say, 'Calm down love, no need to make a fuss,' but all the time he stared at me with cold, furious eyes and his friend, who had become bored with my bike, turned and grabbed hold of his arm.

'*On y va! On y va!*' said his friend, and without looking at me he hauled him away off the train, leaving me sitting there trembling.

Mercifully I was left alone once we started moving again, and after a couple of hours the weed finally had the effect I had hoped for and my companions started to mellow out. Reassured by the calmer mood among the soldiers, I made a tentative move towards my panniers, where a packet of chocolate biscuits awaited me. It was late afternoon, I hadn't eaten since breakfast and I was feeling distinctly weak with hunger. Although I was still nervous about attracting attention to myself, my hunger prevailed over my fear. It was bad enough that I wouldn't be able to go to the loo for nine hours, but I was damned if I was going to let these meathead buffoons come between me and my chocolate biscuits.

I moved slowly and quietly, turning round in my seated position until I could reach the buckles of my pannier bags. Unfastening them as gently as possible, I rummaged around inside until I felt the cylindrical foil packet in my hand. Oh joy! I secreted it swiftly inside my jacket, hoping that the noise of the train would drown out the telltale crackly sound of my opening the packet. But I had underestimated the eagle eyes of my travelling companions, and my covert operation had not passed unnoticed. What did I expect? These men were trained to kill, to stake out their enemies in the impenetrable jungle of the Congo Basin. Did I really think I would get away with such a clumsy manoeuvre?

As I nibbled away on the first biscuit I could feel my blood sugar levels returning to normal, but my relief was tempered by the fact that an enormous soldier sitting opposite me was watching my every mouthful. I avoided his gaze and crammed in a couple more biscuits, staring down at the floor while I chewed, but although I was pretending to ignore him, I could feel his eyes boring into me. Reassured by the fact that I had managed to at least get the biscuits out of the pannier without causing too much commotion among the troops, I thought I might as well try to make the most of this train journey and read a book while it was still light. I went back into my luggage and dug out my current read, which Pete had given to me in Lambaréné, a paperback about a murderous Colombian drugs baron who, in comparison to my current travelling companions, seemed like quite a mild-mannered fellow. A good book and a packet of choccie biccies, what more could a girl want? It was pure Bridget Jones, but I just couldn't relax with the brutal eyes of the soldier opposite trained on my biscuits.

The mammoth joints were still doing the rounds, and as the soldiers became more stoned they were predictably getting the munchies. Eventually it was too much to bear for my giant hulking soldier. He stood up, stepped towards me, and without speaking pointed to where my biscuits were stashed beneath my jacket. I resented his bullying approach and couldn't bring myself to indulge him so readily, so I pretended I didn't understand what he wanted. Towering over me, he pointed again at the location of my hidden biscuits and stared at me with a look so intimidating that my skin prickled in cold fear. I shrugged my shoulders in false incomprehension and he resorted to his ultimate tactic. With a shimmy of his powerful shoulders, he swung his Kalashnikov round from his back so that it was now dangling by his side and with a light movement he flipped it into his right hand so that it was swinging, not exactly pointing, but swinging in front of my face. 'You only had to ask,' I wanted to say, but I handed over the biscuits silently.

On the road, some people worry about when they'll next find a toilet, or the next place to have a wash, but I lived in fear of running out of food and with my emergency supplies now snatched away from me I began panicking about where my next meal was coming from. It would be hours before we reached Brazzaville, and even then, where would I go, what would I do? My plan had been to arrive in daylight and either find a map of the city or hail a cab and tell it to take me to some cheapo hotel, as I had done upon my arrival in Yaounde. I supposed I could still do that, but the darkness changes everything, and what might be a regular, if chaotic, capital city by day turns into a shadowy, seamy underworld by night. African cities after dark were not for the fainthearted, and I had never felt more fainthearted than at this moment. I tried to concentrate on my book, but the images of Colombia's drug wars were constantly interrupted by my overactive imagination setting the scene of my arrival at Brazzaville station, handing over wads of cash to have my bike lifted off the train, striking out into the murky depths of the city, fending off hustlers, petty, and not so petty criminals as I tried to negotiate my way through the unlit streets, searching for a bed and a packet of biscuits. The idea filled me with dread. Eventually it became too dark to read and I put my book away, allowing my mind to run free with doomy images as the train continued its steady rhythmic clatter through the Congo jungle towards Brazzaville, that dark city of severed heads.

The sky turned to black and with the onset of night a tropical storm opened fire. Electric-blue lightning flashed across the sky, deafening thunder almost drowned out the shouting and singing of the soldiers, and the rain poured down in buckets. I huddled under the corner of a tarpaulin, but it was no match for this equatorial deluge and the water lashed in from every direction, soaking me to the skin. The soldiers, used to such occurrences, made no attempt to keep themselves dry, only attempting to protect their spliffs, which continued to be passed among them, a tiny red glow in the black night, moving slowly around the wagon.

Maybe dampened by the rain and the onset of night, the soldiers' bumptiousness simmered down to no more than a murmur of voices, occasionally interjected with the occasional laugh or shout. Four hours later, though, there was a roar of excitement and I looked up from beneath the tarpaulin to see what the fuss was about. I could just make out that the train was coming round a bend, and far off in the distance I could see a glow of pale orange lights.

'Brazzaville!' shouted one of the soldiers, nudging me and pointing. 'Brazzaville! You see, madame, you are nearly there!' he said to me in French.

With all eyes fixed on the city's lights, we rattled on slowly towards them, every clickety-clack bringing this nightmare to an end, but also opening up a new one, as far as I was concerned. The soldiers were back on form now, singing, chanting and shouting with the same gusto as at the beginning of the journey, but I was now panicking silently about what I was going to do when we arrived.

My question was answered for me when the train came to a halt next to a level crossing and without a word the soldiers began untying my bike. Knowing better than to protest, or enter into any sort of discussion, I watched them as they undid the ropes and lowered my bike into the ditch below. Jumping down after it and scrambling down the bank, I swung my leg over the saddle and fired up the engine, almost crying with relief and joy at this sweet sound of freedom. At last, my destiny was in my own hands! But where the hell was I going? The chief of the soldiers was wondering the same thing.

'I don't know,' I admitted, when he asked me. 'I don't know where I am. Are we in Brazzaville, here?'

'Yes, this is the edge of Brazzaville.' He pointed towards the road at the level crossing. There were no street lights, and from what I could make out with my headlight, I was in the middle of nowhere.

'Well, um, I just want to find a hotel,' I said. '*Un bon hotel*,' I added, allowing myself to indulge in forbidden fantasies about running water and electricity.

'Follow me,' he said, walking towards the level crossing.

I rode along the ditch and up the bank on to the road. We waited for a minute or two until headlights appeared in the distance. As they approached, the soldier stepped out into the middle of the road and flagged down the car with his AK47, the accepted way of getting what you want in the Congo. There was a brief conversation with the driver.

'You follow him,' he instructed me. 'He will take you to a hotel.'

'Thank you, thank you,' I gushed, picking up his scraps of assistance with pathetic gratefulness and thrusting a 10,000-franc note into his hand, the accepted way of showing gratitude in the Congo.

'*De rien,*' he said, and with his gun hanging over his shoulder he climbed back on to the waiting train.

I followed the anonymous car through anonymous streets. The train entered Brazzaville from the west, so I guessed we were heading roughly south, but even this meant very little in terms of where I was going to end up tonight. It was strange to have absolutely no idea where I was or where I was going, to leave my fate in the hands of some random stranger, whose name I didn't know and whose face I hadn't even seen. But I was light-headed with relief that the train journey was over, and compared to how I had felt nine hours previously, when I had climbed reluctantly on to the flatbed wagon to the whoops and whistles of the soldiers, I was ecstatic. I was alive, unharmed and free.

We passed along potholed streets through shanty towns, where fires along the edge of the road lit up the rusty iron shacks and the faces of their inhabitants, crowded around street corners or cooking over the glowing coals. Then the streets became wider, passing tower blocks and then moving into a quiet district where luxury villas lay behind high walls, painted white and topped with barbed wire. As I rode through this contradictory landscape I remembered that Brazzaville, as well as being the capital city of Africa's first Marxist state, had also served as the capital of Free France during the Second World War, and in the last ten years had played out its own country's bloody civil wars. It had certainly seen some action in its chequered history. Now here I was; I had never even intended coming here when I had plotted out my route, all those months ago back home. I had planned on taking the easy option: the boat from Cabinda that would have deposited me halfway down the Angolan coast. How different things would have been if that had worked out. But it hadn't, and despite my yo-yoing emotions and the trials of the last few days I was glad about that. Sometimes, I reminded myself, it was good when things didn't go to plan.

The car turned into a driveway and I stuck close to the bumper, passing under a metal barrier and past what looked to be an exceptionally well-tended lawn. This wasn't a road, unless it was a private road, and I wondered where on earth this mysterious man was leading me. The answer came as we rounded a corner and he pulled up outside the gleaming entrance of the five-star Brazzaville Meridien. I almost fainted with shock; this was not what I had expected. There were uniformed doormen, and valet parking, and a swimming pool, and a business centre. And probably cable TV and room service and a big squishy bed and hot water and fluffy towels and . . . I felt giddy with greed and guilt. Through the glass doors I could see well-heeled, important people milling about in the lobby wearing designer clothes. And I was hovering outside with a filthy trail bike, soaked to the skin, stinking of diesel and covered in mud. I had been deposited at the most expensive hotel in Brazzaville, in the Congo, probably in Central Africa, and goddammit, I was staying! If there was ever a credit card moment, this was it.

FIFTEEN

Safe at last within the walls of the Brazzaville Meridien, I entered a strange state of delayed shock. It was almost as if these incongruously civilised surroundings – the fluffy towels, the room service, the cable TV and all the other trappings of comfort – brought the reality of the last twelve hours home to me in glaring Technicolor. I could barely believe I had come through it unscathed, but still, I shuddered at the thought of what could have happened, even though nothing actually *had*. Out in the real world of the Congo, whether in the jungle wilderness or the savage city streets, I wore, unwittingly, a protective shell, a metaphorical tin hat and flak jacket, which provided me with the necessary edge to get by; it allowed me to act tough, to not care about being dirty and smelly, to stand up for myself and barter with people, all the things that didn't really come naturally to me. But away from all that, tucked up in bed, watching telly and sipping hot chocolate, I couldn't summon up my hard edge any more, and the very thought of having to take on the outside world again filled me with dread. Even the sight of my muddy clothes, boots and crash helmet piled up on the floor made me shudder, reminding me not only of the events of the last few days but also of what lay ahead; the tricky bit wasn't over, it had only just begun. I needed comfort, both physically and emotionally. The Meridien could take care of the former, but the latter was harder to come by. It couldn't be bought with any number of Visa cards, and I ached with a painful longing to be wrapped in Austin's arms.

The hotel was filled with Africa's élite and I guessed I was not alone in developing a siege mentality inside its secure, clean and tidy confines. The management had successfully tapped into the paranoia of their guests and created a little world for them which meant they never needed to leave the hotel boundaries. There was an internet café and a swimming pool, several restaurants, a conference centre, meeting rooms, boutiques and gift shops in the foyer, laundry services and, outside the door, taxis to whisk you away, so you never had to actually set foot in Brazzaville's streets or rub shoulders with its million residents. Only in Africa had I seen the haves and the have-nots separated in such an unapologetic, almost clinical fashion.

The Meridien was ludicrously expensive but, I reminded myself, I hadn't chosen to come here, I'd just got dumped here by the stranger in the car. What was I meant to do? Tell him to take me somewhere else? Spend the night driving round Brazzaville looking for a hotel within my budget? But I didn't quite manage to convince myself and I cleansed my guilt with toil, hand-washing my clothes in the bath, thereby saving money by not using the vastly overpriced laundry service. It took ages, used up all the little bottles of shampoo and bars of soap, made a terrible mess in the bathroom, and after three washes and some violent scrubbing with my nailbrush I still couldn't get the smell of diesel out of my knickers.

Back in the big, squishy bed, I tucked in to a crème caramel, flicked through the TV channels and considered my options. I could stay at the Meridien for ages, I mused; I could live here, like some eccentric ex-pat recluse. I could run up a huge bill, do a runner, say my card was stolen. But then what? I still had to get to Cape Town and from here that meant going to Kinshasa, riding through DRC and then Angola. Despite my hours of rumination, it never occurred to me to jack it all in and fly home. In the end I decided to give myself a day off and wait for my itchy feet to make their presence known. They'd be back, they always came back in the end; they were just a little weary, that was all.

I slept right through to lunchtime the next day, and when I made it down into the lobby I was greeted with much interest by the bellboys, the security guards and the receptionists. They held doors open for me, pressed the buttons on the elevator, called me Madame Lois, and commented on how, er, different I looked from when I had arrived the night before. I wanted to go into the city centre, pick up a few provisions and check out the port to find out the sailing times of the ferry to Kinshasa, but despite the hotel's many charms, it could not supply me with a map of Brazzaville. So, in the style of a true Meridien guest, I enlisted one of the yellow taxis waiting outside the hotel door to take me there.

My cabbie was a wily character called Jules, who, when I

gave my instructions, failed to inform me that everything is shut in Brazzaville between midday and three in the afternoon, one legacy of French colonialism they're not in a hurry to get rid of. This useful nugget of information was only elicited when we'd been driving around the city for fifteen minutes. Rather than tell me to come back in three hours' time, Jules had decided to take me on a spontaneous tour of Brazzaville which would last until three o'clock, when everything opened again, and no doubt cost me a fortune. I tried to protest, but he made out he couldn't understand what I was saying and in the end I decided to give up, sit back and enjoy the ride. But not for the first time in this country, I felt as though I'd been slightly kidnapped.

By day, the city was far less intimidating than when I'd arrived here in the pitch dark. It had been designed and laid out by the French, with wide streets, trees and roundabouts, and was largely free of the horn-honking, snarled-up madness of other African cities. We passed by the Nabemba tower, Brazzaville's famous landmark, a futuristic structure shaped like an elongated cooling tower which holds the title of the tallest building in Central Africa, before driving out of the city centre alongside the Congo river.

'You must see the rapids, very famous,' said Jules as he turned down a side street and parked up next to a little bar on the river's edge.

He took a seat at a table overlooking the river and called to the waitress. He hadn't suggested stopping for a drink, but seeing as he had a compliant white girl in his cab who didn't speak very good French, he might as well make the most of it. The events of the last few days, especially the train journey, had altered me somehow, and I felt less inclined to make a fuss

301

or try to control every element of my trip. It was too much effort to get into an altercation, and my newfound laissez-faire approach meant that I didn't really care what happened, I would just go along with it. It was almost a relief to have someone else in charge for a change.

I ordered a Coke, and Jules ordered an enormous bottle of the local beer, Ngok, with a label featuring a green crocodile with a sly, toothy grin, not unlike that of Jules himself.

'Look! Look!' he called, pointing over at the river. Among the furious rapids were a couple of young men, swimming at incredible speeds, their muscular arms shooting in and out of the water, powering them along through the turbulence.

'Wow! That looks pretty scary. Do people ever die, doing that?' I asked.

'Oh yes, many boys are killed, swimming in the rapids,' Jules replied, with his crocodile smile, before taking a large swig of beer.

Immediately below us was a group of women, crouched on the rocky bank, employed in the less risky business of doing the family wash. Considering the task in hand and the location, they were dressed to the nines, the younger ones sporting coordinated hair accessories and elaborate earrings which swung back and forth as they scrubbed away, laughing among themselves, laying out the wet clothes on the hot rocks. A few yards upstream an entire family had arrived to wash themselves, but the teenage son was more interested in diving off a high rock, much to the consternation of his mother. And across the water, ten miles away on the opposite bank, stood the high-rise blocks of Kinshasa, the two capital cities separated by the rapids of the great Congo River, as wild, turbulent and violent as the two nations themselves.

'Have you ever been to Kinshasa?' I asked Jules.

'Yes, several times.' He paused to call over the waitress and order another bottle of Ngok. 'My family, we went there in 1997, during our civil war. And when Kinshasa is in trouble, they all come to Brazzaville.' He laughed, but he didn't look amused.

'I am going there tomorrow,' I said.

'Alone?'

'Er, yes, well, I'm meeting my husband there,' I added quickly.

Jules looked relieved at this news.

'Oh, that is good. You would not want to go to Kinshasa alone, not a good place for a white woman. The people there, they are hard people, very hard.' He made a vicious crocodile face to illustrate the temperament of Kinshasa's eight-million residents. 'Not like the people in Brazzaville. We are friendly people here, easy-going.'

I almost choked on my Coke, wondering how people who impale severed human heads on their car aerials could be described as friendly and easy-going. I put Jules's social commentary down to the usual neighbourly jingoism, but as I glanced over the water towards Kinshasa I felt my stomach tighten in knots. I was going there tomorrow morning, and there was no husband waiting for me, it was just me, on my own.

After Jules had downed his third bottle of Ngok, I made the tentative suggestion that I'd like to visit the port now. Not only was it gone three o'clock, but if we stayed here any longer I feared that he would be in no fit state to drive anywhere. He ambled off to the car, predictably leaving me to settle the bill. The port, or the Beach, as it is known locally, and somewhat optimistically, was a circus of entrepreneurial Brazzavilleans, mostly big, busty women, shouting, pushing and hustling. Even my quick visit to check out the times of the boat involved a non-stop stream of polite, '*Non, non, merci, non merci*,' as I dodged the hawkers selling cigarettes, sweets, barbecued corn, nuts and mobile phone accessories.

I was plucked out of the crowd by a couple of young fixer guys who introduced themselves as Ricky and Kevin. I wasn't convinced they had been christened with such names, and suspected that they watched *EastEnders* on cable TV and were trying to curry favour with me; if I had been German they would have probably been called Hans and Rudolf. But they seemed friendly enough and made me promise that I would enlist their help tomorrow for the merry dance around the customs, immigration and police that would precede my ferry journey; and with my newfound happy-go-lucky approach, I agreed. My carefree attitude may have convinced Ricky and Kevin, but it wasn't fooling me, and after I had paid off Jules, a little too handsomely in my opinion, I made for my room and spent my last night in the Meridien fretting, unable to sleep and feeling physically sick as I tossed and turned, twisting myself into knots among the freshly starched sheets.

I busied myself by reading, watching TV and writing my diary, but when it came time to sleep I couldn't stop the catalogue of facts and figures rolling through my mind. More people killed in DRC's war than in World War II, widespread sexual slavery by the armed forces, the highest rate of rape in the world, young boys taken from their homes to be child soldiers, not to mention the regular armed attacks on vehicles, some recently reported on the road from Kinshasa to Matadi, the very road I would be riding along tomorrow. Recent news reports brought details of the Rastas, a new armed group in the country, painting a gory yet bizarre picture of this dreadlocked militia, living in the jungle, wearing shiny tracksuits and LA Lakers shirts and routinely burning babies, kidnapping women and literally chopping to pieces people who stand in their way. What the hell was I thinking of, going to this inhuman country tomorrow morning?

In the middle of the night, still unable to sleep, I switched on the TV in an attempt to still my troubled mind, only to be faced with the weather report for Kinshasa of all places. Heavy rain and thunderstorms were predicted, with the accompanying graphic of the grey cloud with two heavy raindrops and a bolt of yellow lightning. Never had a weather forecast so accurately reflected my feelings about a destination.

I must have managed some sleep as I awoke, as predicted, to a grey sky heavy with rain which did little to boost morale. From the window of my air-conditioned room it looked, to a resident of the northern hemisphere, like a cold and gloomy January day, but when I stepped outside to pack up my bike, I was immediately hit by the claustrophobic, muggy air of the tropics. The hotel staff all turned out to give me a rousing send-off, as well as plenty of warnings about Kinshasa.

'Goodbye, Madame Lois, please come back soon!' they called out in halting English, and in my friendless state I felt touched, even by this shred of corporate hospitality. I rode down to the river with my stomach churning to find Ricky and Kevin waiting for me, flagging me down as I rode into the port.

The usual hoo-hah involving small men with big rubber stamps was particularly drawn out and painful, requiring a constant stream of cash and an industrial scale of photo-copying. We lost Kevin somewhere along the way when he got

305

roughed up and thrown out of an office by an angry, hulk of a man in a grey uniform. By the end of it even Ricky was starting to look a bit stressed, but he eventually beckoned me to follow him on board the ferry, and I rode up the rickety gangplank, clanking my way on to the boat. It was a rusting old iron heap that comprised no more than a covered deck and a few rows of seats for passengers. I parked my bike facing out towards Kinshasa and stared over the water, feeling more apprehensive than ever before on my journey.

There were plenty of men and women coming aboard, carrying enormous sacks of grain on their heads, several men who were already drunk at nine in the morning and a surprisingly large number of cripples dragging themselves around on their withered limbs, or being pushed on board in homemade Heath Robinson style wheelchairs. I asked Ricky why there were so many of them and he sneered distastefully.

'They are trouble, big trouble. They can travel cheap on the ferry, so they go back and forth, selling and buying between Brazzaville and Kinshasa, they sell cheaper then everyone else, and they smuggle things too. They are trouble, very aggressive when they are all together like that. You must not talk to them.'

I watched them arranging themselves and their strange collection of wheelchairs and tricycles, piled up with goods. Africa is probably the worst place in the world to be disabled, but they were getting on with it, survivors making something of their pitiful lives. But they all had the look that I now knew so well, the cold, empty eyes of the Congo.

A few able-bodied chancers were diving off the wharf into the brown swirling water and swimming round to the other side of the boat, where they clambered aboard to avoid paying for a ticket. One of them was even carrying a sack of rice while he carried out this manoeuvre, holding it on his head and swimming with his free arm. Then a burst of shouting and banging drew my attention away to the top of the gangplank, where an elderly woman and one of the deckhands were in the midst of a fist fight. She punched him in the chest, then he shoved her up against a bulkhead, her skull making a dull clanking sound as it came into contact with the rusty iron wall. Fortunately she was wearing a large and elaborate headdress which hopefully softened the blow. But she was not to be deterred and came back at him with a right hook in the face, which he returned immediately. It was the Rumble in the Jungle for the twenty-first century; Ali and Foreman had nothing on these two as they continued to batter each other, sometimes rolling on the floor but always coming up for more. It was turning into quite a commotion as more passengers boarded the ferry, pushing their way past the scrapping couple. In the end some of the heftier-looking males on board, including Ricky, steamed in and successfully pulled them apart.

'What was all that about?' I asked Ricky when the excitement had died down. The elderly woman was sitting alone, perched on a sack of rice, her face clouded with fury.

'Oh, nothing, she is his mother, they are always fighting,' he explained with a shrug.

Ricky bade me farewell – he had other business to attend to, more scams and fixes to take care of, and no doubt, more fights to break up.

'Good luck in Kinshasa,' he said, shaking his head.

Now that Ricky had gone and the drama of the fight had subsided, the attention was turned towards me, and I was soon surrounded by a curious crowd. They formed a circle around me and the bike and stood there staring, except for one particular man who was steaming drunk and insisted on lurching towards me and draping his arm round my shoulders. Each time he did this I would hop round the other side of the bike, but he always followed, staggering and slurring after me, sending me skipping off back to the other side until I was trotting non-stop around the bike with him in hot pursuit. It was straight out of Benny Hill; the only thing missing was a novelty theme tune. This ridiculous carry-on continued for some time until one of the young men in the crowd hauled him away with a few choice words and a look of disgust. Drunks, the disabled, old women; there was no respect for these weak, lowly members of society in the Congo. It was survival of the fittest, quite literally the law of the jungle.

I thanked the man for coming to my rescue and this dialogue prompted a wave of questions from the crowd. As each one spoke, it encouraged the others and soon I was under siege from a non-stop interrogation. *Where was my husband? Where was I from? Where was I going?* And again and again: *Where was my husband?* I told various lies by way of response, but my inquisitors were quick to warn me that I shouldn't even be thinking of going to Kinshasa, repeating Jules's warning: it was 'very dangerous for a woman alone'. I made up a lie that my husband was waiting for me there, but they wanted to know why he wasn't with me, where he was exactly, where would we be staying? I was thinking on my feet and made up a fantastically elaborate story which they seemed to buy, but I still felt thoroughly unnerved, and as the crowd swelled, moving in closer, and the questions and warnings came thicker and faster, I felt distinctly panicky. Overcome with dizziness and nausea, I forced myself to breathe slowly and deeply and stay calm, but it was easier said than done. It seemed to me that by taking this ferry to Kinshasa, I was jumping out of the frying pan and into the blazing, fiery depths of Hades. When the boat cast off from the dock my heart was thumping fast at the thought of what awaited me on the other side of the river.

The crowd continued to stare at me, but the questions subsided and mercifully everyone's attention was diverted to a scuffle on the roof, where one of the ticketless chancers was hiding out. I had seen him swim round, climb aboard and then leg it up a pole on to the corrugated iron roof, but the deck-hands had seen all the tricks before and it wasn't long before he was rumbled. There was burst of shouting above us and then a lithe black body sailed past, landing like a bomb in the churned-up water. Whether he jumped or was pushed, I didn't know, but he broke into a fast front crawl and it looked highly likely that he would make it to Kinshasa before the rest of us.

The crossing of the river took half an hour, and in some ways I wished it would never end, that I could float indefinitely in limbo, that I would never have to make my nerve-racking entry into this most awful of African nations. As we left Brazzaville behind and the hazy image of Kinshasa's tower blocks became steadily clearer, I became more and more fraught. Now I wished the boat would just hurry up and get on with it and spare me this slow and dreadful countdown.

I could see the chaos of Kinshasa port before we even touched the bank. As the boat edged in to moor, people were already jumping on from the quayside, making daredevil leaps across the water. The port officials were screaming orders to no avail: everyone was yelling at each other and throwing their sacks of rice and bulging Chinese laundry bags on and off the boat. I sat on the bike and waited for the mayhem to subside before making a speedy run up the ramp. But I didn't get very far. My passage was quickly blocked by a mob of aggressive, shouting men who were grabbing hold of my arm, waving fake IDs in my face and yelling orders at me: '*Show me your passport! Get over there! Where are you going? Stay there! Show me your papers!*'

If they were attempting to intimidate me, they were succeeding. I knew immediately, as with the soldiers on the train, that my usual tactic of smiling patiently and being extra polite would have no currency in this situation, and I'd long since realised that damsel-in-distress mode doesn't work in this part of the world. Chivalry is a rare commodity in Africa, and the women are as tough as the guys; they have to be, considering their position in the pecking order, which is somewhere above the animals, but below the men. As I sat there on the bike with my engine running, slipping the clutch on the steep ramp, I knew there was only one way I was going to get out of this situation unscathed. It was time to dig out and dust off my hard-nosed side; if I didn't I was likely to burst into tears, and that would be the worst thing I could do. I got the feeling that people had stopped crying in the Congo a long time ago.

It was a strange sensation to make a conscious decision to act like a seriously stroppy bitch, as there's not much call for this kind of activity in my regular day-to-day life, but it was reassuring to know that I could draw upon it in an emergency. I stayed sitting on the bike, made what I hoped was a don't-mess-with-me-face and started yelling at everyone, telling them where to stick their fake ID cards and to get the hell out of my way. I was almost laughing as I heard myself; I sounded quite ridiculous, but amazingly, it worked. The men made a feeble show of being threatening, but then slowly, one by one, they skulked off into the crowd, leaving me free to ride up the ramp and into the fenced-off yard where the real trouble would begin; dealing with the men with the genuine ID cards.

There were no signs suggesting where I should go, all the buildings were unmarked and equally shabby, and to make matters more confusing none of the men who claimed to be customs and immigration officials were wearing any kind of uniform. There was no way of telling them from the hordes of dodgy fixers that I had successfully banished at the quayside, and once again I found myself at the mercy of yet more shifty, steely-eyed men. To add to the fun, there was now the added delight of being mobbed by legions of money-changers waving wads of Congolese francs in my face.

Luckily I was taken in hand by a young chap by the name of Jean-Paul, who I liked immediately, partly because he spoke English and partly because he was a bit chubby and showed the beginnings of a slight paunch under his too tight T-shirt. There was something quite sweet about him, but I was forever wary about who to trust and once again had only my instinct on which to rely. But my instinct had been getting a good workout lately and it came up trumps again. Jean-Paul never left my side, guiding me over the hot coals of the DRC's entry formalities, most of which were conducted on the bonnet of a decrepit 70s Mercedes under a fierce midday sun.

Customs went pretty smoothly, aside from the unwanted attentions of a one-legged officer who called me into a vast, gloomy hangar on the pretext of examining my bike and made various lascivious suggestions, some of which involved me sitting on his stump. Mercifully, Jean-Paul came to the rescue and steered me back outside into the glaring sunlight, where a man from immigration wanted to have a word with me.

Perched on the bonnet of the Mercedes, he appeared to be proof-reading every page in my passport. He turned to me, his eyes hidden behind mirrored sunglasses for maximum intimidation, and I could see the reflection of my pale, anxious face staring back at me. It occurred to me that I couldn't be more out of place.

'So, where were you before you came here?' he said.

'I was in Brazzaville, in Congo.'

'And before that?'

'Gabon.'

'And before that?'

'Cameroon.'

He said nothing, but flicked through the pages in silence, studying the dates of my visas and stamps to see if they matched my story.

'Let me see your vehicle papers,' he demanded.

I fished them out of my luggage and he laid everything out on the bonnet, double-checking and cross-referencing every single date, right back to when I had entered Tunisia, before copying it all down into a book.

'But you say you come from England. Where did you go from England, not to Tunisia, no?'

'I took a boat to France, and then another boat to Tunis.'

'There is nothing in here of France!' He slammed my passport down on the bonnet triumphantly, and I realised how the car had become so dented.

'If you're English you don't get stamped in France, it's in the EU,' I said, trying not to sound too much of a smartarse. I wanted to add 'Duh!' at the end of my statement, but I feared it would not help my cause.

He obviously had no idea what I was talking about and

312

continued picking through my papers, determined to find something – anything – untoward that would provide him with the evidence he needed to extract a big, juicy bribe. Meanwhile, sensing that cash would soon be changing hands, the vulture-like money-changers were circling again, and as Jean-Paul shooed one away another would appear in his place. Oh, sweet civilised Europe! I thought, with a sudden pang for its open borders, its temperate climate and its single monetary policy.

Confounded by the European question, the immigration officer instead quibbled over smudged visa stamps, questioned the sloppy handwriting of the Nigerian officials, tested me to see if I could remember what dates I had entered and exited each country, and accused me of lying when I failed to recall each one correctly. Jean-Paul was hopping around, trying to reason with him on my behalf, but was blatantly ignored or barked at occasionally. The sun was blazing high in the sky now – even the broken-up tarmac beneath my feet was radiating heat – but our man from immigration was immune to the fierce rays burning down on us and continued to interrogate me as I perched on the car bonnet, feeling distinctly weak and light-headed under the glare of the cruel Kinshasa sun and its equally cruel bureaucracy. How is it possible, I marvelled, that this amount of attention to detail is lavished on completely unnecessary red tape and bullshit while the rest of this country's affairs are in a state of complete meltdown?

The immigration officer didn't like it, but eventually he had to admit it: there was nothing he could get me on. My papers were whiter than white, except for the faked Cameroon exit date which had sailed past his supposedly eagle eyes. He slammed my documents down on the car bonnet and made an invisible nod that meant I was free to go. I smiled at him, enjoying my mini victory; my spotless admin had triumphed over corruption! But my euphoria was short-lived, as it was now the turn of the policemen, and they wanted to see the contents of my luggage laid out on the ground.

Jean-Paul began a plea in my defence, but was banished to the sidelines as they picked over my belongings. The money-changers were still hovering but they were blending into the crowd that had come to watch me unpack my kit. I recognised some of the faces; the one-legged customs man and a few of the guys that had questioned me on the ferry were there, as well as some of the disabled men in their hand-pedalled carts. With a quick glance I approximated that my audience averaged about 1.75 legs per person.

'This is for me, yes, a gift for me?' said one of the officers, an older guy with a cunning, lined face. He was holding up a bottle of liquid soap.

'Er, yes, I s'pose so.' I shrugged. If soap was all he was after, I had got away lightly.

'And this,' said his younger sidekick, flicking through my French/English dictionary. 'I like this, I learn English, yes?' He giggled.

'Yeah, sure, knock yourself out.' If all went to plan I would be in Angola in a couple of days and my French dictionary would be redundant. In fact, these guys were doing me a favour, lightening my load, just as long as they left me my Portuguese phrase book.

'Why are you here in Kinshasa, where are you going?' the older officer asked me with a hint of suspicion. 'You are married, yes?' He seized my left hand and stared at my wedding ring. I was getting used to being grabbed by complete strangers, and I barely flinched.

'I'm meeting my husband, he's here in Kinshasa,' I replied, rolling out the old line.

'But where is he? Why is he not with you?'

I started to launch into my elaborate cover story, but I couldn't remember the full details. To make matters worse, I was surrounded by various people to whom I had already told all sorts of lies, and with the overbearing heat and the pressure of the situation, I was becoming confused about what I had said to whom. Thankfully one of the guys from the ferry unknowingly came to my rescue.

'Her husband is at the embassy, the embassy for Great Britain,' he shouted to the policeman. This was just the cue I needed.

'Er . . . yes, yes, he's at the embassy,' I concurred.

'But why is he not with you?' The officer simply couldn't understand how this could be.

It was all coming back to me now, and my fabrications tripped off my tongue. Luckily, the finicky immigration officer was not present to challenge my quickly rewritten history.

'We were travelling together, but when we were in Brazzaville, I had to go back to England, and while I was away, his visa ran out, so he came here. Then I flew back to Brazzaville and now I am catching up with him.'

'So he came through here, through Kinshasa?' The policeman sounded suspicious.

'Er, yes.'

'He is riding a motorcycle, like you?'

'Yes,' I said, a little uncertainly. This was one nosy police officer.

'I have not seen an English man on a motorcycle here,' he said, his eyes narrowing.

315

'Uh . . .' I tried to avoid his stare, not knowing what to say. But I was saved by his colleague piping up.

'Yes, yes! I see him, he is with a friend, yes?' he said, turning to me. 'Two motorcycles, big motorcycles, one is red, yes? They are here two weeks ago!'

What on earth was he on about? Then the realisation dawned on me: he was talking about the two motorcyclists from Portsmouth that Sherry-Kay and then Pete and Katrin had told me about. They were ahead of me by about two weeks, and unbeknownst to them, they had saved my bacon in a most miraculous fashion.

'Yes, yes, that was him!' I agreed a little too eagerly.

The policemen both nodded, reassured, and I suppressed a roar of laughter at this coincidental stroke of good fortune.

'But why do you go back to England without him?' asked the older officer.

'Well,' I said, putting on a sad face and lowering my voice, 'my grandmother died over Christmas so I had to go back home for her funeral.'

It worked every time. A murmur of sympathy passed through the crowd and this band of cruel, hard men poured out their condolences. One thing they knew about in this country was death.

'Ah, I am very sorry. Very sorry about your grandmother,' said the older policeman, now gripping both of my hands.

I nodded and thanked them for their kindness, trying to look suitably grief-stricken. I didn't feel too guilty, as both my grandmothers had been dead for years, and I'm sure they wouldn't have objected to me misusing their identities to help me out of a hole such as this.

Despite their burst of compassion, no amount of dead

grandmothers was going to stop the police getting on with the business in hand and they continued to rifle through the rest of my clobber, choosing a few more 'gifts', a cigarette lighter and a marker pen, but I didn't mind too much – I was just relieved they possessed such humble tastes. Looking pleased with their haul, they wandered off, examining their prizes, leaving me to pack up and go. The Democratic Republic of Congo was mine for the taking.

'OK, OK!' said Jean-Paul. 'Now you follow me and my friend here. I will take you to your embassy, yes?'

He had commandeered a car and driver from somewhere; the engine was running, and I was caught on the hop. It was too late to start my journey to Matadi today, so I had planned on finding somewhere to stay in Kinshasa and then taking a tentative stroll around the city before it got dark, but my web of lies meant that I had to be seen to be going to the British embassy to be reunited with my husband. If I did anything else, it would look strangely suspicious.

'OK, let's go!' Jean-Paul was calling out of the passenger window. The car was a battered green Citroën, but the driver had ideas above his station and was dressed as an airline pilot, complete with uniform, cap and aviator shades. He was also wearing a headset which, as far as I could make out, was strictly for show, as when I followed the lead that dangled down over his shoulder I realised it was not connected to any device in the car. Maybe he was a pilot, moonlighting as a taxi driver, or was he just a cabbie with an ego problem? I had no way of telling; I had only been here a few hours but I suspected that no explanation was too far-fetched for Kinshasa, this bizarre city that teetered permanently on the tightrope between absurdity and disaster.

There was nothing else for it but to follow Jean-Paul and his friend to the British embassy, and I wove my way through the raucous, densely packed streets, trying not to lose them in the chaos. With eight times the population of Brazzaville, Kinshasa made its twin city across the river look like a village, but there was something about it that drew me in, something exhilaratingly, if morbidly, appealing. As I rode along, enjoying the act of being on the move again, what amazed me most was the very fact that I was here, and that I was unscathed, and that I was riding my motorcycle through Kinshasa! It was so easy to get bogged down by nerves and the nitty-gritty that sometimes I had to remind myself of what I was doing, and why it was so darned exciting! I had wanted an adventure, and I was getting one, of that there was no doubt.

The usual clues marked our entrance into the embassy district, wide, empty tree-lined streets, high walls, fluttering flags and expensive cars, all watched over by uniformed security guards. The Citroen came to a stop and Jean-Paul jumped out.

'Here is your embassy!' he announced with the flourish of a game-show host, smiling as if he'd pulled off an amazing coup. He was really rather sweet, with his podgy tummy and boyish enthusiasm, and I liked the way he called it 'my embassy', as if it had been built for this very visit. I shoved a bunch of US dollars in his hand.

'Jean-Paul,' I said, 'you know you could do pretty well looking after visitors in Kinshasa. It's got a bad reputation and most white people are quite nervous about coming here, but what they need is someone like you who's straight-up and doesn't rip them off. I'm really grateful, thank you.'

He looked a bit bashful and shoved the cash in his jeans pocket.

'There's not many white people come here any more,' he said, getting back into the car, 'but thank you.'

They drove away, and it was only as I walked up to the entrance that I remembered that I didn't actually have a husband waiting for me here. I was beginning to believe my own lies. Well, I might as well go in, I thought; the DRC is definitely one of those countries where you're meant to register with your embassy, and besides, I've never been to a British embassy abroad before. And, I hoped secretly, I might even get a decent cup of tea.

SIXTEEN

Once I'd convinced the sentry that I was a legitimate British passport holder, I was given the go-ahead to pass through the high-security gate and wander around the embassy in search of a man called Claude, who would make a note of my presence, just in case I disappeared into the jungle, never to be seen again. The embassy complex was bigger than I expected, and as I strolled across an inner courtyard I came upon a middle-aged man in a brown suit walking towards me at a brisk pace, carrying an armful of folders. His wispy, sandy hair and pallid complexion gave him a twitchy, pink-eyed, rabbity look, but despite his unassuming appearance he carried himself with the self-possessed air that comes as a birthright to a certain type of Englishman.

'Oh! Um, er, hello,' he said, obviously surprised at my presence but too well-mannered to ask, 'Who on earth are you and what are you doing here?'

'Hi, I'm British,' I said, somewhat unnecessarily. 'My name's Lois, I'm just passing through and I thought I should register with the embassy, while I'm in Kinshasa.'

'Oh, yes. Very good. Yes. Not a bad idea at all. Well. Let's see, er . . .' He spoke in short staccato sentences in a voice reminiscent of wartime wireless broadcasts.

'They said I need to see someone called Claude.'

'Ah, yes. Yes. Claude. Well, oh dear, excuse me . . .' He shifted his folders under his left arm and offered me the smooth, limp hand of a lifelong pen-pusher.

'Roger,' he announced.

He didn't state his rank, or even his surname, and I wondered if this was because he expected me to know who he was. Maybe he was the top bod here, the Ambassador himself? And maybe, I pondered, when you're that important you no longer need a surname, like Elvis, or Madonna, or Jesus.

'So. Er, well, er, what brings you to Kinshasa? Working here, are you?' he said in an obviously forced attempt at small talk.

'No, I'm just on my way to Matadi, but I felt a bit nervous about coming here on my own, to DRC I mean, not the embassy . . .'

He let out an awkward chuckle.

'So I thought I might as well check in.'

'Ha! Yes, I see. Yes, well, it's not all that bad here, really,' he said, as if he was letting me on a top secret. 'So who are you with? One of the NGOs?'

'No, no, it's just me, I'm travelling down to Cape Town, on my bike.' I waved my helmet around for his benefit.

'Oh! What! Sorry, I'm not sure I . . . er, what? So, you're here on a motorcycle? With a tour, are you?'

'No, no, I'm riding my bike from England to South Africa so I'm just passing through.'

He looked flummoxed and little red patches appeared on his sallow cheeks.

'On your own? Riding a motorcycle? Gosh, how odd. Oh, well, I see. Well, yes, we'd better find Claude, I suppose.'

I followed him into one of the buildings and through grey corridors where noticeboards displayed photocopied memos about revised policies and changes to procedure. I could feel the blandness draining the life out of me, and I wondered if I was finally going native. The outside world of Kinshasa's colourful, if crazy, merry-go-round seemed preferable to this stifling monochrome world of British bureaucracy. Roger was hurrying along ahead of me with an ungainly shuffle that made his prominent buttocks wobble up and down. He was clearly a busy man and his job description did not include dealing with the hoi polloi that walks in off the street; and as we scurried along behind him I realised that the more lowly jobs – the clerks, the secretaries, the security guards – were taken by black, English-speaking Kinshasans.

'Wow, this place is huge!' I said, catching up with him and trying to make conversation.

'Yes, of course. Kinshasa is a very important place for us,' he said in a tone of voice that suggested I was extremely stupid for not being aware of this fact.

We eventually entered a small office where a smartly dressed young black man was tapping away at a computer.

'Ah! Claude . . . er . . .' Roger faltered slightly as the other man looked up from his work with a bemused expression. 'Er . . . it is Claude, isn't it?' And for a moment I thought Roger was going to turn to me and remark how they all looked alike, but his breeding and innate self-assurance allowed him to blunder his way through his gaffe.

'Young lady. British citizen. Wants to register. Yes? Jolly good. This young man will take your details,' he said, turning to me. 'I hope you enjoy your stay,' he added as an after-thought, as if this expression was something that he had heard other people say and was trying it out.

The cup of tea was obviously not going to be forthcoming, but I thought I might as well plug him for some info while I had the chance.

'Can you recommend somewhere to stay in Kinshasa, and also, do you have a map of the city that would show me how to get out of town on the road to Matadi?'

'Our chap here can provide you with a map,' he said awkwardly, motioning to the man who might or might not be Claude. 'As for somewhere to stay, er, a hotel, you mean? Ah, well . . .' – he looked a mite awkward – 'er, it depends on your, er, budget. We usually put up guests at the Memling but there's the Grand too, although to be perfectly honest, I find it a little shabby.'

I had the feeling that mine and Roger's concept of shabby might differ slightly, so I thanked him for his suggestions and finally let him go, free to shuffle around his dreary domain in peace.

The group of security guards outside the embassy proved to be a lot more useful, not to mention better company too, and I ended up hanging out with them for a while, chatting about my journey and about England, and giving them rides on the bike, shattering the aura of diplomatic hush with bursts of laughter and the rumble of the engine as we zipped up and down the tree-lined street.

It was late afternoon now; I had yet to find somewhere to stay, and although I felt considerably more relaxed about being in Kinshasa than when I had arrived just six hours earlier, I had not completely shaken off my underlying sense of unease about being alone in Africa's most dangerous city, especially at night. It was time to get going and find somewhere to hide out and batten down the hatches before darkness fell. Fortunately the security guards gave me directions to a hotel that came under my definition of shabbiness and I holed up for the night, feeling frustrated that my circumstances and inherent sensibleness prevented me from exploring Kinshasa's nightlife, but also relieved that I had made it this far with no major drama.

I awoke uncharacteristically early, buzzing with nervous anticipation about my 200-mile ride to Matadi; I had no idea what the road or the terrain would be like, and I envisaged miles upon miles of mud, interspersed with intimidating police roadblocks and military checkpoints. But first, before any of that began, I had to find my way out of the city, a challenge that always inspired in me a mild dread. Thankfully, the man who might be Claude had done a fantastic job of photocopying a detailed street map of Kinshasa, although he had then gone on to do that curious thing of talking me through the route in minute detail, having already given me the map. I always wonder why people do this, as surely a map negates any need for verbal instruction, but never mind, he had been very kind and helpful, so I had listened patiently, not wanting to pour water on his cartographical fire.

As I packed up the bike and performed my usual checks of the oil level and chain tension, I felt quite pleased that I had survived a night and a day in Kinshasa. It gave me confidence for the next leg of my journey: a huge hurdle had been surmounted and I wondered how much of the hurdle had been largely a product of my own making. With the combination of an overactive imagination and a few bloodthirsty, attention-grabbing news stories, it had been easy to believe that just by coming to DRC I was risking my life; that I would be robbed, raped or murdered, possibly eaten, or at best, have my hands cut off – a notorious Congolese punishment, albeit one that was introduced by the colonial Belgians. But aside from a few of the heavies at the port, everyone else I had met had been welcoming, helpful and friendly. In fact, the least hospitable person I had encountered was my fellow countryman, Roger in the British embassy, and as I fired up the bike I couldn't help but laugh at the irony of this, before setting off into Kinshasa's rush hour.

I forced my way into the traffic, sharing the city's frenzied streets with ramshackle overloaded buses, blacked-out 4 × 4s and UN tanks. Of all the African towns and cities I had passed through over the last few months, Kinshasa was the most chaotic. The city centre was packed solid, thick with exhaust fumes, the traffic creeping along slowly just like any other capital city, but the noise was deafening, with the relentless blasting of horns, the roar of thousands of clapped-out cars and the raucous sales pitch of Kinshasa's entrepreneurial street vendors flogging their wares at every junction. I slowed down as I approached a busy intersection and noticed that a man standing on the corner was selling the heads of huge tropical fish mounted in wooden frames, I guessed as a souvenir, should you be so inclined as to pretend you had caught such a massive and exotic beast. I stopped for a moment to study them closer and was hit by a vile waft, the unmistakable odour of rotten fish.

'*Bonjour*, madame! Real fish, from the great Congo River!' said the nattily dressed proprietor of these bizarre specimens. 'I catch them myself' – he pointed both index fingers at me in the style of a gunslinger – 'so you don't have to!'

He delivered his punchline like a pro, and I wondered where on earth he had learnt his sales patter. The smell of the mounted fish was overpowering, even in Kinshasa's rush hour smog, and my wrinkled nose did not go unnoticed.

'Do not worry, madame, the smell, it will go away after few days, then you have beautiful fish to put on your wall and impress your friends and family.'

I looked closer and realised with a mixture of disgust and amusement that he had not made any attempt to gut, clean or embalm the fish; he had literally lopped off their heads, nailed them to a picture frame and coated the whole thing with varnish.

'Tiger fish, madame, very rare, you take home to England.'

The idea of carting a framed varnished rotting fish-head across half of Africa and then on a plane to Heathrow was so brilliantly absurd that for a moment I almost considered it, but my sensible side won out and I used my usual excuse.

'*Pas d'espace*,' I said, pointing at my over-stuffed panniers, and he nodded.

'Maybe your husband buy, yes?'

'Yes, yes, I'll tell him,' I promised, and set off into the traffic with the stink of dead fish eventually extinguished by exhaust fumes.

It wasn't until I left the city centre and entered the straggling outskirts that the real Kinshasa showed its squalid, desperate true face. I had seen millions of dilapidated vehicles since setting foot on this continent, and I barely noticed them any more, but the Kinshasans had taken it to a new level. Every car, van, truck, pick-up, minibus and motorcycle was a skeletal image of its former self; smashed up, rusted away, dented, missing its doors and windows, or occasionally, in a vague attempt at repair, with the windows replaced by plastic bags and gaffer tape. Exhausts scraped and bounced along the ground, thick black smoke lingered like fog in the hot humid air, flat tyres limped along painfully; but just like the paraplegics on the Kinshasa ferry, these vehicles were defying the odds and making the best of their bad lot. Despite everything, they were doing what they were designed for: transporting enormous amounts of people.

It had rained heavily overnight and the streets were awash with mud and slurry, concealing massive potholes under the dirty brown water which made for several unplanned jolts and splashes. As I was ploughing slowly through a stretch of flooded road, a minibus in front of me stopped without warning, forcing me to slam on the brakes. The driver jumped out and came round to open the rear doors and I could see that every seat in the bus was taken. Nonetheless, he was stopping to pick up more passengers, and the very second he opened the door a bunch of about forty men and women waiting by the side of the road charged inside, pushing each other out of the way, shouting and shoving and climbing on top of each other, elbowing their way inside. In less than a minute the minibus was at bursting point and I could no longer see any of the interior, just a mass of humans piled high: arms, legs, a pair of trainers, the occasional flash of teeth or the whites of someone's eyes. The driver went to shut the doors but there were still eight women from the crowd who had not managed to elbow their way inside the bus. Undeterred by the reality that was staring them in the face, they hitched up their ankle-length dresses and began clambering up the bodies of their travelling companions, using the random collection of limbs as a ladder. They squeezed their heads into tiny gaps, grabbed hold of feet and hands and balanced themselves on any spare square inch of human they could find. The driver, realising there was no way he was going to be able to shut the doors now, returned to his seat and peeled out into the traffic, soaking me with a spray of muddy water in the process but leaving me with the fantastic view of eight brightly coloured, shapely bottoms sticking out of the rear doors, bouncing and wobbling as the minibus bumped away up the road.

It was this dogged persistence and inventive resourcefulness that characterised the people of DRC – the crippled salesmen on the ferry exploiting their discounted fare to undercut the competition; the airline pilot appearing out of nowhere as my cabbie; the policemen taking their 'gifts' from my luggage; the man selling framed fish-heads; and now the women who refused to be left behind by the bus, not to mention its driver, happy to keep stuffing them in for a few extra francs. But this national trait was no accident, it was written into the constitution. Article 15: *Vous êtes chez vous, debrouillez vous* – this is your home, so fend for yourself – a phrase coined by a former emperor weary of his poverty-stricken subjects begging him for help; the very antithesis of the welfare state. It was further compounded as the country's modus operandi when the pink-champagne-glugging dictator Mobutu announced at a party conference that it was 'OK to steal a little', and thus a way of life was born.

Strangely enough, Article 15 had touched my life two years before I set foot in the Congo, before I had even come up with the plan of visiting this corrupt, crumbling African nation. An asylum-seeker from DRC working as a postman in London had rustled up £20 million by stealing every chequebook he came across and setting up an elaborate money-laundering empire. £4,000 of his haul was mine, or to be more accurate, my bank's, as my stolen cheque sent me flying into the red to the tune of about £3,999. No doubt Mobutu would have been proud of his countryman's ingenuity, for as a Congo proverb so wisely points out, a mouse that goes hungry in the groundnut store has only himself to blame.

Kinshasa's shanty-towns and makeshift shops and markets that stretched along the road continued for twenty miles, but I was left to ride along in peace, as the ever-industrial inhabitants of Kinshasa were too busy bringing Article 15 to life with their non-stop homespun commerce to notice a white woman on a motorcycle in their midst. Eventually the traffic thinned out, the last rickety market stalls and tin shacks ebbed away, and I broke out into beautiful open country of green rolling hills. After the hemmed-in claustrophobia of the jungle that had accompanied me since Cameroon, this undulating landscape and the panoramic views over the Congo River came as both a joy and a relief.

Another source of joy and relief was that the road to Matadi was tarmac and in immaculate condition, winding through this almost pastoral scene in gentle curves with a dreamy serenity that felt strangely at odds with the country's horrific, violent history. The explanation for this incongruously good road came in the shape of the steady stream of trucks that thundered along in both directions, transporting goods between Kinshasa and Matadi, the country's major port at the mouth of the Congo River. Although relishing the pleasures of the open road, my journey to Matadi was tinged with uncertainty. This was where I was hoping to enter Angola, but I had no Angolan visa and Matadi was my last hope for this elusive stamp. However, the only evidence for this was hearsay, picked up from other travellers. If I failed here, I didn't know what I would do; I had no back-up plan, but I shoved this thought to the back of my mind, knowing better than to worry about things that hadn't happened.

The ride to Matadi was surprisingly pleasant and, more shockingly, uneventful. A police checkpoint pulled me over, but upon realising I was '*une touriste*', they waved me along with no further ado, and when I arrived in Matadi a few hours later I warmed to the place immediately. It was a busy, hilly port town built on the steep bank of the river, and tucked among its twisty streets were several grand buildings dating back to the colonial era, including the striking, five-storey Hotel Metropole, built in 1928, with its impressive façade and airy, tiled courtyard. These days, the hotel was still a going concern, but only just, and a peek inside revealed an air of faded glamour gracing its marble staircases and mahogany-lined corridors, suggesting a long-lost heyday when seafaring merchants and Belgian plantation owners would have graced its top floor dining room, smoking cigars and sipping brandy, keeping an eye on the comings and going of the port and no doubt discussing which of the workshy layabouts would be getting his hands cut off this week. I snapped a few photos of the hotel's Gothic charms, but when I turned my camera out of the dining-room window to the view of Matadi's docks a waiter rushed over in a flap.

'No, madame! No! You must not take these pictures, not of the port, not of the bridge. If the police see you, you are in big trouble. Big, big trouble. They will arrest you, they will take your camera.'

I was the only person in the semi-derelict, fifth-floor dining room; there was no way anyone could see me, but still, the fear was evident in his face and I stuffed my camera away in my bag, apologising. The Belgians and their iron rule may have left a long time ago but they had been replaced with a new spectre, of a home-grown variety.

Not having the first idea where I should go to seek out an Angolan visa, I headed straight to the border post, which was on the far side of town. I was met with much interest and friendliness by the officials and the few hangers-on that congregate in such places. As border crossings go, it was remarkably low-key, nothing more than a collection of shabby one-room buildings perched on the brow of a hill, and certainly not the intimidating frontier between two of Africa's most troubled nations that I had expected. An inspection of my passport soon flagged up my lack of Angolan ink and I was sent back into town.

'You must go to the Angolan consulate,' the immigration officer told me.

I asked him for directions and my question prompted the band of merry men who were hanging around to pitch in with their directions. I soon realised that although they all knew its location, they didn't know how to explain it. Maps and street names were not part of life here, and they directed using local landmarks, which was of little help to a stranger like me. The only useful piece of info I elicited from them was that it was next to a market.

'You take a taxi,' said one of them, 'he will know, you tell him *le marché Damar*.'

I took their advice and rode back into town, hailed a cab and gave my vague instructions. Sure enough, the cabbie deposited me at the entrance to the Angolan consulate, a plain metal gate set into the *de rigueur* diplomatic high wall, and as predicted, situated next to a busy market. In keeping with embassies the world over, it kept infuriatingly illogical opening times and was currently shut. I roused a sleepy security guard, who told me to return at eight-thirty the next morning, and I wandered back to my bike, stopping in the market to pick up some supplies.

The *marché Damar* was a colourful affair, with fruit and vegetables piled up all over the muddy ground, some that I recognised and others that I had never seen before, but all of which would have been condemned by any British supermarket for their physical imperfections. The place was heaving with women who were buying and selling and chatting with each other as they wandered among the produce at a leisurely pace. In a corner a tempting smell drifted over from a big cast-iron pot balanced precariously on a fire, and as I followed my nose, I saw that a man was serving up spaghetti and tomato sauce in polystyrene cartons; it was the nearest thing to fast food that I had seen in a long while. I bought a portion and then chose some fruit from an elderly woman next to him. She was barefoot and dressed, like all the women in the market, in a brightly coloured, printed wrap with a headdress made from matching material; she was sitting on a blanket on the ground, surrounded by her wares. As I crouched down to pick out a mango and a couple of bananas, I noticed she had a large black handbag next to her feet; it was open and I could see that whatever it contained was moving. As I peered inside, she noticed my curiosity and pushed it towards me for a closer look. It was filled with a squirming mass of live, fuzzy, black caterpillars, an inch long with little brown heads.

'Are these for eating?' I asked her in French.

'Yes,' she replied, 'you can fry them or eat them like this.'

'Really?' I said, incredulous, and not a little revolted. If this was considered a national delicacy, it was no wonder there were reports of cannibalism in this country.

'*Ah, oui, oui! Beaucoup de vitamines!*' she declared, a big smile breaking out over her wizened features as she scooped a handful out of the bag and offered them to me. I declined politely, sticking instead to a preferable, if less adventurous diet of condemned fruit.

I was back at the Angolan consulate at 8.30 on the dot the next morning, but the consul himself did not share my eagerness for his duties, and his Mercedes rolled up around nine. I had been ordered to wait in the street outside the sentry's hut, but now that the main man had arrived, I was allowed inside the compound. Not very far though; my next resting place was a small concrete room just inside the gates, but thankfully it contained a portable air-conditioning unit rattling away in the corner. Half an hour later an aide beckoned me to follow him; now I was allowed inside the consulate building, where I was plonked in a slightly better equipped room, this time with a few chairs. A stiff, haughty woman appeared after about twenty minutes and demanded to know my business. Thankfully, she spoke English, as my Portuguese phrasebook had still not received the attention it deserved.

'I'm travelling to South Africa, overland,' I explained, 'and I would like to apply for a visa for Angola.'

'Your passport,' was all she said in response, holding out her

333

hand before disappearing again, leaving me to stew in my anxious juices for a little while longer.

When she hadn't returned in half an hour, I was beginning to think the worst, but the door creaked open and a small, besuited man instructed me to follow him into yet another room, slightly grander, containing a desk and some hopelessly out-of-date photographs of Angola's beauty spots and cityscapes.

'You wish to travel to Angola?' he said, fixing me with a birdlike stare. 'Why?'

I explained the details of my journey again, trying not to sound too weary of this ridiculous farce.

'We do not issue tourist visas. We can issue you with a transit visa only. It is for five days. You must cross the border into Namibia five days from now. The visa will start today.'

Five days! To travel the length of Angola! I didn't how many miles it was off the top of my head, but I mentally pictured my map of Africa and gulped. Angola was one of the big ones, and by all accounts it had no proper roads any more; they had all been destroyed in the civil war, along with the rest of the country's infrastructure. It was going to be tough.

'The transit visa is eighty US dollars,' added the little man. I wondered if he was trying to talk me out of it.

I handed over the cash and he took me into my next waiting room, a bigger and grander affair that was making an unconvincing stab at 'dictator chic'. Fussy soft furnishings and gilt repro antique furniture stood awkwardly on the concrete floor next to a clattering white plastic fan, and strands of fake pink flowers and ivy hung in clumsy festoons around the French windows, which looked out on to a back yard filled with rubble.

Fortunately I had my book about the Colombian drug baron, which kept me occupied for another half hour or so before the haughty woman who had relieved me of my passport entered the room.

'Please, come with me,' she said, and jumping up quickly I followed her down a gloomy corridor and into the most intimidating room so far. The walls and high ceiling were lined in dark wood, with just one weak light above our heads, giving off a sickly yellow glow. The room was empty except for a large table and two ridiculously ornate and enormous banqueting chairs, painted in what surely appears on Dulux's colour charts as Classic Despot Gold. The only other item in the room was an immense portrait in oils of the Angolan president, which loomed over the table.

The haughty woman motioned for me to take a chair, which succeeded in its job of making me feel very small. She sat opposite, opened a big leather-bound book at a blank page and proceeded to quiz me in minute detail about pretty much everything she could think of, slowly transcribing my answers into her weighty ledger. We covered the usual subjects first: full name, address, my profession (I opted for my standard unthreatening default: a secretary), where was I going, where had I been?

'What is your age?'

'Thirty-three.'

'Are you married?' she said, glancing at my wedding ring.

'Yes.'

'So where is your husband?' came the predictable response, the question I had heard so many times on this continent.

'He is in England.'

She was trying to remain detached and impartial but I could sense a whiff of disapproval.

'Do you have children?'

'No.'

The whiff was a little more pronounced this time; it said: thirty-three, married, with no children? What's wrong with you?

'What is your religion?'

'Er . . .' Oh Gawd. My mind galloped through my options. If I say 'atheist' that whiff is going to get a whole lot more pungent. 'Agnostic' maybe? No, that's for wimps. So help me Richard Dawkins! What would you do? There's always Jedi. No, no, I need to claw back some favour after leaving my husband at home and not having gone forth and multiplied.

'Roman Catholic!' I blurted out. It was the first thing that came into my head that sounded suitably austere and a bit scary. She seemed to approve.

Next we came on to the subject of my family, the names of my parents and my brothers, their dates of birth, their addresses. I wondered if this was actually an elaborate attempt at identity theft.

'Does your father have any brothers?' She was beginning to sound bored now.

'No, just sisters.'

She wasn't interested in them.

'Does your mother have any brothers?'

'Yes, two.'

'What are their names, where do they live?'

I felt quite ridiculous sitting there, dwarfed by the colossal gold chair, under a giant painting of the Angolan president, saying, 'Well, Uncle Graham lives in Wolverhampton and Uncle Roderick lives in Norwich.'

'Wol-ver-hamp-ton,' she repeated awkwardly as she scribbled in her ledger. 'Is that a country?'

'No,' I replied, shaking my head, 'it's another world.'

We left the interrogation room and walked back to her office. I had been here for two hours now and I thought we were finally through, but no, there was yet more admin.

'Now, you make five photocopies of your passport,' she said, almost yawning with the tedium of it all.

I wanted to scream. Every second that was ticking away now was one less second that I would get to spend in Angola. If, as the little man had informed me, my visa started today, I was already wasting valuable time.

'OK,' I sighed, trying to stay calm. 'Where's the photocopier?'

'No, not here. There is a place in the town, near the . . .' She was so utterly uninterested that she drifted off halfway through telling me. 'He will show you,' she said, collaring a random aide who happened to walking past at that moment.

He was a young guy by the name of Gerard who was new to the job and had yet to acquire the embassy employee's traditional snooty inefficiency; in fact, he was glad of the excuse to get out of the consulate and go for a jolly in town. On our way to the photocopy place he kept popping into various shops and stalls to say hello to his friends, pick up some supplies for his mum and chase up his cousin, who owed him some money.

Meanwhile, I was becoming increasingly twitchy. Although it was good news indeed that I was going to get an Angolan visa, I now had a new challenge on my hands: to ride the length of the entire country in five days, only at this rate it wasn't going to be five days. I was already halfway through day one, and I hadn't even got the darn thing. The illogicality of the situation astounded me, even after all this time in Africa, the least logical continent in the world. I tried to hurry Gerard along, but even when we'd done the photocopying and I'd got the precious stamp in my passport, I still had the convoluted pantomime of an African border crossing ahead of me. Dusk was around six, so by the time I would be hitting the road I feared that most of the daylight would be gone.

'Er, right then, Gerard,' I suggested again gently, as he stopped to partake in a frenzy of hi-fiving and elaborate handshakes with his mates, 'shall we get on with this photocopying then?'

'Oh, yes, yes!' he said, as if he had forgotten all about it, and led me to a little tumbledown stall where an ancient photocopying machine was sitting on a chair outside the door. But it was not to be. The stall owner was shaking his head.

'No paper,' Gerard translated to me. 'No worry! I know somewhere.'

Across the road another monolithic photocopier was taking up most of the pavement outside a grocery shop. Gerard ducked inside and for a while it was looking promising but once again, my hopes were dashed.

'No ink,' he explained, shaking his head.

I groaned in despair.

'No worry!' said Gerard again. 'Come with me.'

I followed him down the road and into the stately entrance of a neglected nineteenth-century building. Gerard bounced up the wide staircase, two steps at a time, and as I followed him I could hear music drifting down from above. On the first floor, in a empty, cavernous room, among piles of wood and building materials, were a couple of men sitting listening to a cassette of Koffi Olomide on a paint-spattered 80s tape player. I guessed they were renovating the building, and I wasn't quite sure why Gerard had brought me here, but then, much to my relief, I spotted a photocopier in the corner.

The two men greeted Gerard with much bonhomie, and after they had exchanged effusive greetings, asked after each other's extended families and sung along to the tape, Gerard uttered the words I wanted to hear.

'Yes, yes, it is good, this photocopy, it is good!'

At last! Now hurry up! I screamed silently as I handed over my passport.

Gerard lifted the lid of the photocopier and splayed the passport out flat on the photo page, but just as he was about to press the green button, Koffi Olomide's light-hearted tones slowed, then slurred, and then mutated into a deep strangulated growl before falling ominously silent. The light bulb above our heads went out and the photocopier was no more. Matadi was having a power cut.

'Haaaaa!' roared the three men in amusement, while I swore inwardly and wished that some of this African ability to laugh at every misfortune would start rubbing off on me soon.

'Heehee!' giggled Gerard. 'No electricity, electricity gone! But do not worry, look!'

He pointed to where his two friends were hauling a massive petrol generator out of a cupboard.

It took a while to get it started and there was much pulling of the cord, and shouting and laughing. A few more men appeared from somewhere and soon they were all getting stuck in, while I stood there watching, knowing better than to get involved; this was most definitely man's work. Finally, with a cheer from the assembled gang, the generator roared into action just as the light bulb came back on, and everyone, including me this time, howled with laughter at this impeccable comedy timing.

We were back in the consulate ten minutes later. I handed over the photocopies and took a seat in one of the waiting rooms, fidgeting impatiently, unable to concentrate on my book and trying not to look at the clock. When the small beady-eyed man came out, holding my passport, I leapt out of my chair, snatched it from his hand, thanked him and pegged it outside to my bike, allowing myself a quick glance at the time. It was half-past one.

I made my way to the border as fast as possible, which wasn't very fast at all, due to the smashed-up roads and heavy traffic. But I wove my way through the busy town centre and headed out towards the border with the port on my right, where towering cranes and rows upon rows of shipping containers dominated the landscape. I was trying to remember my route from when I had come here the day before, looking out for a left turn that led up the hill to the border post, but just as I spotted it, I heard the shrill screech of a whistle and a policeman stepped out into my path, holding up a white-gloved hand as I skidded to a halt.

Oh Jesus! Why now? Literally 100 yards from the border! I knew it was too good to be true; I was a fool to think I could ride through the Congo without a run-in with the cops.

'Where are you going? Where are you from?'

It was the usual questions, and I answered as politely as I could muster, itching to get going again. Then a policewoman joined him, and with a smile that was supposed to be ingratiating but just looked sinister she delicately suggested that maybe I should give them *un cadeau*. I sighed, resigned to the inevitability of it all.

'What kind of gift were you thinking of?' I asked her in French.

'*Oh, je ne sais pas, peut-être de l'eau, un biscuit?*' she said with a shrug, looking hopeful.

Some water, a biscuit? What a sad request! I almost felt sorry for her. Here she was, a member of a police force that has a worldwide reputation for corruption and brutality on an inhuman scale, and the best she can do is ask for a drink of water and a biscuit.

'Maybe, you have, ah . . . a souvenir for us?' suggested her male companion.

What? Like a baseball hat that says 'I ♥ the Congo'? Or maybe a T-shirt with the slogan, 'I work for the Congo police and the only bribe I managed to get was this lousy T-shirt.'

They must be working up to something, I decided. They're just warming up, then they're going to go for the jugular. OK, well, let's see what happens.

I dug out my ever-ready packet of chocolate biscuits and their eyes lit up. Then, with flash of inspiration, I remembered something else and rummaged in my jacket pockets. Before I left, Austin had given me a handful of the button badges he had made featuring a cartoon of me on my bike; his idea being that I give them to children and people I met along the way. I was a bit nervous about offering them to two grown-up police officers in the Congo, they might take offence – in fact, they'd probably throw them back in my face and demand some hard cash, and who could blame them? But I took the risk and held out two badges in the palm of my hand.

The policewoman squealed with glee and her male companion looked almost as excited. They picked them out of my hand and examined them in great detail before fixing them to their jackets. The woman was beaming with delight.

'*Merci beaucoup!*' She giggled like a little girl. '*Quel est votre nom, mademoiselle?*'

'Lois, *je m'appelle* Lois.'

'Lois! *C'est vous, oui?*' She pointed to the badge and smiled even more. 'Lois! *Merci beaucoup*, Lois!'

'*Oui, oui, merci beaucoup!*' added her colleague, arranging his badge among the more official insignia on his lapel.

'*Au revoir! Bon voyage! Bonne chance!*' they called out in between mouthfuls of chocolate biscuit.

And with that bittersweet finale to my Congo adventure I was free to go, forever southwards, and now racing against the clock, into Angola.

SEVENTEEN

After making a reasonably speedy exodus from DRC, thanks to the guys at the frontier who remembered me from the day before, I rolled up at Noqui, the Angolan entry post, at three o'clock only to find it abandoned. The doors to the offices were open, but there was nobody around. The border between the two countries was on a col, and my position commanded a sweeping view of the valley below on the Angolan side. There was little sign of human activity down there, no towns or any roads slicing through the green wilderness, just the occasional group of huts and the faint grey scar of the track that lead away from here, winding its way down the hill. Still twitching with the thought of my visa deadline, I considered just blasting straight through the deserted border post, but as I was weighing up the pros and cons of this idea, a lame black dog appeared from round the back of a pile of rubbish, spotted me and launched into a volley of barking which acted as a summons to the keepers of this faraway outpost. In the style of a Spaghetti Western, various men appeared out of nowhere, striding slowly but purposefully towards me. They emerged from behind buildings, out of the trees and from the shadows. All it needed was an Ennio Morricone strings arrangement and a spot of haunting whistling.

'*Olá*,' they said, and as they approached, the Sergio Leone showdown never materialised and they were shaking my hand, greeting me like a long-lost relative, admiring the bike and chatting away unintelligibly in Portuguese. It was strange to be hearing this new language and when I opened my mouth to return the greeting, an involuntary splutter of French came out.

'*Bonjou* . . . uh, I mean, uh, *Olá!*'

They all laughed, and led me into the tiny immigration office for exactly the same round of questions I'd answered at the embassy just a few hours previously. I got the feeling that not many people came through this way, because when I moved into the customs building the officer floundered around, dusting off old box files, searching for the correct paperwork and scribbling out his frequent mistakes, as if he'd done something like this once upon a time, but it was all a bit hazy. As he scribbled and scratched his head and threw spoiled form after spoiled form in the bin, I sat in the corner and used the time productively, writing out a list of useful expressions from my Portuguese phrasebook.

The pocket-sized book provided me with all the necessary niceties, but its target market was clearly, and quite rightly, holidaying families in Portugal, not motorcyclists in Angola. It included certain *bons mots* such as, 'This campsite is too

344

muddy' and 'This firewood is wet,' which I supposed might come in useful, but to whom I was going to be complaining about such inconveniences, I had no idea. It was also deafeningly silent on the subject of landmines, which admittedly aren't much of a cause for concern in the Algarve. They were, however, a huge concern of mine. I knew that despite Princess Di's best efforts Angola was still littered with mines and that the verges of roads were the favourite hotspots. Unfortunately, these same verges were also my favourite hotspots for just about every activity, from checking the map and having a quick snack to answering the call of nature. There would be no more ducking behind a tree for me, and I had spent an inordinate amount of time over the last few days wondering what new method I should employ.

Once I'd jotted down yes, no, please, thank you, I don't understand, bread, water, oil and the old staples, 'Fill 'er up!' and 'Do you speak English?' I made myself face up to the facts about my forthcoming dash across Angola. I unfolded my map and totted up the distance from here to Oshikango, the Namibian entry post at Angola's southern border. It was 1,200 miles. I had four full days plus a couple of hours of daylight left today, but realistically I was looking at 300 miles a day. On good tarmac roads it would have been fine, even at my top speed of sixty miles an hour. But if the reports were true, and Angola's roads had been literally blasted away, destroyed by twenty-seven years of civil war, then I probably wouldn't make it.

By half-past three the customs officer had filled his wastepaper basket but had also managed to make some sense of his forms and I was given the all-clear. My bike was legit, I was a Roman Catholic secretary, and Angola was mine for the taking. All that was left for me to do was ride as fast as I could for the next four and a quarter days. As I buckled up my helmet and prepared to leave, the immigration man came out after me, babbling away and waving his hands up and down, wiggling his fingers. I listened and watched and listened some more, but in the end I had to admit defeat. Shaking my head, I consulted my new list.

'*Não compreendo*,' I said, a phrase I feared I would be using rather a lot over the next few days.

'Woosh! Woosh!' he said, adding sound effects to aid my comprehension and pointing to the sky.

'Ah! Woosh, woosh!' I said, suddenly grasping his meaning.

He was providing me with a weather forecast, but the exact details remained unclear. I dug out my phrasebook and flicked to the dictionary section at the back. I tried wind and rain and storm, but while he nodded vigorously at all of these suggestions, there was still something else he was trying to tell me. At a loss, I turned to the chapter about weather and showed him the page.

'*Sim! Sim!*' he said. Yes! Yes! He was pointing to one particular phrase. *A inundacão repentina*. He looked at me apologetically, as if he himself was responsible for Angola's weather systems. I looked at the book. It translated as 'a flash flood'.

But even this ominous exchange wasn't enough to dampen the excitement that always accompanies the entry into a new country. An invisible line in the ground is crossed and everything changes; another language to grapple and stutter with, strange names, new places and people, another currency to count and convert and confuse, banknotes bearing portraits of national heroes you've never heard of; a whole new set of mores to absorb, to be befuddled by and to attempt to understand. It was like being a kid again, gazing around and lapping up the novelty; my tongue was practically hanging out, panting for more. This is the stuff that drives me, I realised, and I was reassured that my zeal for the new and the unknown and the weird was still safely intact. There had been moments when I feared the Congo had knocked it out of me, when I'd lain awake at night in some grotty flophouse, dirty and doused in sweat, listening to the scrabble of cockroaches or to strange men's voices shouting in alien languages outside my door; and I'd promised myself a future of holiday cottages in Dorset, cream teas and sedate ambles around National Trust gardens, if I only made it home. But Dorset could wait, Angola couldn't.

I had two and a half hours of daylight left, no idea where I was going to end up and no idea what lay ahead of me once I had descended into the valley below. I was way out in the sticks here, and there wasn't a decent-sized town for a couple of hundred miles. The route started out as a broken concrete path, but that didn't last long and soon I was crawling along on a track rougher than anything I had encountered before. For the first time since my ride through Algeria's Hoggar Massif I was in high country, and the track crawled repeatedly up and down the steep hills, strewn with rocks and so washed-out that where rainwater had poured downhill, it had cut a trench several feet deep, effectively slicing the track in two down the middle.

Steep rocky descents had always been my dirt-biking *bête noire*, and perched at the top of a particularly long, steep hill, I felt the pounding heart and churning stomach I knew so well. The bottom looked an awfully long way down, and to make matters worse, immediately at the bottom the track crossed a small stream on a half-rotted log bridge, which to my fearful eyes looked horribly slippery and unstable. I sat poised at the top, studying my options carefully, but there was no clear route down the hill: rocks and craggy outcrops littered every possible path. My cautious side wanted to go gently, footing it down if necessary, but in my heart of hearts I knew this was the worst thing I could do: I could only touch the ground with my tiptoes and that was a fast route to losing my balance and taking a tumble. I knew there was only one thing for it: keep my eyes focused on where I wanted to go and roll down as fast as I dared, letting gravity and momentum do the work. I took a deep breath and made the leap of faith.

The hill whizzed by in a flash, and before I knew it I was at the bottom; the log bridge barely registered and I was still flying along, heading towards another identical hill, only this time I was going up it. There was no time to stop and consider my options; I just opened up the throttle and gunned my way to the top, bouncing over the rocks and throwing my body weight to the left to avoid sliding down into the wheel-swallowing trench that lay in wait for a careless sideways slip.

I have to admit that I'm not much of an adrenalin junkie. I don't really like being scared for the sake of it and am more likely to be found enjoying the aforementioned cream tea in Dorset than dangling at the end of a bungee rope. So if I'm going to make myself heart-thumpingly, knuckle-whiteningly scared there's got to be a very good reason, and although I wasn't quite sure what the reason was at this precise moment, there was no denying that there was something extremely rewarding about this riding. But the thrill wasn't about dicing with danger or going fast – if I had stopped to analyse it at that moment I would probably have said that it was more about putting myself in a situation that forced me to overcome my nerves.

As a kid I had possessed an irrational fear of lighting

matches, and when I joined the Brownies I was horrified to discover that the initiation ceremony would involve me traipsing up in front of my parents and all my fellow Brownies and their parents, and lighting a candle with, horror of horrors, a match. Eek! The very thought of it gave me sleepless nights for weeks before the event and when the day finally arrived I was quaking with dread. But of course, when my name was called I marched up there, struck the match and lit the candle. And that was the end of that phobia. I considered all this as I plunged up and down this rocky track, and figured that there might be an easier way of overcoming one's fears than going motorcycling alone in a former African war zone scattered with landmines, but hey ho, I was here now and, just like the little girl with the box of matches, there was nothing else to do but get on with it.

Despite my gung-ho attempts, I was still making piteously slow progress and by quarter-past five I had clocked up just fifty miles. The land had levelled out a bit now and the track had become a flooded, muddy strip, passing through tiny villages of mud brick buildings with thatched roofs where families huddled around a communal fire, cooking their dinner. After my experience of arriving in the Congo and being chased by shouting natives waving sticks I was a little wary about even making eye contact with these people, but my qualms couldn't have been further off the mark. At almost every village they stood up and greeted me as I rode past, always waving and smiling, and gradually my fears were allayed.

The light was starting to fade and I knew I would have to call it a day soon, but I had no idea about where I should lay my head for the night. Bush camping was out, thanks to the land-mines, and there were certainly no hostels of any kind out here in this remote corner of Angola; there weren't even any structures more substantial than a mud hut. My only option was to call in at one of the villages and refer to my phrasebook: 'Podermos a camper aqui para passer a noite?' Please can we camp here overnight? OK, it made me sound like I had an imaginary friend, or, worse, like a schizophrenic, but I didn't know how to change the plural into the singular and I figured they would get the gist.

I made my decision on which village to choose by riding past and gauging the enthusiasm of the inhabitants' greeting. After a couple of warmish, but still decidedly average responses I was beginning to wonder if I was being too fussy; it was getting dark and sooner or later I was going to have stop somewhere. Then another little settlement appeared and it was as if I was Princess Di, back from the dead. The children ran towards me shrieking with excitement, a cheery-looking chap standing next to a truck with a few young men waved with reassuring heartiness and a winning smile, and the women, often the least effusive, flashed shy but friendly smiles and raised their hands. This was the village for me.

I swung a wide turn, pulled up to the group of men and reeled off my practised line. The older of them, the cheery-looking one, who I guessed to be the truck's owner, gave me the warmest smile I had received in weeks and answered me in my own tongue.

'Yes, yes, of course! You sleep here tonight. We sleep here too, you will be safe here.'

'You speak English!' I said in surprise.

'A little, I speak French and Portuguese better, I drive my truck between Congo and Angola, so I have learnt to speak both languages and I speak a little Lingala too.' He took my hand. 'My name is Sabe,' he said, still smiling.

Sabe had pretty much exhausted his English with his greeting and we and his three companions slipped into French, with him translating into Portuguese for the benefit of the villagers, who had by now formed a curious circle around me. The village consisted of only four huts, but there were an enormous amount of children for such a small community and just a few women, most of whom were busy preparing the night's meal. Noticeably absent from the scene were any men, and I wondered if this was the cruel legacy of Angola's war.

I set about pitching my tent and with plenty of helping hands it was up in record time. Sabe's three companions were probably the sweetest, most helpful teenage boys I have ever met. Dressed in scruffy Adidas and Nike cast-offs and even sporting a touch of gold bling, these boys, going solely on appearance, were lifted straight out of a middle-Englander's nightmare. Plonk them down on a street corner in Peckham and you'd have the perfect cover shot for a hysterical *Evening Standard* exposé about London gang culture. But if Sabe was my guardian angel for the night, these three boys were his cherubs, perched on my shoulder and flitting around me, ready to lend a hand at a moment's notice.

Strange as it sounds, I did feel as if Sabe had been sent to watch over me. Maybe this was merely an over-reaction on my part, due to the inevitable vulnerability that always accompanies the first tentative steps into a new country. Everything is strange and new, and lacking any reference points or familiarity; you have to throw yourself out there and see what happens, and that is exactly what I had done. Turning up alone at dusk in an African village and asking to be taken in for the night had required me to make another leap of faith, but something had drawn me towards this little collection of huts, and towards Sabe particularly; it was something I had sensed even as I passed by at twenty-five miles an hour.

Sabe himself would have put this down to a divine intervention by our good Lord, as after we had been chatting for a few minutes he handed me a slightly worn, dog-eared pamphlet written by an American Evangelist.

'I am one of his disciples,' he explained simply.

I thanked him and made a show of reading the literature. It was not the first time on this journey that my atheist self had benefited from a stranger's religious beliefs, but I still felt as awkward as ever. Can't people be nice to each other without God being involved? I wondered, but there was no way I was going to get into a debate on that thorny subject. I was tired and muddy and all I wanted to do was eat and sleep.

I threw in a packet of biscuits and the remains of a loaf of bread as my contribution to the meal, and we sat around on the ground eating the porridgey stew that the women had made. They were still a little shy towards me, but I knew that in their eyes I might as well have come from another planet: in Africa a woman without a man or children is eyed with suspicion, or, at best, pity. The kids, on the other hand, still untainted by such ideas, were hysterically excited by every move I made, watching in wide-eyed wonder as I went about my usual mundane tasks of setting up camp, unpacking my panniers and checking over the bike. But when I rounded everyone up for a photo call, even the women overcame their shyness and the whole village, all twenty of them, gathered together in an excitable gaggle.

'Where are you going tomorrow?' Sabe asked me while we were sitting around after dinner.

'I'm hoping to reach Luanda, but I'm not sure if I'll make it.'

The capital was about 260 miles away, and if the road was anything like the fifty miles I had ridden today, it was going to be a hard day's ride.

'What do you think?' I asked him.

'Maybe. We are going to Luanda too, but for us it will be two days. On a motorcycle you will go faster. In the truck, it is very, very slow, some time it will get stuck in the mud, or there is another truck that is stuck and we cannot move. Why must you go to Luanda tomorrow? Are you meeting someone there?'

I explained about the visa and my five-day dash across the country.

'Do you think I could get away with taking longer?' I asked Sabe. 'Would there be trouble at the border when I leave?'

Sabe reflected on this for a moment.

'Possible, possible. Yes, they may make trouble, because you are a woman alone. You understand what the police are like. Maybe they make you pay money, maybe worse.'

This wasn't the answer I'd hoped for. I'd considered forging my visa exit date as I had done in Cameroon, but the Angolan visa was a proper printed piece of paper, glued into my passport, not a smudged inky stamp. I resigned myself to the fact that I was going to have to stick to the time limit, and I decided to view it as a challenge, a race against the clock.

'What time will you leave in the morning?' I asked him.

'When it is light, six o'clock. And you know about *los minas*, the mines?'

'Yes, is it still a big problem?'

'Not so bad as before, some have been cleared, but still there are many more. Stay on the track always,' he warned.

353

I thanked him for his advice and we agreed to leave at the same time tomorrow; I needed every scrap of daylight I could get. It was pitch black now and the only light was from the embers of the fire; the night was strangely still and cool after my hot sticky nights in the Congo, but the sky was cloudy and I remembered the immigration officer's forecast of flash floods. With 1,200 muddy miles ahead of me, that was the last thing I needed. With the thought of an early start tomorrow I bid everyone good night and crawled into my tent. The murmurs of conversation outside eventually dwindled away and were replaced by a quiet but continuous sound of scratching and snuffling outside the tent. My overactive imagination was cooking up all sorts of explanations, and in the end I had to sate my curiosity. I unzipped my tent and was relieved to find nothing more menacing than a couple of goats and a pig trotting around the tent, making inquisitive sniffs at this alien structure that had appeared in the middle of their village. I slipped back into my sleeping bag feeling relieved. It wasn't exactly the pitter-patter of tiny feet that my mum had hoped would be keeping me awake aged thirty-three, but it suited me just fine.

I was woken the next morning by the sound of the women making a fire and preparing the first meal of the day. It was still quite dark, and when I looked out of my tent at the bleak surroundings that made up the backdrop to their life, I couldn't help but wonder what kept them going, what got them up in the morning day after day. They had no life outside this patch of muddy ground, no radio or TV, no running water or electricity to make their daily duties a little easier, no car, or even bicycle, to broaden their horizons. But still they were up at the crack of dawn, spurred on, I assumed, by the need to take care of their children, the only focus on which to concentrate their energy and efforts. No wonder they felt sorry for me in my childless state, I thought; they must think I have a terribly sad, empty life!

Sabe and the boys were up and about and ready to leave, but they waited for me as I packed up.

'We will leave together,' Sabe explained, 'but you must go first. You will be faster than us, but if we are behind and something happens to you then we will find you. So you are not alone,' he said, his kindly eyes twinkling. He must sleep with a smile on his face, I thought.

'Thank you, that is very kind. Thank you for everything.'

As Sabe had predicted, the truck was reduced to near walking pace and I soon left them behind, but as I rode on alone, tackling the rugged terrain, it was a comforting thought that my guardian angel was following along. The track was as hellish as the previous day, rocky and washed-out, climbing through steep hills, but as I moved towards the Atlantic coast, heading for the town of N'zeto, the sparsely populated wilderness of the north ebbed away and the first signs of a war-ravaged civilisation began to show its ugly face. The rocky trail ended, turning into an ancient, broken-up concrete track which made for harder and even slower riding, as my body and bike were shaken to pieces from the endless agonising jolts. Bomb craters had seen off large sections of the road, creating muddy swamps and puddles big enough and deep enough to sink a truck. It was all right for me, I could pick my route around the edges, pushing through banks of tall, stiff reeds, but I wondered what Sabe would do in his big truck, although he plied this route often and I'm sure he was used to such trials by now.

N'zeto looked promising on the map. It was a sizeable black

dot in a black circle, which according to Michelin meant a town brimming with services for the traveller. '*Toutes ces ressources*', stated the map legend with great confidence, promising hotels, restaurants and petrol stations; but Michelin's cartographers had not taken into account twenty-seven year of vicious fighting. Their map still showed Angola as having tarmac roads, railways, airstrips and national parks, all those trappings of a modern, peaceful country. There was nothing of the kind, and when I rolled into N'zeto I knew that I would have to lower my expectations for my short time in Angola and stop looking to the map for hope and promise.

It was an undeniably depressing place, its half dirt, half concrete streets laid out in a grid and lined with squat, grey buildings. As far as I could make out there were none of the usual elements that gave a town character – a central square, a town hall or a park – in fact there was not a single tree or patch of greenery anywhere. Not that I cared particularly about these things at this moment, what I wanted was a petrol station, but even this basic institution was missing from N'zeto's dismal streets. I rode through the town to the coast, but even the sight of the ocean failed to raise my spirits. The Atlantic was as dull, grey and lifeless as the town.

I stopped a girl who was walking past and read out my request for petrol from my list. Amazingly she seemed to understand, and with a big smile she beckoned for me to follow her. A couple of streets away she called out to a boy who was sitting on the steps of a little grocery store. He took over as my guide and I followed him, riding at walking pace to his house a few blocks away, where in the front yard was a twenty-five-gallon drum, full of petrol. The price was high but I couldn't blame him – he had a monopoly in this neck of the woods. I hadn't seen a single petrol station since I'd entered the country, 150 miles back, and if I hadn't found him I would have been stuffed, and worse, stuck in N'zeto. Predictably a crowd gathered around me as he filled up my bike, pouring litre after litre into the tank using an old water bottle. But there was no hostility among the onlookers, just lots of questions, some valiant attempts at English, less valiant attempts at Portuguese from me, and lots of laughter.

'It is very good! I am very happy to see you!' said a middle-aged man who was carrying his small son on his back.

'Oh! Thank you,' I replied a little nonplussed. Did I know this man?

He took my hands in his and gripped them tight.

'I never think I see tourist again in Angola. It is so good you are here! You make me think Angola has future. Thank you for coming here, thank you.'

Crikey! I was so touched I had to choke back a tear. Of all the people I had met and the countless fleeting contacts I had made with strangers on my journey, I had never expected to incite a reaction quite like this, and I left N'zeto with a full tank of fuel and a warmer feeling than when I had arrived. I had been in Angola for less than a day, but I had the distinct sensation that there was something special here and I cursed the stupid Angolan consulate and its five-day transit visa for hurrying me through.

It was midday now, and I had enough petrol to get me the 160 miles to the capital, Luanda, but I had no idea whether I could make it or not. The state of Angola's roads meant it was impossible to make any definite plans about where I was heading, or where I would stay; the only thing I could do was to keep going and play it by ear. It didn't take long for my

357

warm feeling to evaporate as I slogged through 160 miles of thick sludge. At least the rocky trails of this morning and last night had been in some way fun, and challenging in an enjoyable way. But this was sheer, utter, gruelling misery. Moving slowly south, I was now leaving the tropics and moving into a more gentle land of grassy plains, but the heat remained intolerable and made the physical exertion of manhandling the bike through the mud even harder.

There were few villages or towns along the way to break up the tedium, and, tormented by my pressing schedule and the ever-present fear of landmines, I didn't feel as though I could pull over on to the verge and take a break. This was especially annoying when it came to the small matter of toilet breaks, and I decided eventually that my only option was to make sure the coast was clear and hurriedly crouch down in the middle of the muddy road behind my bike, listening out for any approaching vehicles. Fortunately, there was hardly a soul on this lonely mud motorway, just the occasional truck coming the other way, plodding along at a snail's pace. I was desperate to make it to Luanda before nightfall, not being too keen on tackling an African capital city in the dark, and with the combination of the punishing, slow riding and the visa deadline hanging over me, I couldn't allow myself to waste a single second. Concurrent activity was necessary, I decided, and at one point I found myself having a piss, eating a banana and checking the map, all at the same time. 'Lois, are you actually enjoying this? Would you describe this as fun?' I asked myself as I performed this bizarre example of multi-tasking, but that question opened a whole giant vat of worms, and I decided to postpone my philosophising until I got home. I had more practical matters to worry about now.

By late afternoon it was apparent that I was not going to make it to Luanda before dark. It had started raining now, a heavy, persistent rain that turned the track to a muddy river and made ingress through clothes and bags that until now I had considered waterproof. I was riding as fast as I could, but the soaking and the pounding I was taking was making me increasingly exhausted, and for the first time on this journey I feared that I was unable to physically cope with what I had set out to do, a thought that had never troubled me before, even in the Sahara and the Congo.

The puddles, which were already sizeable affairs, were increasing in size and depth before my very eyes, and often the route would stretch out before me in a long brown line of water with not a patch of dry land to be seen, even far away in the distance. After my Congo spill, I was now a little wary of shimmying around the edges of flooded sections, and decided that straight through the middle was definitely the technique of choice. This had been working fine so far, but as I entered one particularly long stretch of muddy water I realised within a few feet that if I continued any further this one was going to drown the bike. The water was already halfway up the cylinder head and hovering just inches away from the sparkplug.

I couldn't paddle the bike backwards with my tiptoes, so there was nothing else for it but to jump off and haul it back. Up to my thighs in water, with the rain hammering down, I heaved my fully loaded motorcycle with all my might, panting and groaning with the effort required to pull it out of the mud. Soaked through with sweat and rain, I managed to successfully drag it back out of the water, but as I went to lower the side stand I slipped on the muddy ground, lost my balance and the bike fell away from me, landing with a squelchy thud. A torrent of swear words poured forth from my mouth, for no one's benefit but my own, and I stared at my supine bike in absolute despair. I wanted to cry, and a few sobs came out but no tears were forthcoming. It was a strange sensation. I felt like crying, I wanted to, but I couldn't, and I wondered if I had already used up my tears quota for this trip. But I also knew that there was no point in crying, it didn't help matters, and it certainly didn't get my bike vertical again. There was only one way of doing that, and, summoning up my final shreds of strength, I gripped the handlebars and the rear grab handle and with the kind of horrible grunting noises that weightlifters make in the gym, I righted my fallen steed.

Both my bike and I were now completely covered in mud, but I'd long since stopped caring about such things. I hadn't been properly clean for weeks and my clothes positively stank. I climbed back on the bike and, without thinking, cut an off-piste route for myself through the waist-high beds of reeds alongside the road. Oh my God! Landmines! I suddenly remembered, and I recalled Sabe's words from last night: 'Stay on the track, always.' It was too late now, I was most definitely off the track. A drowned bike or a leg blown off? That was the decision, and the leg was going to win over the bike every time. I steered back into the flooded trench, creeping along the edge of the water, trying to lean over to stop the bike sliding into the deep channel in the middle.

'What the hell am I doing here?' I shouted aloud to myself. 'What is the bloody point of it all?'

But I didn't have the answers, and in the end I settled instead on yelling a simple statement that I repeated ad nauseam.

'Never again!' I cried. 'Never again!'

EIGHTEEN

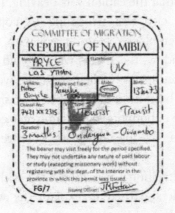

COMMITTEE OF MIGRATION
REPUBLIC OF NAMIBIA

Name: BRYCE LOS YTHAN	Statehood: UK
Vehicle: Motor Bicycle	Make and Type: Yamaha 100	Male/Female: Female	Birth: 13 Jan 73
Chassis No: 7421 XX 2315	Visa Type: Tourist Transit
Duration: 3 months	Point of entry: Ondangwa – Owambo

The bearer may visit freely for the period specified.
They may not undertake any nature of paid labour
or study (excepting missionary work) without
registering with the dept. of the interior in the
province in which this permit was issued.

FG/7   Issuing Officer: J.K.Unitman

As I predicted, I arrived in Luanda in the dark. As the mud
bath turned to broken concrete and then potholed tarmac,
the murky fringes of the city crept up on me, crowded and
choked with fumes. The lack of street lighting made it hard
to navigate, and with my map of the city centre being of little
use in the outskirts, I pulled into a petrol station to orientate
myself. Despite my filthy state, being thoroughly worn out
and not having a clue where I was, or where I was going, I
was surprisingly glad to be here. Around dusk, while still
battling through the mud, I had considered finding another
village in which to camp, but I was so weary that I couldn't
face the thought of being on show, surrounded by staring
faces and answering question after question. I craved the
anonymity of a big city where I could blend into the shadows,
find some faceless place to stay and collapse, where I

didn't have to perform or force a conversation in a foreign language.

Luanda's population had been swollen by an influx of rural Angolans, forced into the city by the civil war, and there was a palpable sense that the capital was heaving, that this relatively small colonial city was struggling to cope with its new residents. Tower blocks were strewn with washing hanging from every window, the streets were stuffed solid with traffic and the displaced masses milled about all over the pavements. It should have been intimidating, but it wasn't, and there was a tangible sense of bonhomie, the same relaxed good cheer that had existed in the bleak streets of N'zeto, multiplied a thousand-fold.

At the petrol station I was inundated with passers-by who stopped to talk and tried to explain the way into the city centre, but my lack of Portuguese was hindering me and I was becoming more and more bewildered. Then a voice cut through the babble.

'Do you need some help? I speak English.'

A dapper young man with bright, intelligent eyes introduced himself as David and took me under his wing. It was a Saturday night and I'm sure he had better things to do, but he hailed a cab, jumped in and told me to follow him. We were heading for a hotel in the centre that he recommended, but on the way we made various unplanned stops where he would step out of the car and point out significant sights and attractions of his city.

'This is the cathedral . . . and here we have the port where the . . . and this is a good view over the . . .' And so it went on.

I was shattered, soaking wet, covered in mud and starving hungry, the latter being largely due to the fact that my supplies of bananas, bread and tomatoes had been pulverised into an unappetising purée over the course of the day's riding. I wanted nothing more than to wash, eat and sleep, and not necessarily in that order, but David was so kind that I went along with his impromptu sightseeing tour.

'D'you think they'll let me in?' I asked David when we finally pulled up outside the hotel. It certainly wasn't posh, but they had every good reason to refuse me entry, considering the state I was in.

'Of course!' he assured me.

The security guard did a double-take as we stepped through the door. We made an odd couple: David, a spruce young man about town, accompanied by Swamp Thing. The receptionist, however, was a consummate professional and he barely raised an eyebrow, treating me like a VIP. David arranged everything, even organised parking for my bike, and before leaving wrote down his address and phone number.

'Please call me if you need anything while you are here,' he said with his lovely, patient smile. I could have hugged him, but I didn't want to spoil his natty duds with a muddy embrace. Instead I settled for a marginally cleaner handshake.

'Thank you so much! I really appreciate your help, thank you,' I told him from the very depth of my heart. Another guardian angel had been sent to me and I knew how lucky I had been.

'*De nada!*' he said with another gentle smile, and with that he was off. No hassle, no sleazy come-ons, no demands for money. Just the kindness of a stranger. I hoped that a little bit of David's magic had rubbed off on me, and that I could keep hold of it long after I returned home, and pass it on to someone else.

The misery of the day's trials soon dissipated when in the hotel bar I met a group of Norwegian oil workers, celebrating one of their birthdays, and the day was rounded off with a fun and rowdy drinking session in their company. I went to bed feeling pretty buoyant, largely thanks to a few bottles of Cuca beer, but also because I had clocked up 260 miles of truly demanding riding. Day two of my Angolan dash was over and here I was in Luanda, on time and on target. It had been hard, though not impossible, but there was to be no slacking off: I still had over 900 miles to cover in three days. It was feasible, but only if everything went to plan.

When I paid up at reception at eight o'clock the next morning, the young chap behind the desk gave me instructions on how to find the necessary road out of town, naming landmarks to look out for on the way. His English was patchy, but I thought I had understood his directions; coupled with my own street map of the city centre, I felt pretty sure I could pull it off. As I was packing my bags and making a final check of the map, the receptionist came running out after me.

'*Oh, senhora!* I am so glad you still here!' he cried in heavily accented English. He was holding a bunch of bank notes. 'You give me too much! I think you gone and I never see you again!'

Always a bit slow with the numbers, I was still getting to grips with the Angolan *kwanza*, and it wasn't helped by the fact that most institutions in Luanda preferred to be paid in US dollars or Euros. I was constantly getting confused with the exchange rates and I had unwittingly overpaid for my room. He stuffed the handful of notes into my hands and I marvelled once again at the wonderful people of this nation.

What I didn't marvel at, however, was its weather. The rain was lashing down, and Luanda on a wet Sunday was not a particularly inspiring place. The predicted floods had arrived, and torrents of rainwater poured down the hilly streets towards the port. Oh, how I yearned to stay in the hotel and curl up with a good book, but it was tough luck: I had to get going, floods or no floods. I rode up the street, wiping my goggles every few seconds, looking for junctions, roundabouts and landmarks to aid my navigation. I could see the museum, and the statue that the receptionist had told me to look out for, but when I looked at the street name on the wall I was not where I'd thought I was. The map never lies, I reminded myself, knowing how easy it is to persuade oneself that the map is wrong, and I went back to the hotel, to start again. I tried a different route, but again I ended up on a road that I couldn't find on the map and I continued riding around in circles, trying to locate a street or a landmark that I could definitely pinpoint, from which to start my journey out of the city.

Thoroughly bewildered and dispirited by the torrential rain and my pathetic inability to find my way, I rode down to the old port, where a beautiful street of colonial buildings ran along the water's edge. The majestic Banco de Angola took pole position and was marked on my map. Right, I said to myself sternly, stop getting in a tizz, take a logical approach, orientate yourself, and follow the map. You know what to do! But once again, after just a few turn-offs, I was completely confused. I was riding down streets that weren't on the map and my map bore no relation to where I'd thought I was. It must be wrong, the map must be wrong, said my despairing inner voice. But the map never lies, countered my rational side. I don't understand! I cried aloud.

The streets in this part of the city were largely deserted, but cowering from the rain in the doorway of a church I spotted a group of four men. My Portuguese was far from up to the job, but I had nobody else to whom I could turn. I pulled up next to them, offered a greeting and uttered a few words and the name of the main street that I was looking for, hoping that they would understand my plea.

'Are you lost?' said one of them in English.

Hurrah! My heart leapt with joy. Thank you British Empire for colouring the world pink, thank you America for foisting your TV shows on the world, thank you Britannia for ruling the waves and forcing most of the world to speak my language!

I explained my predicament and they huddled around my map, then the English-speaking one let out a laugh.

'Your map is old, these are all different now. When the new president came in, he changed the names of all the streets in Luanda.'

Bloody egotistical politicians! I thought. Do they know how much trouble they cause, renaming roads after themselves and their cronies and their families? Lordy! How's a girl meant to get around in this city? But I was laughing too, never failing to be amazed at yet another example of African illogic.

It took me three hours to get out of Luanda, mainly due to my map fiasco but also due to the outskirts of the city being brought to a near standstill by the heavy rainfall that had flooded the already congested streets. I filtered my way through the cars, feeling waves of dirty water slosh over my feet, but the clock was ticking and I kept moving as fast as I could through the gridlock. I had lost most of the morning already and I needed to make up the time.

Heading away from the coast now and into the heartlands of the country, the tropics were just a memory as I climbed to a plateau that reminded me more of wild parts of Wales than of anything I had seen in Africa. It was hilly and grassy, dotted with trees and big outcrops of rock, and for the first time in ages I felt cold. It was a strange, long-forgotten sensation after so long in the sticky heat of the jungle and, before that, the harsh baking sun of the Sahara. The miserable cocktail of rain, mud and non-stop riding continued, but when I wasn't feeling sorry for myself, I was feeling sorry for the poor Angolans. Out here in this more populated part of the country, reminders of their long and tragic civil war were evident wherever I looked.

Every town was a bombsite: people were living in their half-demolished homes, and the walls of houses, shops, banks, even churches, were smattered with bullet-holes. Abandoned tanks lay by the side of the road, victims of landmines hobbled through the streets with half a leg missing, and children played with bullets in the mud. This had once been a real, functioning nation; you could see the remains of it in the abandoned, bullet-sprayed hotels and the shops whose neon signs no longer flashed, in the road signs, rendered almost illegible with machine-gun fire and the overgrown, rusty tracks of the railways. When the civil war had kicked off in 1975 following independence, the Portuguese had upped and left in a huge airlift, one of the biggest mass exoduses in history, leaving the native Angolans to fight among themselves, which is exactly what they did for the next twenty-seven years. But with the Portuguese went all the knowledge, skills and expertise of running a country, and the black Angolans were left in something of a fix. It was not dissimilar to a couple of parents deciding their squabbling children are too much trouble after all and baling out of the family home, leaving the kids to grow up without them.

Considering this terrible past, I couldn't understand for the life of me how the Angolan people were the kindest, most hospitable bunch of folk I had encountered in Africa. Everywhere I stopped I was met with a friendly smile, sometimes with an attempt at a greeting in English, but always with genuine warmth and curiosity. There was none of the hustling, or scamming or begging, that I had encountered in other African countries. Most startlingly, they weren't interested in what I could do for them, but what they could for me, and this humbling show of humanity helped to put my own tribulations into perspective.

My third night in Angola was spent in the small town of Quibala. I had once again broken the golden rule and was riding in the dark. Quibala was barely discernible in the pitch black of an Angolan night, with its total absence of street lighting, and it was strange arriving in a town in darkness, having no sense of what the place looked like or its layout, feeling my way along the main street, trying to suss out where to go. Like a moth I gravitated towards the brightest point, an unusually well-stocked and illuminated grocery store, where, as if my guardian angel was at work again, I was immediately befriended by the owner's young son, a bright, serious boy with the appropriate name of Ernesto, who was studying English as if his life depended on it. When he discovered I was a real, living English person, from London, standing right here, in his dad's shop, he could barely contain his joy.

'Oh, England! One day I will go there! My biggest dream is to go to England!' he exclaimed.

Yeah, you and me both, I thought to myself, standing there dripping on the floor in my now customary end-of-day state: wet, knackered, filthy and hungry.

'Is there anywhere in town where I can stay the night?' I asked him.

He went silent for a moment, thinking, then jumped up as if struck by an idea.

'Follow me!' he said, and we stepped out into the dark. I pushed my bike, walking next to him as we crossed the main street and took a turning down a side road.

'We are having our carnival tomorrow, why don't you stay and join us. It is a very great day in Quibala, I think you will enjoy it very much.'

Yet again I was stymied by my confounded transit visa and I explained my predicament to him, but he looked a bit vague and I don't think he really understood what I was saying. He nodded absently and I felt strangely envious of his innocence, nostalgic for those teenage years when life is uncomplicated by pointless red tape and stupid rules. Well, he would find out all about it when the time came for him to visit England, but I kept quiet about this, feeling the need to protect him from the millstone of bureaucracy at his tender age.

'Here we are,' he said, stopping outside what was quite clearly a building site.

'Oh!' I said, looking at the half-constructed structure in front of me. It had steps leading into a hall but there was no back wall and the hall looked out on to a pile of rubble and pallets of breezeblocks. But leading off from the hall was a corridor with numbered rooms. Maybe this was going to be a hotel one day. Or maybe it had been and was damaged in the war, and was now being repaired.

'Um, what is this place?' I asked Ernesto.

'My father owns it,' was all he said, making no reference to the work in progress, and calmly led me to room number four, which was pitch black and smelt of wet plaster. 'Just one moment,' he said, disappearing down the corridor, returning a minute later holding a candle in a Wee Willie Winkie style holder.

'Here!' he said, holding it out to me and illuminating the room. I looked around in the flickering light and saw that the room was completely empty. Not a bed, not a mattress, not a chair, not a curtain, nothing.

'Ah! Er, great. This'll be just fine,' I assured him, and I meant what I said. I was happy to sleep anywhere that was dry.

'The bathroom is at the end of the hall,' said Ernesto.

That sounds promising, I thought, but I was very much mistaken. The bathroom only had three walls and there was no running water, just a loo, a bucket and a bath tub full of water. The method was self-explanatory so we didn't linger long in there.

As we made our way back from the bathroom, the door of room number three opened and a big stocky man covered in plaster dust stepped out, greeting Ernesto. A conversation in Portuguese followed and I realised that this was the resident builder and he was insisting in a most gentlemanly fashion that we swap rooms, his being lavishly equipped with not only a mattress, but an electric light too! I entered into a polite British refusal – 'No, really, no, no, I'll be fine, no really.' But the builder wasn't having any of it and began carting my bags into his room.

'I must return to the shop now,' said Ernesto. 'Will you need something from there, some food, water?'

'Yes, but I'll come by tomorrow,' I said, thanking him for his help, and he trotted off down the steps into the night.

It was only eight o'clock, but I collapsed on to the mattress and briefly considered the fact that on the face of it things looked decidedly dodgy, sleeping in a half-built hotel with a random builder in the next room and no locks on the doors. But I was too tired to worry very much and I soon drifted off to sleep. It wasn't long before I was roused from my slumber, but as it turned out, it wasn't the builder who was going to trouble me that night, but another occupant of the hotel. As well as boasting a mattress and a light bulb, room number two also had its very own resident bird living in the rafters, which flapped and squawked continually all night, almost drowning out the next-door neighbours whose carnival spirit had kicked in early and were blasting out music at such a volume that even my earplugs had to admit defeat. Thus I awoke the next morning, on the fourth day of my Angolan sprint, more shattered than ever before.

What with all this talk of carnivals, hotels being built and Ernesto's polite eloquence and Anglophilia, I had imagined Quibala to be some charming little town, a cultural stronghold among the mindless violence, an Angolan Hay-on-Wye maybe. The light of day shattered my bourgeois fantasy. It was a bombsite. Opposite my half-built hotel was a large, three-storey house that had had its entire front wall destroyed, leaving a cross-section of the building on display. This would not have been an uncommon sight but for the fact that the family had continued to live in it as if nothing untoward had occurred. Like an open doll's house, I could see the carpeted living room complete with chairs and a sofa, the stairs going down to the kitchen where a woman was busying herself with pots and pans, and a bedroom on the top floor housing several beds. It was business as usual.

At the grocery store I was met with a sad and hurt expression from Ernesto.

'I thought you were coming back here last night!' he cried. 'I waited and waited for you!'

'Oh no! I'm sorry! I said I would come back in the morning, not last night.'

It was just a case of crossed wires, but his face looked so let down that I felt awful and by way of recompense I bought an excess of supplies from his dad's shop, stuffing my panniers with tins of sardines, chickpeas and green beans.

Things were looking good for the day's ride. For a start, it wasn't raining, so I set off from Ernesto's store thankful for this small morale-boosting mercy. My late start yesterday had knocked me back and I now had just two days to cover 700 miles. My body ached from the incessant pummelling of riding on these dire roads, but I didn't care about that, just as long my bike was holding out, which much to my amazement, it was. It started on the button, and no matter what dramas unfolded and what punishment I foisted upon it, it just kept going. As for myself, I had learnt to expect very little now from each day and if it ended with the bike and me in one piece, I considered it to be successful. I wasn't really sure if I was exactly enjoying myself, I was merely existing, operating like a machine: ride, eat, sleep, ride, eat, sleep . . .

I made good progress in the morning along roads of bomb-damaged tarmac and half-decent dirt, and at lunchtime, arriving in the town of Huamba earlier than expected, I made the decision to press on without stopping. I had clocked an amazing 170 miles already today, and if I kept going at that progress, I was quietly confident that I would make it to the border in time. But my good fortune was not set to continue, and soon the heavy grey skies exploded in a furious storm. Thunder rumbled in the distance and jagged flashes of bluish-white lightning streaked across the sky. The storm coincided with the road entering a pine forest, which gave a degree of protection from the pouring rain, but the densely packed trees blocked out any sunlight and in the dank heart of the forest the ground had turned to a swamp, never having known the drying warmth of the sun's rays. The forest was ancient and dark, thick with the rich scent of pine, but the trail that led me through the woods was muddy beyond anything I had encountered, even in the Congo, and my progress slowed to a crawl as I battled my way along the churned-up track.

It was hard to believe that this barely navigable trail, which would probably constitute a remote bridleway in England, was the main route between two of Angola's major cities, a thick red line on the map. A few miles into the forest I happened upon three truck drivers whose valiant attempt to ply their trade along this road had been well and truly thwarted. One of the trucks, a ten-ton flatbed, had sunk up to its windscreen in a giant mud-filled bomb crater. A smaller pick-up was trying to pull him out, but to no avail, and the driver of the sinking truck was laying logs across the track to provide some much-needed traction for the pick-up. The third vehicle, an ex-army truck, had attempted an off-piste route through the trees and had come a cropper going down the steep bank, toppling over on its side and shedding its load, the result being the strangely striking, almost pop-art effect of thousands of cans of orange Fanta scattered all over the forest floor.

None of the truckers looked particularly disturbed by their predicament and one of them even offered me a can of the runaway Fanta. There was not much I could do to help, so after exchanging greetings I went to continue, but, with the track blocked by the trucks, I also had to take an off-piste route. There was a definite path, probably trodden over the years by locals on foot, wanting to avoid the bomb-hole, but to a motorcyclist it was more akin to a feet-up, observed trials section. Knowing that a cautious approach would spell disaster, I shot down the muddy bank, over a couple of logs, round a few trees, skidding and sliding around on a few cans of Fanta and back up the bank, feet up the whole way. The truck drivers paused from their own, very different, form of trials to give me a round of applause and I rode on, feeling quite pleased with my Sammy Miller moment.

But good spirits are dashed as easily as they are found in Angola, and soon I was out of the forest and back in the storm that was howling across the desolate plateau. The sky was black and the crashing thunder moved nearer and nearer with every clap. The rain was ceaseless, coming down in sheets, but the ground could no longer absorb it quickly enough and torrents of muddy water flowed past me while huge chunks of the dirt road were disintegrating before my eyes. Overhanging trees and thorn bushes dangled in my path, scratching my face and ripping my waterproofs, allowing yet more rain to soak me, quite literally, to the skin. I was out in wild, high, open country now, with not a glimmer of civilisation in sight; there were no signs of people living here – they had probably been forced out in the civil war's slashing and burning of the villages. I longed to see some sort of evidence of the human hand at work, just a hut or a farmhouse, a truck or a car. But the only signs of man's existence were grim and sinister, in the shape of rusting tanks at the side of the road and the crumbling concrete of improvised roadblocks.

Trying to avoid another flooded crater, I hugged the side of the track, sticking to a gulley, but my front wheel hit a submerged log, the bike jolted and before I could correct the steering it toppled over to the left, taking me with it and trapping my left foot between the crankcase and a rock. The pain sent shockwaves through my leg as I felt the bone-crunching impact of the rock and my ankle being wrenched and twisted as I struggled to free myself. Summoning up some adrenalin-fuelled superhuman strength, I pushed my body-weight against the bike, forcing it upright again. Swinging my right leg over the saddle, I restarted the bike and continued onwards through the mud and rain without a pause. I had reached some weird state of mindless, almost hypnotic doggedness, and I realised with shock that my customary, very vocal, response to such an incident had not been forthcoming. I hadn't howled, screamed or even whimpered in pain when my foot had been crushed; in fact, not a single word had passed my lips, not even a swearword. If I had given up complaining and swearing, things were really bad.

In cruel, glaring contrast to my successful morning, it was now half-past four and I had managed just sixty miles since lunchtime.

Sod this! I thought bitterly. Why didn't I just stay in Huamba at lunchtime, and sod the transit visa? Why don't I just accept that I'll get roughed up at the border for overstaying, pay the bribe, and have done with it? Whatever happens, it can't be as bad as this.

But even if I did decide to take my own advice, it still didn't answer the pressing question of what I was going to do right now, and where I was going to stay tonight. I looked at the map and saw that the town of Caconda was coming up in about forty miles. It would take me at least two hours to get there, I would be riding in the dark yet again and I didn't know what I would find, but it was bound to have somewhere I could shelter for the night, even if it was a bombed-out house.

The rain continued its endless hammering, the thunderclaps moved ever nearer in terrifying crescendos, and the lightning ripped across the darkening sky. It was a storm of biblical proportions, and I wondered briefly if it was my punishment for lying about being a Roman Catholic, or maybe for my greater sin of being an atheist in this religion-addled continent. Troubled by such ridiculous notions, I figured I might be losing my mind, and I forced myself to think solid, rational thoughts. I shall triumph through reason and logic! I declared, which was quite handy, as immediately after I had made this statement I came upon a fork in the road which wasn't marked on the map, and with nothing remotely like a road sign to aid the traveller, clear rational thinking was my only hope.

The left fork showed the broken remains of the tarmac leading off into some woods, while the right fork was a most unappealing option; here was the *inundacão repentina* that the border guard had warned me about. It was a rock-strewn, muddy track, but was currently under a foot of fast-flowing water; the heavy rain had turned it into a treacherous river and I hoped, and almost prayed, that this was not the route to Caconda. I dillied and I dallied, and I looked at the map, and the compass, and tried to orientate myself in the dim light and the pouring rain. There were faint tyre-marks in the mud leading to the right fork, but then again, the scraps of old tarmac on the left fork suggested the course of the original road. On the other hand it did look quite overgrown, almost abandoned. What to do? If only there was someone around to ask.

But there was no one and there were no solid clues to help me either. Then, as I stared at the left-hand fork I noticed, among the bushes, that this route was lined with concrete posts about a foot high; they were painted red and white and looked quite official. This must be it, I decided, and secretly thankful to not be riding up the torrential river, I headed off down the old road, following the line of the posts, bumping over the smashed-up blacktop and slaloming around the bigger potholes.

I don't why, but after about 500 yards I had a sensation that something wasn't quite right. I'm not sure what caused me to stop and question my decision, but it was no more than a feeling, some kind of intuition, and nothing whatsoever to do with the reason and logic in which I trusted so deeply for my survival and sanity. Whatever this force was, it persuaded me to go back to the junction and think again. I swung a wide U-turn through the bushes around one of the posts and as I did so, my headlight caught the white painted concrete, illuminating a patch of faded red lettering. I stopped and peered closer and as I read the words my heart froze. Weathered by Angolan rain and sun, it was only just legible, but it told me everything I needed to know. Underneath a crude motif of a skull and crossbones were the words that shook me to the core: *PERIGO MINAS*. But just in case you hadn't got the picture, in small letters there was an English translation too. It said: Danger Mines.

A deafening roar of thunder and an almost simultaneous flash of lightning exploded above me and the rain lashed down harder than ever. I was in the thick of the storm, sitting in the middle of a minefield. What were the chances of that? And what a choice! Struck by lightning or blown apart by a landmine? Or possibly both. At the same time even!

I sat there on the bike, trying to control my thumping heart. All the bad roads, the hard riding, the tumbles in the mud: they all paled into insignificance. Now I really had a situation on my hands. I had ridden 500 yards into a minefield and now I had to ride back out again. The only way to do this was to follow my tyre tracks exactly, but they were dissolving before my very eyes; the rain was washing them away as quickly as I made them. As I rode back the way I had come I felt a strange sense of calm envelop me, as if my fate was out of my hands and I was high above, looking down on my filthy, bedraggled self, pottering through an Angolan minefield in the pouring rain. None of it seemed real.

It wasn't until I reached the junction in one piece that my true state of distress surfaced. Some survival mechanism had aided me through the minefield but now, faced with the far less dangerous task of riding up the river, my peculiarly eerie calm disintegrated and entered some kind of delayed shock. I heard myself calling out, 'Help! Somebody help!' Of course there was no one to hear my plea, and I knew this, but just shouting it seemed to make me feel better and I set forth into the water. But my judgement was failing me and my riding was suffering; it wasn't that the river with its rocks and mud was technically beyond me; I'd ridden worse things in Wales – for fun! But the success of riding up this river lay in picking the right line, and my exhausted, traumatised-verging-on-hysterical brain was no longer functioning properly; stupid mistake followed stupid mistake.

Within a few yards I had ground to a halt with the bike rocking to and fro like a seesaw, marooned where the bottom of the engine had become stuck on a submerged rock. Neither of the wheels was touching the ground and my only option was to climb off into the water and heave the bike backwards off the rock. Perched in this awkward position, the handlebars were level with my shoulders, and with the centre of gravity so high, I could hardly move the bike at all. I certainly didn't feel confident to keep it upright should it start to fall. Dusk was upon me now and the fading light magnified every problem 1,000 times. I was close to tears of sheer desperation now, but adrenalin kicked in and with a massive wrench I hauled the bike off the rock and back into the knee-deep water.

Slumped over the handlebars in utter despair, catching my breath and trying not to think about what I was going to do next, I heard a new noise. Not the noise of the hammering rain or the thunder, or the rushing river. It was a mechanical noise, the gentle splutter of a two-stroke motorcycle engine. I must be imagining things, I thought, but when I turned round, either I was hallucinating or there was a smiley young man wearing fake Gucci sunglasses and spankingly clean white trainers, sitting astride a little two-stroke bike at the junction and watching me with an amused expression.

I was overcome with joy to see this stranger, but I was so distraught that I didn't even greet him, I just started waving my arms around and pointing up the river.

'*Caconda? Caconda? Aqui? Caconda, sim?*' I cried, seeking confirmation of what I already knew.

He nodded calmly, confirming my desperate pointing and hand-waving, that indeed, this torrent of water was the road to Caconda. Then he rode over to me and stopped, still smiling his gently amused smile and still wearing his sunglasses, despite the fact that it was almost dark.

'You are from England?' he said.

'Yes.'

'Aah . . .' He nodded his head knowingly. 'You ride to Cape Town from England, yes?'

'Er, well, actually . . . yes. Yes, I am,' I said, surprised that he had sussed me out so quickly.

He shook his head and smiled in amused pity, as if to say, you crazy white people, you do this for fun, and we have to live like this, day in day out. I felt properly foolish. Then he laughed and patted me on the arm.

'Come on! Follow me!' he called out over his shoulder as he plunged into the flood water.

I couldn't believe it. How many guardian angels did I have in Angola? Or were they all the same one, cropping up in different guises when I needed them most? That was how it seemed to me. This latest one knew all the nifty shortcuts to avoid the rocks and the muddy bits and the deep bits, and when there was no option but to ride through the water, he lifted his feet off the foot-pegs to save his spotless trainers. His bike was a tatty old Yamaha 125; it had worn-out road tyres and his rear wheel-bearings were shot to bits, but he nipped along the river with ease, and I felt suitably humbled as I followed along in his wake. At a track junction he peeled off with a wave, instructing me to carry on straight ahead for Caconda. I was sad to see him go. He rode off into a beautiful sunset strewn across the sky, and I suddenly realised that the rain had stopped, the clouds were clearing and the sky had turned orangey-pink. Once again, I was exhausted, wet, filthy and riding in the dark, but this time, something told me that the worse was over.

Caconda proffered a room in a bar and a meal of rice, chips and salad, complete with my ratty bike sitting next to me at the table, having been lugged up the steps by a couple of eager boys. The Bar Centrale was the only building in town radiating any light, and I gravitated towards the soft glow that illuminated its weatherbeaten sign on this wet, black night. It was presided over by a group of youngsters who didn't look old enough to be allowed inside such an establishment, let alone be running it, but they were certainly enjoying having a go. We spoke very little of each other's language but they happily gooned around in front of my camera after dinner, posing beside my bike and performing stunts on their bicycles in the dining room. After the grind of the last few days it was a delight to indulge in that most joyful of activities: mucking about.

The morning brought the more necessary pursuits of patching up my various clothes and belongings that were beginning to show the wear and tear of four days of Angolan motorcycling. I sat out on the steps of the bar, attracting a group of black-clad, elderly women, who stood in silence at a respectful distance, watching as I patched up my torn water-proofs with gaffer tape and attempted to glue the sole back on my right boot where its state of permanent saturation had rotted away most of the stitching. Finally I checked over the bike, relieved to find it was still going strong, though a few symptoms of weariness were beginning to show. The speedo cable had snapped, the back light was out and the handlebar clamp bolts had worked themselves loose. Nothing major, in fact impressively minor, considering what I had put it through, but I saw it as a warning, and as I checked over every nut and bolt before setting off on the fifth and final day of my visa, I found myself cutting a deal with the bike: 'Just get me to the Namibian border and I'll be really nice to you, I promise, I'll change your oil and clean your filters and do anything, I'll even wash you!' This was all uttered in silence, as I suspected the gaggle of elderly ladies found me weird enough, without me talking to my motorcycle.

I had a whopping day ahead of me if I was to make it to the border by the end of play, but I was determined to do it. In a stupidly masochistic way, I had almost come to relish the challenge of the five-day Angola dash. I knew this was quite silly, but it was a survival mechanism: I had decided to view something that was basically unpleasant as a test of endurance, of both woman and machine, with the ultimate idea being the sense of achievement by the end of it, even if I had almost killed myself in the process. But in truth, what I really wanted to do was to stay here for ages, to explore the country at my leisure and mingle with the Angolan people, who had touched my heart like no other. I would come back one day, when Angola's Big Men woke up and recognised the immense economic power that a few tourist visas could bring. But would that spoil it, I wondered? I didn't want to be one of those snooty traveller types who trot around the world complaining that tourism has ruined everything, too smug and self-absorbed to realise that they are in fact, talking about themselves. Could it be that Angola's charm lay in the fact that the safaris and the backpackers and the gap-year goody-goodies had not yet carved a path through this land? And if so, did it mean that by coming here I was part of Angola's solution, or the beginning of a new problem? I wasn't sure, but I did know that I would be back, one day.

The rain returned to see me on my way, but over the course of the morning the sky changed from black to grey and eventually to a heavenly pale blue. The mud dried out into hard red crusts and the earth became dry and sandy; the trees and grass turned yellow and sparse, and for the first time in days I felt the sun on my face, and my boots and socks began to dry out. Here was the proof that my trials were nearly over; I was heading towards dry, dusty Namibia with its red sand dunes and empty desert plains. In the wonderful way that the Equator works as the earth's geographical mirror, I was seeing the real-time reflection of my northern hemisphere journey as I moved further south, and there was something satisfying about this unshakeable neatness and symmetry on this most chaotic of continents. Here, in my last few hundred miles in Angola, I was as far south of the Equator as Agadez is north, where I had watched the land turn greener as I left the Sahara behind. In a few weeks I would be in Cape Town, Africa's very own Mediterranean-style melting-pot, the perfect mirror image of Marseille, from where, all those months ago, armed with a generous helping of *bonne chance*, I had made that giant leap into Africa. My good luck had served me well and I hoped there was enough left to last me the final 1,000 miles of my journey.

I could hardly allow myself to think that I would make it to the Namibian border, but subconsciously the idea that the end might be in sight was driving me on and I rode as fast as I dared, wincing as my bike slammed in and out of the endless potholes, but hardly caring any more. I was demob end-of-term happy, and despite the fact that every muscle in my body was crying out for rest I rode without stopping until lunch-time, where a small town brought the sweetest reward in the shape of a *pasteleria*, a Portuguese style cake shop stuffed with temptation: sticky custard tarts, cream cakes and all sorts of mouth-watering pastries that I didn't recognise piled up into towering, calorific pyramids in the window. You could almost forgive the Portuguese for dumping the Angolans if this was their legacy. I replaced five days of lost blood sugar in five minutes and continued onwards in fine spirits.

By mid-afternoon, my sugar rush had worn off and, knowing that the end was in sight, I became overwhelmed with such deep exhaustion that it was only the endless jolting that kept me from falling asleep. When the road finally fizzled out at the Namibian frontier, I could hardly believe it was happening. Like weary desert travellers see mirages of oases and palm trees, I wondered in my dreamlike state if this border post was my imagination playing tricks on me. But no, it was all breeze-blocks, barriers and barbed wire – the very real stuff of African border crossings. The various offices were in a fenced-off compound, and before I rode inside I used up the last of my *kwanzas* buying a bunch of bananas from a group of women sitting on the ground, selling fruit and vegetables outside the gate. When I climbed off the bike my legs almost buckled beneath me, but I just managed to croak out a weary greeting in Portuguese as I handed over my last couple of notes. I stuffed the bananas in my top box and went to push the bike through the gate. I was already thinking about the tedious tide of bureaucracy that was about to engulf me, and I was only vaguely aware of the high-pitched screeching behind me.

'Amiga! Amiga!' came the voices, but I continued on towards the immigration building, distracted by thoughts of red tape.

'Amiga! Amiga!' It kept on coming, a chorus of women's voices, but I took no notice until I felt a bony hand on my shoulder.

I turned round to see the women who had sold me my bananas, waving money at me and gabbling in Portuguese. I assumed I had underpaid them so I scrabbled around in my

384

pocket for any extra coins or notes, but their waving and screeching intensified.

'*Não!*' They laughed, shaking their heads. '*Não!*' And one of them crouched down on the ground and drew numbers in the dust with a stick.

When she stood up and shoved a handful of notes and coins in my hand, I suddenly realised what they were trying to tell me. Addled with tiredness and baffled once again by foreign currency, I had overpaid for my bananas. Instead of giving them the equivalent of a pound, I had given them a tenner. And they had chased after me to point out my mistake and give me my change. These kind-hearted, honest women were my final, lasting memory of Angola, and their screeching chorus of '*Amiga!*' was its most fitting swansong.

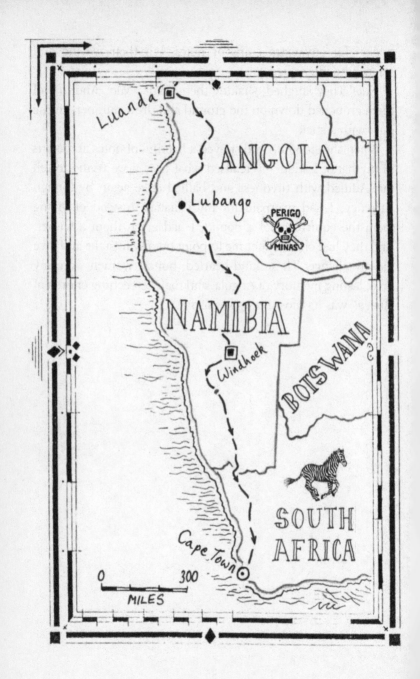

NINETEEN

I staggered through the exit formalities on my last legs and headed across the compound towards the Namibian immigration office. I was so worn out now that I was practically hallucinating, and when I shut my eyes I could still see the road moving towards me, as the vibrations of five days' non-stop dirt-riding continued to rumble through my body, even after I had climbed off the bike. I perked up a bit with the realisation that all communication from now on would be spoken and written in English, but my good mood wavered when I read the sign on the door: Namibian Immigration Department – Open 7 a.m. to 6 p.m. Oh no! I hadn't even considered the idea that they might be shut, that it wasn't a twenty-four-hour border post. When I looked at my watch I used up my last crumb of energy on a whoop of joy. It was eight minutes to six. I had done it! From the top of Angola to the bottom, over 1,200 miles on the worst roads I have ever ridden, in five days! I had really done it!

The Namibian office was neat and tidy and manned by two uniformed officers, a cross-eyed man and a woman with unfeasibly large breasts that she supported by resting them on the counter.

'You have come from Angola? On a motorcycle?' said the man, one eye on my paperwork, the other somewhere on the wall next to him.

I confirmed this to be the case, feeling quite triumphant and secretly hoping he was going to congratulate me on my epic achievement, but it was not to be.

'Motorcycles are very dangerous, no? Why do you not drive a car?' he said. 'Much more comfortable too. But maybe you can not afford a car? It is more money, yes?'

I really couldn't be bothered with the way this conversation was going, so I just said, 'Mmmm,' and nodded vacantly, wanting nothing more than to curl up in the corner of the office and wake up tomorrow. But he obviously wanted to chat.

'Lots of rain, very bad floods,' he said. 'Not very nice on a motorcycle.'

'Mmm, very bad, not very nice,' I agreed.

'Very wet, yes, you must be very wet?'

'Mmm, very wet.'

'It is the worst flooding Angola has seen in twenty years, many people have died,' contributed the woman, turning towards her colleague and sending my paperwork fluttering to the floor with a sweep of her gargantuan bosom.

Once he had used up all his negative comments about motorcycling, a computerised, thoroughly twenty-first-century border crossing followed and I was back on the bike within minutes, spurred on by the sight of a shiny new world beyond the chain-link fence. I could see a strip of glossy black tarmac with road markings and street lights; it was lined with shops and hotels and petrol stations, and there were some road signs with town names and distances: all the hallmarks of civilisation that in my curious state of mind seemed to belong to another, long-forgotten existence. I rode away from the gate in a daze of weary relief, and wondered why there was a line of cars and trucks driving straight towards me. My last remaining scrap of survival instinct kicked into action, and I realised, as I swerved across the road – they drive on the left in Namibia! Why hadn't Boss-Eyes and Big-Tits thought to impart this useful nugget of information to me? The next shock to my befuddled brain was performing a rubber-burning, brake-squealing emergency stop at a red light. I couldn't remember the last time I had seen a set of traffic lights.

Dazed and more than slightly confused, I pulled in at a petrol station to get a grip on myself before I was killed by yet another unexpected facet of modern civilisation. I discovered with delight that the petrol station had a shop attached to it, as well as a cashpoint and public toilets too. No more hovering in the mud for me! Inside, the shop sold not only everything I needed, but also loads of stuff I didn't. There was an entire fridge of smoothies, a revolving display of sunglasses, a bewildering selection of biscuits, crisps, sweets and chocolate, and even *Heat* magazine. A looped tape was playing over the PA, advertising things I had never heard of in a South African accent. I wandered around this consumers' utopia like a recently released prisoner, just picking things up and looking at them, and flicking through lifestyle magazines, discovering, after months in the wilderness, what was currently Hot! and what was Not!

After about twenty minutes the man behind the counter approached me and enquired, in a not particularly gentle fashion, if I needed any help; his tone of voice suggested he meant of the psychiatric variety, rather than with my retail therapy. I stared at him for a second, a little taken aback; I hadn't seen a fair-skinned, blue-eyed blond man for some time, and I guessed he must be of Germanic descent, from when Namibia was a German colony in the late 1800s. As I waffled my excuses about having arrived from Angola and being in a severe, but essentially pleasurable, state of culture shock, I caught sight of myself in the mirror on the revolving sunglasses display as it came past me, and understood why he was slightly chary. My face was plastered in mud and there was a smudge of dried blood where a thorn tree had scratched my cheek this morning. I had removed my crash helmet before entering the shop in a bid to look less intimidating, but it had not had the desired effect. My hair, caked with sweat and more mud, was sticking out at all angles in big clumps like a poorly executed attempt at dreadlocks.

'OK, just checking,' said the man, returning to the counter while keeping a suspicious eye on me.

Outside it was getting dark and I decided to find somewhere nearby to stay the night where I could spend the evening doing something to improve my pitiful appearance. But no sooner had I got going, still marvelling at the traffic lights, road signs and street markings, than I was stopped at a military checkpoint, a timely reminder that I was still in Africa. The big burly black chief studied my papers at length but remained thoroughly confused by my presence. He reminded me of the immigration officer at the Nigerian border and even of Roger at the embassy in Kinshasa; like them, he simply couldn't understand what on earth I was doing here.

'You are from where? From England?' he said, peering at my passport under a searchlight. He had mean eyes and spoke irritably, as if I had been sent specifically to annoy him. 'But how, but what . . . but why are you here?'

I was so tired, and not just physically. I was tired of this conversation; as I opened my mouth I felt as though I had answered these questions a hundred times.

'Um, well, y'know, riding across Africa and all that.' It was all I could manage.

'But, but . . . why?'

Oh no, please! This was verging on an existential question that I was definitely too weary to answer, or even think about at this point.

'Well, I . . . er . . .'

A crowd of his cronies had gathered now, and were staring at me as if I was an animal in a zoo. To be fair, I probably smelled like one.

'But, I mean, how did you get here?' continued the officer, still utterly befuddled.

'On my bike.'

'No, no, but how? I mean, um . . .' He shook his head, totally puzzled. He didn't even know what it was he wanted to know.

'Well, first I took a ferry from England to France,' I began, in a *Listen with Mother* voice, 'then I took another ferry to Tunisia, then I rode into Algeria, then Niger, then Nigeria . . .'

'Yes, yes, yes,' cut in one of his more savvy underlings, already bored with my story. 'She's just a tourist,' he explained to his boss.

But the chief was still shaking his head, squinting at my driving licence and passport.

'But, you are with an organisation, yes?'

'No, it's just me'

'Ah! You are in a competition, a rally?'

'No, I'm just riding my bike, um . . . for fun.'

This was possibly stretching the description of the last few weeks, but never mind.

Meanwhile, two female officers were nudging each other, giggling, and pointing at the sole of my right boot, which had almost come off again and was hanging on by a couple of threads of glue. They spotted the gaffer tape repairs to my waterproof jacket and sniggered some more. The chief handed my documents back to me and stood there shaking his head, looking baffled and extremely irritated, while his colleagues continued to stare at me in sullen silence. After a couple of minutes the chief made a dismissive gesture with his hand, which I took to mean, 'Welcome to Namibia! I wish you a wonderful journey through our beautiful country, and I trust you will enjoy the famous Namibian hospitality,' and they all plodded back to their tin hut.

Feeling like I deserved some comfort, I treated myself to a night in what looked like a pretty decent hotel, one of many advertised by the side of the road. It ticked all the boxes: hot running water, a bath and shower, cable TV, a phone in each room, buffet breakfast the next morning, even a swimming pool. The place was spotless, decorated in a suitably trendy ethnic style which said, 'This is the new face of Africa.' But behind the tribal masks, the zebra-skin furnishings and the eco-waffle lay the dreaded rules and regulations, or 'rigulations' as the Afrikaans woman on the desk called them when she handed me the sheet of laminated A4, listing all the things I wasn't allowed to do during my incarceration.

I must not steal the towels or the dressing gowns; I must leave by ten the next morning, otherwise the 'late check-out surcharge' would be incurred; breakfast must be finished by nine a.m. (nine a.m.! Surely, this was a breach of my human rights); I must be in possession of a valid car park ticket or my vehicle would be clamped; and so it went on. By the time I had read this pathetic list I was so depressed that I wanted to leave, but it was too late; she already had my credit card and according to Rule No. 4 cancelling without twenty-four hours notice incurred the 'late cancellation penalty'. God knows how much a cancellation of less than five minutes would cost me.

'I've parked my bike out the front,' I said to the receptionist. 'Is that all right?'

It was locked up outside the main entrance next to a sign that said 'GEEN LEEGLEERS RYLOPERS EN BEDELAARS WORD OP DIE RYBAAN TOEGELAAT NIE.'

The English translation was printed below: 'NO LOAFERS, HITCHHIKERS AND BEGGARS ARE ALLOWED ON THE DRIVEWAY.'

'No!' said the woman. 'You must park it in the parking area. You must get a ticket from the attendant.'

'Oh, OK, I'll just dump my bags and then I'll move it.'

'You had better do it now, otherwise it may be clamped.' She said the last word as 'climped'.

With the fear of the dreaded wheel climp hanging over me, I pushed the bike round the back of the building and entered into the spectacularly longwinded process of securing a car park ticket.

'You should take all of your belongings in with you,' said the parking attendant as I unpacked just my essentials. 'You don't want them to get stolen.'

The thieves, the wheel climping, the surcharges – this was a pretty scary place, and it seemed the dangers continued inside. As I walked to my room, laden with every single piece of my luggage, I passed the swanky indoor swimming pool, set in the centre of the hotel in a glass dome. Through the glass I could see the inviting sight of the turquoise water, surrounded by exotic plants in big earthenware pots, but the pool was empty; not a single guest was to be seen splashing about or even relaxing on the wooden sun-loungers. The explanation for this came by way of a sign on the door to the pool which read: 'NO SWIMMING'.

Despite all this petty bureaucracy, the novelty of my reverse culture shock was enough to keep me cheerful, and for the next few days I revelled in Namibia's comforts. Life was ordered and efficient again, I didn't feel my stomach tightening at the sight of a policeman, and the roads were so smooth I could have kissed the tarmac every morning. As my aching limbs slowly recovered, I swore to myself that I would never again stray from the blacktop on this journey. Namibia's towns were Germanic in style: neat, clean and organised, complete with street names and house numbers. There were supermarkets which sold everything my heart and stomach desired, and even banks that let you in to change money. But after the anarchic world of Central Africa I struggled with the sudden plethora of rules and regulations. I had crossed an international border and now there were parking restrictions, no-entry signs, fences and gates, and signs that shouted 'PRIVATE PROPERTY' and 'KEEP OUT'.

Namibia was a huge nation with a tiny population, and it

was strange to be back in so much emptiness after the over-populated, hemmed-in countries of the jungle. Here I could ride for 100 miles without seeing another vehicle. The endless straight roads and the dry, rocky landscape beneath a vast sky gave the sensation of an American road trip. But just when I was thinking this could be Arizona, I would be reminded of exactly which continent I was in by the sight of a zebra galloping along beside me, or a family of baboons lolloping across the road. It wasn't only the wildlife that jogged my memory: on the outskirts of the towns there were still the shacks of corrugated iron and the squat, breezeblock huts, the architecture of Africa, clustered around one of the ubiquitous bottle stores, where a couple of old black guys would invariably be sitting outside in the shade, sipping from a paper bag.

For me, life was easy again. The sun shone every day and I flew along through this huge empty country unhindered. But after the full-throttle, high-octane, sheer intensity of riding through the Congo and Angola, I was overcome with a profound sense of anticlimax. There was no challenge, no excitement, no adventure for me here. In my quest to spice things up a bit I sought out the dirt roads and the desert tracks, forgetting all about my pledge to never leave the blacktop, but even this failed to ignite a spark in me; and with more time for thinking, rather than merely surviving, I pined sorely for Austin and home, and, most strangely of all, for Angola, or more accurately, for its spirit.

A couple of days later, on the outskirts of the capital, Windhoek, my journey was pleasantly hijacked by two women who unbeknownst to them did a fine job of snapping me out of this curious mood of mine. They had found me by the side of the road, checking my map on the way to the famous red sand dunes of Sossusvlei. Spotting my British number plate, they had pulled over in their hire car, just to say hello.

Val and Liz were in their early sixties, two trim, grey-haired retired teachers from East Sussex, and they were having the time of their lives. After reading an article about Namibia in a Sunday newspaper, Val had phoned Liz immediately and told her they were going on holiday to Africa.

'We'd been wanting to do something exciting ever since we went to Iceland last year,' Liz explained.

'The country, not the supermarket!' said Val, and they both shrieked with laughter.

Val had then phoned one of her grown-up sons and instructed him to get online and book them on a flight to Windhoek without further ado. 'I don't know how to do all that internet stuff!' she explained with a dismissive wave of her hand and another bark of laughter.

After we'd exchanged our stories and realised that we were heading in the same direction, they suggested we travel together. There was something warm and fun about these two women who were old enough to be my mother, and I was more than happy to tag along.

'This looks like the most scenic route,' said Liz, pointing at their map.

'I think some of it's on dirt tracks though,' I said, unsure if their hired Nissan Micra would be up to the job. 'D'you think the car will be all right?'

'Oh, don't worry about that!' Val shouted out of the driver's window. 'It's not our car anyway! If we get stuck we'll just leave it there and hitch a lift with you!' And the two of them howled with laughter again.

This is more like it, I thought, already feeling their carefree high spirits chipping away at my jaundiced state of mind, and we set off on the four-hour journey to Sossusvlei. Val and Liz refreshed my road-weary eyes and ears with their enthusiasm, which verged on childlike wonder. They stopped the car repeatedly to take in the view or watch the wildlife, and gasped with excitement at the sight of a bird of prey or a baboon in a tree. Val scrambled up rocks and took photos of plants while Liz jotted down notes in her travelogue.

'You don't know how lucky you are, Lois . . .' said Liz, when I commented on how much they were enjoying themselves. We had stopped at the side of the road and she was making a thermos of Twining's Earl Grey. 'What are you, thirty? Thirty-two?'

'Thirty-three.'

'Yes, exactly, when I was your age I had three children to look after, Val had two, and we both had full-time jobs. I was a teacher, Val was a nurse then. And we both had a couple of useless husbands, long gone, thank God! You see, there was no way we could have been gallivanting around Africa or anywhere else. We've had to wait until now for our adventures. The kids have left home and we're going to live it up!'

'Too bloody right!' agreed Val, clambering down a rocky slope for her cup of tea.

'So what happened to your husbands?' I asked, intrigued, and because I didn't think they'd mind me sticking my nose in. I was right, Val warmed to the subject immediately.

'Oh, poor old Andrew, we were watching the telly, would've been nineteen-eighty, eighty-one? I can't remember – anyway, Greenham Common was on the news, and I said to him, "I think I'd like to go there, just for a weekend." He said, "Don't

397

be so bloody stupid." I said, "I'm bloody serious," and he said, "If you go to Greenham Common don't expect me to be here when you get back," so . . .'

'So, she went,' said Liz, continuing what I guessed was a now legendary tale in their double act. 'And she stayed for two years!'

'And what happened to Andrew?'

'Oh, he was still there, two years later, waiting for his shirts to be ironed!' shrieked Val, almost crying with laughter and spilling most of her tea in the process. 'Only joking, only joking,' she said. 'He buggered off, I took the kids to Greenham. He lives in Colchester now.'

'He's a proper Essex boy!' said Liz in the appropriate accent and the two women cackled hysterically, scaring off a nearby baboon that was sniffing around for scraps of food.

'And what about your husband?' I asked Liz when she had regained her composure.

'Oh, nothing half as interesting. I stuck it out for longer than Val, that was what you did in those days, you got married for life. But when all the kids had gone to university I just couldn't stand it. He was so . . . so boring!'

'I hope you do better at it than us,' said Val, tapping my wedding ring with her teaspoon. I was thinking exactly the same thing.

We continued at our gentle pace through the rocky, almost lunar plains of western Namibia, reaching Sossusvlei by early afternoon. It was unbearably hot and we sought out the only refuge along the way, a café seemingly plonked in the middle of nowhere and presided over by an enormous man with a long grey beard who called himself Mr Muggsy. He had the desperate jollity and forced eccentricity of someone who has devoted their life to inventing themselves as that most tragic of roles, the 'local character.'

'Ah! Welcome, lovely ladies, roll up, roll up! What can I do for you this fine day?'

He was wearing a striped butcher's apron covered in stains.

'No doubt you have come to sample Mr Muggsy's Famous Chocolate Cake!' He said the last three words in the style of a ringmaster introducing a circus act.

I groaned inwardly at his reference to himself in the third person, a sure sign of the self-appointed celebrity.

'Yes indeedy! They come from and far and wide for Mr Muggsy's Famous Chocolate Cake, just take a look at the book!'

On the counter was a visitors' book, full of gushing praise and excitable eulogies to the legendary cake. I wondered how much of it he had written himself, but on closer inspection it did seem worryingly genuine, although it was mostly the work of Australian backpackers with girlish handwriting and lots of exclamation marks.

'Hey Mr Muggsy! Your cake is wicked!!! Luv Haley and Jo from Melbourne. XXX.'

'Your choc cake rocks, dude!!! Nikki and Rob from Sydney.'

And, more disconcertingly: 'I can't believe I am here at last! I have heard so much about your famous chocolate cake and I have wanted to taste it for so long! I can't believe I am actually here, eating it at last! It is even better than I ever imagined! This is the greatest day of my life!!! Leo from Lithuania.'

This one had a distinctly bogus air about it and I suspected that the mysterious Leo was in fact Mr Muggsy's Eastern European alter ego.

Val hadn't said a word since we had arrived and was busy

studying the stuffed zebra head mounted on the wall, so it was left up to Liz and me to make polite conversation with Mr Muggsy. Over the next twenty minutes we got the full details of his disastrously short marriage (unsurprising), his stint in the army (unlikely), the list of books in which he is mentioned (two), his appearances on television (one), and the steady stream of fans that come from all over the world to taste his chocolate cake (millions). As is the wont of the local character, he talked about himself almost exclusively, and when he did ask a few questions of Liz and me he didn't bother listening to the answers.

There was no way we were going to get away without tasting the confounded cake, and I considered refusing on principle, although I wasn't quite sure exactly what principle I would be upholding – buying desserts from self-obsessed, crashing bores? In the end we shelled out for a slice each and I was annoyed to discover that it was indeed, extremely tasty. As if this wasn't bad enough, we were then pressganged into contributing to the visitors' book. Thankfully another couple of customers arrived at this moment and, seeing the opportunity to escape, the three of us uttered our hasty farewells and hurried back to our vehicles.

'Jesus! What a prick,' said Val, as she climbed into the car.

We headed for the dunes and there was no denying the beauty of the stunning red Namib desert, but I as far as I was concerned, it had been ruined. There was a visitors' centre and a car park, where you had to buy a ticket to continue through a gate and along a road where signs instructed you not to stray from the tarmac into the desert, and a ranger who drove up and down the road, making sure that nobody was disobeying the rules. The final insult was the expensive campsite, which had to be booked in advance. This wasn't how I wanted my desert! It was utterly bogus, and I remembered the boundless wilderness of the Sahara, the feeling that you could die out there. You couldn't possibly die here, even if you wanted to; some busybody would turn up sooner or later and ask if you had a ticket. No, I had to admit it, Namibia wasn't the place for me.

I left Val and Liz the following morning with not just my energies and enthusiasm renewed, but also a brand new spring in my step. I had borrowed Val's mobile phone the previous evening to call Austin, who had broken the best news I could have hoped for: he would be coming out to meet me in South Africa. I emitted a high-volume squeal of delight, and was so excited that I could barely sleep that night, much to the amusement of my more cynical companions.

Cape Town was beckoning like never before, and I felt the need to finish what I had started. I refolded my map of Africa for the last time, revealing the final few hundred miles of my journey, and there it was, in big bold type, staring out at me from the tip of the continent, the city that marked not only the end of my journey, but now my reunion with Austin too. Since leaving home I had barely allowed myself to think about arriving in Cape Town – it had seemed so far away and, at times, an almost unachievable goal. Now, it was literally down the road, just a few days' ride away.

A couple of days later I crossed the Orange River, which forms the frontier between Namibia and South Africa, and followed the signs and the numbered instructions that led me through the official entry procedure with almost military efficiency. How different from all those other border crossings, I thought, remembering the sinister intimidation of Kinshasa,

401

the riotous stampede into Cameroon and the laidback, whisky-soaked entry into Gabon. The white South African men who stamped my passport and checked my papers seemed happy to live up to their national stereotype, cracking unfunny jokes about the stupidity of women and making boorish allusions as to whether or not I was a real redhead. I briefly wondered what Val would have said to put them in their place, but I couldn't be bothered to rise to the bait, so excited was I by the fact that I had crossed my final African border. This was it! I was in South Africa.

Like southern Namibia, the land here was spectacular but harsh, its rocky hills baked by the fierce sun and only occasionally punctuated with small scrubby bushes. The road wound on forever through this emptiness until I reached the town of Springbok, which was like arriving in 1950s England. It gave me the creeps. Everyone looked old, even the young people. Women wore twinsets and brooches without irony, everything closed at five o'clock and the white Afrikaners spoke in shamelessly racist terms about the 'blacks' and the 'coloureds'. Despite apartheid having officially ended ten years ago, there was still a sense of discomfort hanging in the air; it reminded me of being in the company of a married couple who have recently argued but not yet made up and are still seething with resentment and unspoken anger.

I was heading due south for Cape Town, and if all went to plan I would arrive a couple of days before Austin, leaving me some much needed time to sort out my ragged appearance. But before I settled down to a session with the eyebrow tweezers and the toenail varnish there was one last thing I had to do. I was purposely avoiding entering the city itself until I had made it to the Cape of Good Hope, the south-western tip of the continent, where the Indian Ocean meets the Atlantic. Only then would I feel that I had truly ridden the length of Africa.

Long overland journeys invariably end on some sticky-out bit of land somewhere, often a far-flung outpost that has become a tourist destination merely due to its extreme location. As I approached Cape Town, I ignored signs for the city centre and skirted round to the east, heading for the southern coastal road that would take me to the tip. As the ocean came into view I recalled my arrival at the tip of South America almost three years ago to the day, remembering how I had gazed out at the cold sea, knowing that Antarctica was just a stone's throw away, and marvelling that I had ridden all the way from Alaska. Soon I would be standing on another sticky-out bit of land, once again staring out to sea, with the entire African continent behind me. Although my journey through Africa had been just half the time and distance of my ride through the Americas, it had been ten times as tough, and I felt truly grateful to be here.

It was a suitably glorious day for such a momentous occasion, the sun hot and high in a cloudless sky as I headed along the coast road, itself a dream ride, passing through impossibly quaint fishing ports and tottery Victorian seaside towns. After a few miles the road curved away from the sea, climbing through low, gorse-like open country up on to the headland, where I could hear the sound of the two great oceans meeting, their waves crashing on to the Cape. There was a blustery wind up here and I could taste the salt in the air, blowing in off the sea. It was so perfect, such an exquisite, uplifting place to finish a journey, that I even forgave them for the concrete visitors' centre and the pay and display car park. But only just. Thankfully I left these abominations behind, and as I descended the hill towards the sea I felt a tingle of excitement as I saw, for the first time, the tip of the African continent. The waves were breaking on its rocky shore and a few happy holiday-makers were snapping away with their cameras while their subjects posed in front of the wooden sign that marked this legendary spot. I'm nearly there! I was squealing to myself, I've made it! I've ridden across Africa!

The bike gave a little splutter, but I didn't take much notice. It had been running fine for the last 10,000 thousand miles and I had the utmost faith in it. Then it spluttered again, as if it was running out of fuel, but it couldn't be – I had filled up only a few miles back. But like a painfully predictable scene in a bad sitcom, fifty yards from the Cape of Good Hope it gave one final splutter and ground to a halt.

I couldn't believe what was happening. Of all the places to conk out! I dismounted and started investigating, but there was nothing obviously amiss. There was plenty of petrol in the tank; I pulled off the fuel hose and it was coming through fine, pouring out all over the ground. I quickly shoved it back on before I created an environmental disaster. The electrics were fine, the battery was good, I had ignition, the engine was turning over, but nothing was happening. I fiddled with a few more things and had another go at starting it, but to no avail. Again, the engine turned over, coughed, spluttered and died. After repeating this pitiful process a few times, I resigned myself to the sad truth that I would be pushing my bike to the tip of Africa.

Carrying my helmet, with my jacket draped over my arm, I arrived, slightly out of breath and very pink in the face, at the wooden sign. I was immediately pounced upon by a minibus-load of South African rugby players, who couldn't wait to get stuck into a bit of gung-ho motorcycle mechanics. I tried to explain the symptoms but they weren't interested in listening to my diagnosis and they drowned out my explanation with their own eager banter.

'Come on, let's have a look!'

'I used to have a Yammy dirt bike . . .'

'It's turning over . . .'

'Probably just run out of fuel – typical woman eh?'

This comment caused much merriment among the rugby team. An older man, standing nearby with a pair of binoculars and a book about identifying sea birds, gave me a sympathetic look and I managed a grateful smile.

'Nah mate, there's plenty of fuel . . .'

One of the guys was fiddling with the choke, another with the fuel hose, while I stood there watching them test everything I had just tested five minutes earlier.

'Where've you come from, then?' asked one of them.

'England.'

'What? Not on this bike?'

'Yes.'

'Y'kidding me, you rode this bike from England? Guys, she rode this bike from England!'

'You crazy bird!' said the one who had made the joke about running out of fuel. 'You must be bloody insane!'

'Might be something in the carb, take the float bowl off . . .' one of the others was saying.

'Have you got any tools?' said another to me.

'Of course she hasn't! She's a girl!' said the joker of the pack.

The birdwatcher gave me another look and imperceptibly rolled his eyes this time.

405

'You don't need to use the choke if the engine's warm,' another one was telling me.

Oh really? I didn't know that. Thank God I met you, I muttered silently, incredulous but nevertheless amused by the irony of my grand adventure climaxing in such an unlikely scene.

Eventually I decided to take command of the situation and try the highly unscientific when-all-else-fails technique. Grabbing the handlebars, I gave the bike a vigorous shake and hit the start button. It promptly roared into life, and sat there, ticking over like a dream. There was a bit of cheering and back-slapping among the rugby players, except for the joker, who said, 'Huh! There was nothing wrong with it in the first place!' But I was too overjoyed to care about his dented macho pride.

'Excuse me,' I said to the birdwatcher, 'could I trouble you to take a picture?'

'I'd be delighted,' he replied, and I took my position in front of the Cape of Good Hope sign for the obligatory photo call. It was official: I had made it.

I rode away, waving farewell to the rugby buffoons and the twitcher with my motorcycle mystery remaining unsolved, but I wasn't complaining; the bike was running and I was on the move again, heading north for the first time in months, towards Cape Town and Austin – my glittering prize at the end of a long journey.

A romantic reunion of filmic proportions took place in the airport, and for a little while all thoughts of mud and sweat, grot and grime, mechanical mishaps and motorcycle maintenance floated away. Although I was still 10,000 miles from London, I was back where I belonged.

'So come on! Tell me everything. How was it?' said Austin later that evening, once we'd got the more important preliminaries of our reunion out of the way.

It was a big question that demanded a big answer, and I didn't know where to start. I had barely had time to think about it myself, and when he asked me that simple question it brought the reality home to me; this was the end, my African adventure was over. I wouldn't be getting on to my bike in the morning and setting off into the unknown. But that was OK; I was ready to go home.

I remembered my send-off from home on that chilly October afternoon four months before, and when I thought back to how I had felt at that moment, as I rode away from all my comforts, material and otherwise, I knew that something had shifted in me. Would I still feel that painful exposure on the boat to Tunis? Yes, I probably would, but maybe it wouldn't bother me so much. Would I still worry myself to distraction about heatstroke and riding my bike in the sands of the Sahara? No, I probably wouldn't. Would I still shed tears of fear and frustration at being forced on to a train full of drunk, stoned, marauding Congolese soldiers bearing Kalashnikovs? Yes, I definitely would. Even now, and despite the fact that nothing actually happened on that awful day, I still shudder when a TV news broadcast shows a mob of camouflage-clad soldiers, brandishing their machine guns, fighting yet another of Africa's pointless wars. But I don't want to ever reach the point when I stop being scared of the 'big black men with guns'. I would rather be scared than become one of the dehumanised, with their empty eyes, for whom guns and intimidation and death are part of normal life.

But that one day of fear and misery will never overshadow

407

the pure elation of flying across the incomprehensible emptiness of the Sahara or the incredulous joy and relief at being plucked from the jaws of disaster by one of my Angolan guardian angels. Over the last few months, writing this book and reading through my hundreds of pages of scrawled diary entries, I began to notice a recurring theme running through my journey, a theme that didn't occur to me so clearly while I was in the midst of the action. Reading back through my journal I saw that every time things were looking a bit sticky, someone appeared out of the blue to help me – yes, even in the Congo! I couldn't have planned it any better myself, and that's part of the delight – that none of it was planned. Certainly, things could have gone horribly wrong, but they didn't; in fact most of the time they went wonderfully right.

But it was still hard. Africa is a hard place in which to travel, but for me that brought its own rewards: I wanted real life and that's what I found, in all its beauty and comedy and occasionally in its terrible ugliness too. I'm not going to start making cod-meaningful statements about Africa and its people; that kind of gap-year philosophising always makes me cringe, and I'm painfully aware, too, of the discomfort that surrounds the idea of white Westerners striking out into the Dark Continent for the adventure of tackling its rough roads and surviving its harsh challenges, when the people who live there could probably do with a little less of that kind of 'adventure' in their lives and a bit more tarmac and clean water.

But I will hold up my hand and say that is why I wanted to ride across Africa: I wanted an adventure and I got one, and travelling by motorcycle heightened my adventure a thousand times. Being on a bike throws you out there into the thick of it, whether you want it or not, and makes you more vulnerable as a result. But with that vulnerability comes an intensity; a concentrated high, a sweet, nerve-jangling, heart-thumping, sugar-rush sensation of the kind that only comes from real, down 'n' dirty, life-affirming motorcycling, and I suspect I will always be seeking out that feeling, somehow, somewhere.

'You know, I can tell you now that it's all over,' said Austin, looking serious all of a sudden, after he had listened to my rambling summary of my 10,000-mile ride. 'I was really worried about you, I mean, really terrified when you were in the Congo. I would lie awake at night and pray, to something, or someone, that you would be all right.'

Coming from a man who has made the well-considered leap from altar boy to card-carrying atheist, this was quite a statement. Austin had made such a show of unwavering support and enthusiasm for my African adventure, but now, for the first time, I was seeing the reality of being the one who stays behind.

'I'm so sorry . . .' I started to say, but he interrupted me.

'Don't be silly! I would never have stopped you, and I wasn't worried when you left; I've ridden through Africa, I know what it's like, but when you phoned me from the Congo . . .' He trailed off, looking pained at the memory.

'Next time,' I announced, 'we're going together!' And we punched the air simultaneously, our giggling fuelled by one too many bottles of South African Pinotage. But it wasn't the booze talking; I meant it from the depths of my heart. My solo ride across Africa had got something out of my system; I had pulled it off, and in doing so I had laid something to rest inside me.

'So you haven't got the back-to-reality blues then?' asked Austin when I tried to explain this to him.

'No, not at all!'

'Really? You don't have that empty feeling of "What now?"'

'No!' I assured him. 'In fact, it's more like I'm jumping up and down and shouting: What's next?!'

'Well,' he said with a twinkle of his blue eyes, 'it's funny you should say that, because I've got an idea . . .'